Managing Truancy in Schools

DAVID COLLINS

CASSELL

London and New York

Cassell

Wellington House
125 Strand
London WC2R 0BB

370 Lexington Avenue
New York
NY 10017-6550

www.cassell.co.uk

First published 1998

British Library Cataloguing-in-Publication Data
A catalogue record for this book is available from the British Library.

ISBN 0-304-70300-1 (hardback)
0-304-70301-X (paperback)

Typeset by York House Typographic Ltd, London
Printed and bound in Great Britain by Redwood Books, Trowbridge, Wiltshire

Contents

Acknowledgements

I would like to record my thanks to my former employer, the Central Council for Education and Training in Social Work, who supported my research over a four-year period. The views and opinions expressed in this study are entirely those of the author and are not the views of CCETSW, its management, or the Department of Health.

I am grateful to the schools who so willingly participated in the research at a time of rapid change. I received all the help, encouragement and information that I asked for, always within an atmosphere of openness and honesty. I hope that I have been able to represent accurately the significant issues which were of concern to all of them.

I would like to record my thanks to Professor Peter Ribbins for his helpful guidance throughout the research and in the production of this book.

This book is dedicated to Christine and all other parents who dutifully send their children to school while remembering their own truancy.

Introduction

Nothing is more important to our society ... than the education of our youth.
Nothing in pursuit of educational excellence is more important than studying the
models of things that work ... [and] from which we suspect all of us can learn.
(Peters and Austin, 1985, p. 411)

I have had a long interest in truancy as a probation officer, as a teacher, as an
education adviser, and as a researcher. The interest may have come from a
frustrated wish to be a truant myself, but as a boarder at a private school it
appeared impossible because I faced immediate detection and there were no
excuses for not being 'in place' at any time, day or night. My activities were
so controlled by others that I had to find alternative ways of rebelling; but
that's another story! But control is what successive governments have tried to
apply to children and parents in the state sector since the introduction of
compulsory schooling, in order to have full attendance and everyone in their
place. Controls might work if there is 24-hour surveillance, but that is not
possible in the state day school, and there has been no call to turn state
schools into prisons.

Governments have used the fear of the anti-social actions of children who
are 'out of place' to make the controls legitimate, claiming that truancy leads
to juvenile crime and unemployment. Increasingly government has emphasized the contribution that schools make to reducing truancy, thereby
reducing crime and unemployment. This was illustrated in the Conservative
government's white paper *Choice and Diversity* (DfE, 1992), which resulted in
the Education Act 1993 and which appeared to give considerable control to
both the school and parents. One result of the 1993 Act was that schools had
to publish their rates of truancy, thus helping parents to avoid selecting
'underperforming' schools for their child.

But experience suggests that many parents do not get involved in selecting
a school; research suggests that control, in the form of the law, is often
misunderstood, inconsistently applied and fails to produce co-operation.
There is no conclusive evidence that truancy causes crime or unemployment, although the three might have a common cause. The composition of

the intake to a school may have as much to do with its truancy rates as its management, ethos or curriculum. Truancy is, then, a rich seam for research: it has been with us since children have been sent to school (well before the introduction of compulsory state schooling) and there was, and is, no 'quick fix' for it.

This book tries to set the framework for flexible, innovative and individual responses from schools to truancy: responses that are firmly based on policies made within the school, which reflect a clear grasp of the law and use research evidence wisely. I hope that the book will help in the formation of practical policies; it does not set out to prescribe action.

The focus is 'truancy', by which I mean that it is about pupils who, having been registered with a school, have been identified as not attending when it, and therefore the law, says that they should. Thus the focus is on unauthorized absence of any type. Whether it is called truancy, post-registration truancy, or unauthorized absence, schools often regard it as a disciplinary matter for which the pupil is punished (notwithstanding the fact that the offence is committed by the parent). It is also seen as a predictor of yet more trouble in the future, and in some cases this is undoubtedly true. But research evidence shows that much truancy happens in the final years of schooling, where it appears to be widespread among low-ability pupils; that many truants come from low-income families where their services at home are more important than schooling, and that these truants may be no more involved with crime than those who attend regularly. The truant should not exclusively be seen as coming from a particular social underclass[1] and always engaged in illegal or anti-social activities.

The book focuses on truancy from maintained mainstream secondary schooling (11 years to 16 years). In part this is because this age group is the focus of considerable media interest and political intervention, in part because most truancy takes place in secondary school, and in part because of the link that has been made with juvenile crime. The book also considers absence in general. This is because both absence and truancy result in the loss of educational opportunity, because the correct classification of the two causes schools considerable difficulty, and because absence rates may be a more significant indicator of the success of a school in motivating pupils than unauthorized absence alone.

The book draws together a wide range of evidence from research and practice including findings from my own research into aspects of truancy in 20 Midlands secondary schools undertaken between 1994 and 1996.

Chapter 1 sets current concerns over unauthorized absence into an historical context; a context which tends to show that these concerns are not new and have, as yet, not been resolved. The chapter considers the gradual and piecemeal introduction of compulsory education along with the development of methods to enforce attendance using the criminal code. Attention is given to those aspects of the enforcement that involve the role of the attendance officer, a forerunner of the Education Welfare Officer of today. The chapter concludes with a model for understanding some of the attitudes of teachers, parents and pupils to compulsory education, through which unauthorized absence may be better understood.

Chapter 2 is epidemiological in nature and presents evidence of the amounts of attendance at schools, the amount of absence from them, and the reasons for that absence. Consideration is given to the amount of unauthorized absence that actually takes place and whether any generalizations can be made about which pupils are absent, when they are absent and for how long. Evidence from longitudinal studies of the criminal careers of young offenders is considered, along with a review of the influence schools have on protecting young people from criminality. Evidence of the important influence of social background is included. The chapter concludes with a discussion on the relationship of unauthorized absence to criminality, arguing that because there is an association between them the one does not necessarily cause the other.

Chapter 3 considers the legal duties which LEAs and secondary schools have to perform in relation to unauthorized absence and matters related to attendance, and how they both carry out their duties when seeking to enforce attendance. The chapter is divided into three sections: the first considers the relevant duties of the LEA, the second the duties laid on the school, and the third the requirements laid on the LEA by statute and regulation when carrying out its enforcement function.

Chapter 4 reviews research material and present-day examples on how schools and other agencies might approach the problem of dealing with attendance and unauthorized absence, and what might motivate pupils to maintain or improve attendance. The chapter is divided into three main sections. The first considers the ways in which schools can best be managed so as to reduce the rate of occurrence of unauthorized absence, and the actions that the school can take to deal with unauthorized absence when it occurs. The second focuses on those services supplied by outside agencies to help the school deal with more persistent cases of non-attendance. The third section considers the work of the Social Services Departments in relation to behaviour problems in school and unauthorized absence from school, and considers the difficulties of co-operation between schools and social workers.

Chapter 5 summarizes the findings from my research into current practice within 20 Midlands schools. Section one considers the schools' communication with parents and others over attendance matters, section two considers aspects of the methods used by schools to motivate pupils to attend. The third section uses ideas from transactional analysis to help understand the way schools deal with absence, and this provided the basis for the selection of four of the schools for further research.

Chapter 6 presents a summary of the transactions evident in each of the four schools and issues common to them all. Chapter 7 presents six themes that are intended to be of help to any school reviewing policy and practice in relation to absence and truancy, and emphasizes the need for a whole-school attendance policy.

Note

1   For a debate on the existence of an underclass in Britain, see Mann, 1994, p. 86.

## CHAPTER 1

Compulsory Education and Unauthorized Absence

'I'm glad we've got that boy at last,' says the officer, looking at the names on his list. 'The father had to go to prison for him for seven days, and I believe it was pretty nearly as much the lad's fault as anybody's.'

('A Walk with a School Board Officer', *Manchester Guardian*, Wednesday, September 17, 1873)

Between 22 October and 5 November, 1990, TV-am presented a series of programmes called *Missing Out*, devoted to the problem of truancy in British schools. The series was advertised in the *Guardian* on 23 October with the following statement:

Missing Sums: Do you know what your children are doing today? Graph plotting? Map reading? Purse snatching? With 500,000 pupils regularly skipping school, we look at tomorrow's destitutes, drop outs and criminals.

(Quoted in Carlen *et al.*, 1992, p. 41)

Guests on the programmes ranged from HRH Prince Edward through cabinet ministers to professional educators, Education Welfare Officers, pop artists, parents and pupils. Sixty people staffed a helpline each day and logged nearly 2500 calls over the period, about 30 per cent from truants, most of the rest from the parents (mostly mothers) of truants. The producer of the programmes, writing of their effects, said:

The Home Secretary's Special Adviser asked for a copy of the entire series with back-up papers stating that, as a result of the series, the Government now wanted to re-examine its proposals to bind over the parents of truants as outlined at October's Conservative Party Conference. The outcome was that no such provision went into the Criminal Justice Bill.

(Hastings, 1991, p. 2)

The issue of absence from school, and particularly unauthorized absence was, once again, 'firmly on the political agenda' (Carlen *et al.*, 1992, p. 41).

A number of events followed. The (then) DES issued the *Education (Pupils' Attendance Records) Regulations 1991,*[1] which updated the 1956 regulations and also put the problem of unauthorized absence into a modern context. In July 1992 the government issued the white paper *Choice and Diversity, a New Framework for Schools* (DfE, 1992), which included a chapter on pupil admission and attendance (Chapter 5, p. 28). The white paper proposed legislation which resulted in the Education Act 1993.[2] In the financial year 1993/4 the DfE made £9 million available to Local Authorities under the GEST funding scheme to finance schemes to tackle truancy and disaffection, and in 1994/5 the amount was increased to £14 million.[3] In May 1994 the DfE issued six linked circulars under the general title *Pupils with Problems* (DfE, 1994); all six circulars bear on issues relating to attendance.

Just like the TV-am advert, the 1992 white paper assumed a link between criminality and truancy, and by implication made a link between truancy and a lack of readiness for citizenship and employment.

> Boys or girls who stay away from school, or who have been entered on the register then absent themselves for substantial parts of the day, are more likely to grow up unhappy and unfulfilled, leave school much less qualified tnan they might otherwise be and worst of all sometimes get drawn into a life of crime.
>
> (DfE, 1992, section 1.25)

Subsequent legislation provided powers of control, and punishment, for those parents whose children fail to attend, and regulations and circulars set the context within which schools should work to motivate pupils to attend.

The TV-am broadcast touched on many issues of concern to parents, pupils, policy makers and professionals: there were 'deep-seated concerns about order and control, proper parenting, the work ethic, crime and much else' (Carlen *et al.*, 1992, p. 39). These concerns are about preventing deviance from societal norms if possible, or adequate control if not, and can be seen as an extension of the 'law and order' debate (with the state as victim). Five years on similar concerns were expressed by the Labour government in their white paper *Excellence in Schools*:

> Pupils who fail to attend regularly are blighting their chance of future success, may put themselves at risk of abuse, and can be drawn into anti-social or criminal behaviour.
>
> (DfEE, 1997, p. 56)

The purpose of this chapter is to set these modern concerns into an historical context: a context which shows that they are not new and are yet to be resolved. The chapter considers the gradual and piecemeal introduction of compulsory education, the development of methods to enforce attendance based on the criminal code and the enforcement role of the attendance officer, a forerunner of the Education Welfare Officer of today. The chapter concludes with a model for understanding some of the attitudes of teachers, parents and pupils to compulsory education, through which truancy may be better understood.

Unwillingly to school

There is little doubt that children who were sent to school by their parents even before the introduction of compulsory schooling did not always want to go and from time to time 'wagged' it, like Robin Toodle in *Dombey and Son* (Dickens, 1848, p. 305). But before the introduction of compulsory education neither Toodle nor his parents would have been classed as criminals just because he wagged it. However, if the children of those times offended against the law, and there were many who 'eked out a precarious livelihood … [by] begging and petty crime in the jungles of mid-Victorian England' (Hurt, 1979, p. 58), then they could be sent to prison. Following imprisonment they were sent to reformatory school under the provisions of the Reformatory Schools Act, 1854. For them schooling became compulsory as a result of offending. However, successive legislation after 1870 began the process of requiring the attendance at school of the children of the poor and unemployed, those on relief, casual workers and the unskilled. Many of them did not go willingly, and many absented themselves. Legislation had the effect of increasing the numbers of waggers, and defining them, and their parents, as criminals. As the quotation at the head of this chapter indicates, by 1873 some poor parents in some parts of the country were being sent to prison because their children would not go to school. The effect of legislation was a change from providing compulsory schooling for young offenders to producing offenders from those who avoided compulsory schooling.

Elementary education for all

Education at elementary levels and above had been available for those who could pay for it, or who sought out free schooling, for hundreds of years. Much of that schooling was in the Classics, had a religious motivation and was aimed at achieving entry to university (Roderick and Stephens, 1982, p. 17). Very little schooling was generally available to the working class and what there was tended to be piecemeal, often part-time and unco-ordinated, being 'under the auspices of various agencies' (Roderick and Stephens, 1982, p. 16). What schools there were often had their origin in a wish to provide welfare for religious reasons (the missionary motive) and a wish to help people to learn to conform to their 'position' in life (the social control motive).

> But in Spitalfields, in the period under review (1812–1824), the establishment of schools was part of a large-scale programme of the charitable provision of food, clothing and money and the distribution of Bibles and tracts, undertaken by the largely Evangelical and Dissenting upper and middle class with the aim of controlling the populace in the interests of social and economic stability. A study of Spitalfields at this date thus throws into relief one of the most important aspects of the early history of popular education – its function as a means of countering social change and as an agent of the socialisation of the children of the poor for a life in a stratified, exploitive industrial society.
>
> (McCann, 1977, p. 2)

State control of education was slow to develop for two reasons. First there was the fear 'that an educated populace might turn to subversion, refuse to obey superiors, or desert their menial tasks' (Murphy, 1972, p. 9). It seems as though those with power in society required education for the poor to combine the missionary motive (and the fear of God) with the social control motive (and the fear of deportation) for it to be considered successful. The second reason for the slow development was the struggle between the churches. The nonconformist and established churches fought to be the primary influence over the poor; neither church wished to see the other, or the state, become the sole provider of education to the working classes. As a result, the development of education was delayed, uneven and met with resistance.

> The development of a national public system of education in England and Wales lagged behind the continental states by a good half century. Nothing like a full public system existed before 1870, compulsory attendance was not effected in most areas until the 1880s, and elementary schools were not entirely free until 1891 ... The majority of schools were owned and controlled by the National Society and the British and Foreign Schools Society, representing, respectively, the Anglican and Non-conformist churches. It is true that from 1833 onwards governments did give some financial support to the societies but this remained a small fraction of their finance until 1870.
>
> (Green, 1990, pp. 6–7)

A significant development in the process of making English elementary schooling compulsory took place in 1870. The Forster Education Act, 1870 had the effect of consolidating the previously piecemeal pattern of education provision across the country and setting in place a national system for which the government provided some of the finance. The number of locally elected school boards was increased and government took powers to regulate school districts, supervise the inspectorate and monitor the provision of school accommodation. School boards were given bye-law making powers, were required to manage the schools under their control, administer the grants made available by government, as well as to raise local rates to finance the schools. However, as Hurt points out, local administration gave rise to a variety of local solutions, and encouraged local deviance:

> The 1870 Act had done no more than give school boards the power to introduce bye-laws. For the next six years the boards were under no necessity to enforce them. Until the Education Department drafted model bye-laws in the same year, 1876, the boards produced a bewildering mosaic of rules that gave employers, parents, and children every reason to feel contempt for the law and every excuse to evade it.
>
> (Hurt, 1979, p. 188)

Although some school boards functioned poorly, others produced remarkable results. The London School Board, elected in November 1870, was held by Sydney Webb to have the credit for 'one of the most remarkable chapters in social history ... the transformation effected in the course of three-quarters of a century in the manners and morals of the London manual worker' (Webb, quoted in Rubenstein, 1977, p. 231). However, enforcing the attendance of London's children was not easy. The poor, the unskilled and the casual resisted interference in the fragile balance of their lives; to them education was irrelevant and reduced income. Nevertheless there was a powerful incentive as far as the teachers were concerned to get as many into the school as possible:

> Teachers had the strongest incentive to establish and maintain high rates of attendance. Irregular attendance was of course a source of both apathy and rebellion against the attempted discipline of the class room. But, more important, until the end of 1883 teachers' salaries in London directly depended on good attendance, as the revised code of 1862 intended that they should. Children who did not attend for a prescribed period each year could not be examined and hence they could not earn government grants. . . . If average attendance dropped schools were regraded, and this meant a reduction of the head teachers' salaries.
>
> (Rubenstein, 1969, quoted in Carlen *et al.*, 1992, p. 15)

Since teacher pay and school finances depended on the roll some school boards, notably London, used their bye-law making powers to enforce the attendance of children; section 36 of the Forster Act stated:

> Every school board may, if it thinks fit, appoint an officer or officers to enforce any bye-laws under this act with reference to the attendance of children at school, and to bring children, who are liable under the Industrial Schools Act, 1866, to be sent to a certified school, before two justices in order to their being sent, and any expenses incurred under this section may be paid out of the school fund.

Where officers were appointed they became known as attendance officers, or school board officers, or, in London, 'visitors'. A flavour of their work can be gained from the *Manchester Guardian* article quoted at the head of the chapter. From that article it can be seen that failure to comply with the bye-laws could result in the imprisonment of parents. However, not all the boards enforced full-time attendance, because child labour was important to local manufacturing industries and to agriculture. Locally elected school boards reflected the wishes of local business and allowed many children exemption from schooling in order that they could work. This had not been the intention of the Forster Act and in 1876 the Elementary Education Act was passed, making attendance compulsory. Section 4 of the Act stated:

> It shall be the duty of the parent of every child to cause such child to receive elementary instruction in reading, writing and arithmetic, and if such parent fail to perform such duty he shall be liable to such orders and penalties as are provided by this Act.

Once it had become a requirement to go to school, boards could direct children to enrol, and parents who failed in their duty to send their children to school could be penalized under the criminal code.

As a result of previous legislation a child aged under ten could not be employed. For those between ten and fourteen, if they obtained a certificate of proficiency, employment was legal. The 1876 Act had the effect of requiring education from five to ten at least, and to fourteen in most circumstances. As a result compulsory schooling had three costs. First, employers could no longer rely on cheap labour from children and had to pay adult rates instead (opportunity cost). Second, poor families that relied on their children's earnings now had to lose that money while the child was at school (negative cost). Third, in most areas school fees were payable and very little relief from payment was available (direct cost). It was not surprising that in families where children were unlikely to obtain a proficiency certificate, mostly the poor ones, parents took little notice of the law. Many employers, especially those who employed unskilled casual labour, were elected to the boards (or School Attendance Committees, where these existed). Some board members clearly had a vested interest in colluding with parents who could not afford to send their children to school.

Local boards used their bye-law making powers variously and in ways that reflected local needs and wishes. The Education Act, 1880 attempted to produce some conformity and required boards to adopt the Education Department's 'model' bye-laws and common conditions for the legal employment of children. The majority of the boards used their powers under section 36 of the Forster Act to appoint attendance officers to enforce the law, but in some areas those officers tended not to report the non-attenders, or their parents, to the courts, although unauthorized absence was a criminal offence. The reluctance to use the courts may have come from the attitude of many magistrates of the time who believed 'that particular categories of young person would gain more benefit from working in the home or factory, particularly if it relieved the state of otherwise supporting families in need' (Carlen *et al.*, 1992, p. 16). Such an attitude indicates that an important, middle-class element of the establishment was in major disagreement with the introduction of compulsory schooling of the poor.

Most boards appointed ex-servicemen or ex-policemen as attendance officers with a task that 'may have been conceived as the archetype for enforcing social control' (MacMillan, 1977, p. 27). In some areas this function was carried out with remarkable disregard for the legal rights of the poor.

> Some boards conducted raids of doubtful legality to round up the children and haul them off to school. In Manchester these sorties into the urban jungle had led to affrays when parents had tried to rescue the captives. Police had to be summoned to rescue the would be captors.
>
> (Hurt, 1979, p. 156)

Hurt also points out that the school board officers were strongly disliked and their power to intervene in the lives of poor families considerable (Hurt, p. 156). The strength of feeling can be judged by the fact that although school boards were replaced by Education Authorities in 1902, the title 'school board man', used in a disparaging way, is still current in Birmingham. However, their involvement with poor families, whether resisted or not, resulted in the emergence of a welfare function:

> The waiving of school fees at local discretion had to rely on the investigation of home circumstances, and charitable organisations soon found the school attendance officer knowledgeable about where need was greatest. Some officers on their own initiative approached charities and local suppliers to secure food, fuel and clothing for the poorest families. Some officers were able, by their own efforts, to sustain six cots for poor children in a sanatorium by 1897 and arrange seaside holidays for over 2,000 children.
>
> (Grimoldby, 1970, quoted in MacMillan, 1977, pp. 26–7)

The attendance officer's welfare function became 'accepted practice long before welfare legislation was initiated' (MacMillan, p. 27), and was probably an interpretation of the requirements of the job that was different from that intended by government. There is evidence that compulsory education was motivated by the need to control 'a potentially volatile working class. In other words the English working class in its making posed the question of how the consent of the majority was now to be won' (Carlen *et al.*, 1992, p. 17), and their consent was to a form of capitalism within which the rewards of enterprise were not to be equally distributed. The intention was to 'civilise the barbarians' (Costin, 1972, quoted in MacMillan, p. 27), in such a way that the established class divisions did not break down. The schooling to be offered was coercive, and teachers, especially the teachers of the poor, used harsh, punishing regimes in order to obtain results with an emphasis on drill, discipline, and corporal punishment. In developing their welfare function attendance officers responded to the needs of the poor, and rather less to the wishes of the government. Their response was a form of 'care' rather than 'control'.

> As officers I think the specific purpose of our calling is to give particular attention to the more unfortunate class of children whom no-one cares about. Our office, therefore, is contrary perhaps to general estimation one of the most responsible and one of the most difficult to fulfil. The responsibility arises from the fact that so many poor, half starved, neglected little creatures depend on our fidelity to their cause and our determination to secure for them all the rights which law has provided for them.
>
> (Sleg, 1905, quoted in MacMillan, 1977, p. 27)

The purpose is seen as welfare not regulation, rights not control, liberalism not capitalism. The appeal is for sympathy, understanding, and reclamation under the law. MacMillan points out that having established a need for welfare they sought to improve provision:

> Even before the end of the nineteenth century school attendance officers had been pressing for the increased welfare provision to support the education of children. Food and clothing allowances were urged for poor children and officers were at the forefront in both supplying data for the poverty surveys of the time and calling for the improvement of housing conditions which were believed to be the basic cause of ill-health, crime and poor school attendance.
>
> (MacMillan, 1977, pp. 27–8)

Despite a caring approach the attendance officer was not averse to handing over the 'truant' to the head teacher for chastisement (Hurt, 1979, p. 162).

Thus attendance officers originally employed to enforce an element of law came to recognize, along with many others, the effects of what in later years was to become known as the 'cycle of deprivation', and that both care and control were needed to deal with it.

Free elementary education

Some poor parents did not have enough money to pay the school fees and kept their children away from school. Some school boards recognized this problem and remitted the fees so that the children could attend. Other boards required the parents of children who were absent because fees had not been paid to appear before school managers to give reason why they should not be summoned. In so doing they gave the parents a chance to plead their poverty (Hurt, 1979, p. 159). As the extent of poverty became known, and the burden of payment for schooling recognized, the pressure for free elementary education grew. The Education Act, 1891 made education free, but in so doing it removed any control that poor parents may have had as purchasers of a service (Hurt, 1979, p. 161). One barrier to a child's attendance had been removed but at the expense of the teacher's independence of action. The consensus of sorts that had been forged between parents and teachers thus gave way to 'a new form of authority imposed ... by the state, (and) ... bred further conflict especially when children were punished' (Hurt, 1979, p. 162).

The Balfour Education Act, 1902 abolished the school boards and established 'virtually a single pattern of education authorities, based on the county and county borough councils' (Middleton and Weitzman, 1976, p. 112). The act was brought about by the work of Robert Morant (then the vice president of the Board of Education) because of his concern that there was an absence of government policy at a time when the system was in imminent danger of collapse. In particular, church schools (providing places for over half the country's children, mostly in rural areas) were closing at the rate of 60 or so each year through lack of funds (Middleton and Weitzman, 1976, p. 111). In such a situation attendance at school was becoming more and more difficult to ensure. This was particularly so in rural areas where the journey to school could be long and there was no system of public transport.

That Act also raised the school-leaving age to fourteen and provided free schooling for those fourteen- to sixteen-year-old pupils who wished to stay on. Further attempts by committees of enquiry (Hadow in 1926 and Spens in 1938) to improve the circumstances of the poor and thus remove obstacles to attendance were hampered by 'cuts in public expenditure ... unsophisticated economic management on the part of the government ... [and] official restraint on the resources available' (MacMillan, 1977, p. 28). This is not an unfamiliar scenario in the 1990s.

Employment

It was noted earlier in this chapter that the loss of a child's earnings had been a significant reason for non-attendance. The introduction of compulsory education meant the loss of either all or part of the child's earnings and the raising of the school-leaving age could have been strongly resisted on the grounds of a further reduction in income for the poorest families. However, the earning power of children began to decline during the late nineteenth and early twentieth centuries as British industry became more mechanized, agricultural machinery more complex, and 'out work' declined due to changes in manufacturing technique and cheap imports. Although many children continued to find ways of making money, particularly at harvest time, one reason for non-attendance was gradually removed (Hurt, 1979, p. 198). The greater efficiency of police and attendance officers combined with changing attitudes to employment meant that attendance rates improved. The Employment of Children Act, 1903:

> ... allowed local authorities to frame bye-laws regulating street trading and other juvenile forms of employment. Since the Act was adoptive it proved of little value. Out of a total of 329 authorities there were still 98 without bye-laws regulating general employment and 198 without restrictions on street trading in 1914.
>
> (Hurt, 1979, p. 206)

During and after the First World War the employment of school-aged children continued, and it was not until the passing of the Children's and Young Persons' Act, 1933 that there were greater legislative powers. That Act continued the power of the local authority to make bye-laws, and it also required that all working children be registered and their conditions of work monitored. This Act remains the primary legislation today; recently local authority bye-laws based on that legislation were found to be out of date and poorly enforced, and little real protection is offered to the estimated two million school-aged children now in employment (Pond and Searle, 1991). This issue will be taken up again in Chapter 2.

A consensus of sorts

Previous sections have shown that compulsory elementary education had a considerable effect upon the poor working class, many of whom had no great wish for its introduction. In particular it removed the earning power of children and imposed a form of social control on the activities of the poor. Gradually, however, some sort of grudging consensus from the poor was established.

> Last, one may ask just when did the practice of sending a child to school with daily regularity finally become established. Whereas one is not surprised to find a rise in the incidence of illegal juvenile employment in the First World War, by 1939 another generation had gone through the schools. Yet with the disruption of the normal pattern of life there was a resurgence of older attitudes especially in some of those

> agricultural areas where observance of the law had been lax before 1914. . . . Thus almost three-quarters of a century after Forster's bill had become law, some parents still acquiesced in rather than accepted the legal requirements that had changed the pattern of family life that dated back to a pre-industrial society. What to one social group had appeared to be remedial legislation had added a burden to another.
>
> (Hurt, 1979, pp. 212–13)

Willing co-operation was slow to follow legal coercion, with some parents resistant to what has been described as a collective middle-class attempt to 'transform working class belief, attitude and behaviour' (Carlen et al., 1992, p. 20).

Compulsory secondary education

The Education Act, 1944 added an additional burden to the load carried by the unwilling poor by raising the school leaving age to fifteen. Neither did it seem to be doing much to improve the life chances of the poor. Compulsory education for those between the ages of eleven and fifteen was offered in enlarged secondary schools that had developed a tradition of academic excellence based on the models of endowed grammar and 'public' schools. The Act itself allowed the development of a 'comprehensive' system, but the National government, and the Labour government that followed it in 1945, encouraged the development of a tripartite system of grammar, technical and secondary modern schools. Access to the grammar and technical schools was by competitive testing at age eleven, and since the Act made no provision for an increase in grammar schools the opportunities for working-class children were restricted (Reynolds et al., 1987, pp. 5–6). The tripartite system operated to the disadvantage of some class groups:

> The work of Halsey and Gardner (1953) and Floud (1957) demonstrated that children of manual workers who possessed grammar school ability according to the criteria then used were under-represented in grammar schools and that the children of middle class parents were over represented. The National Foundation for Educational Research (NFER) claimed also that even the best available tests which sought to measure ability at 11 had a 10 per cent margin of error in the selection of children to one type or other of secondary school. The Crowther Report (1959) published results of a survey carried out among recruits to the armed services, which showed that a substantial number of the sons of manual workers in their sample had been wrongly placed at the secondary school stage. All these findings suggested that the intelligence tests used to sort the academic sheep from the non-academic goats were massively unequal to the task.
>
> (Reynolds et al., 1987, pp. 11–12)

A system that promised equality but maintained class differences was hardly likely to be welcomed by the working class; a system that demanded the attendance of their children then failed to recognize their talents had the potential for adding to their disaffection.

The tripartite system did produce a limited amount of mobility between classes. A recent reworking of the material collected for the Nuffield Mobility

Study in 1972 has shown that with more sophisticated statistical techniques some mobility can be identified:

> Reanalysing the data ... a clear pattern emerges; growing inequality before 1944, movement towards equality in the first decade after, but sharply increased inequality thereafter.
>
> (Blackburn and Marsh, 1991, p. 1)

Whilst the criticisms of the tripartite system may have been many, the move towards comprehensive schools was not brought about for egalitarian reasons alone. Comprehensive schooling, introduced in the late 1940s in a few parts of England, was applied to the whole system in 1965 by the newly elected Labour government. That government was committed to greater social unity, but according to Reynolds *et al.* (1987, p. 27) they also 'saw it as a more efficient and effective institution for generating children with unequal qualifications'. Education policy had once again been about the working class, rather than for them.

ROSLA

The raising of the school-leaving age to sixteen in 1973 extended the period that children were dependent on their parents, delayed any possible move into full-time employment, and increased the demand for part-time employment, which, as noted previously, is often illegal and without the protection of registration. For many non-academic children the additional year was not productive and both they and some teachers resented the waste of time (Carlen *et al.*, 1992, p. 100). The result was that the trend towards high levels of absence, noted in the fourth year prior to ROSLA, increased sharply in the fifth year (Galloway, 1985, p. 177).

The legal duty to educate

The Education Act 1996 continues to the present day the principles laid down in the legislation of 1876, 1902, 1944 and 1993 in that it requires parents to secure education for their children, and makes the parents subject to criminal penalties if they do not. Section 7 of the 1996 Act states:

> The parent of every child of compulsory school age shall cause him to receive efficient full-time education suitable –
> (a) to his age ability and aptitude, and
> (b) to any special educational needs he may have,
> either by regular attendance at school or otherwise.

This section makes education compulsory, not schooling (DES, 1989a, p. 40). See Chapter 3 for a full discussion of the current legal duties and rights of LEAs, schools and parents.

The vast majority of parents send their children to state schools; a minority of parents choose to send their children to private schools. A very few parents choose to educate their children themselves. This form of education, one of the meanings of 'otherwise' in the above quotation, is difficult to organize, is unfunded by the state, and set about with bureaucratic obstacles. All parents who educate their children at home will eventually have to satisfy the local LEA that their children are receiving efficient, full-time education as defined by law. It is claimed that there has been a marked reluctance for schools, LEAs and Education Welfare Services to help parents fulfil their legal duty by deregistering a pupil and supporting their efforts to teach the child themselves (Education Otherwise, 1983, pp. 18–19). None of the schools or LEAs in the sample that I studied gave parents any information about education 'otherwise', and, therefore, no parents were offered help if they wanted educate their child themselves. A more surprising finding was that only one authority published a statement to parents about their legal obligations. It stated:

> Parents, schools and the City Council share the legal responsibilities for the education of children. The Education Department and schools must provide suitable education for all the children in the City and under the Education Act 1993 parents must ensure that their children receive a full time education.

This statement was not an adequate description of the law as it then stood, although it was preferable to not offering one at all. It carries the expectation that parents will send their children to one of that LEA's schools; no explanation of the legal alternative is offered.

The consensus/gratification model

So far in this chapter it has been argued that compulsory education was primarily aimed at schooling the children of the poor. Since the poor were often unwilling and unco-operative, coercion in the form of legal controls was applied. The middle and upper classes did not always agree with the need for change and some were resentful of the requirement to share their schools with the poor. Although it remains to be determined whether most of today's unauthorized absentees come from the poor unworking working class, in the past this seems to have been the case.

A model is now proposed that provides a classification of the attitudes, or 'frames of reference' (Brown, 1987, p. 32) of those involved to better understand their response to compulsory schooling and to absence from it, particularly that form of absence that is unauthorized. This model, described below, is based on the interaction of two bipolar continua, the one being consensus through to non-consensus, the other deferred gratification through to immediate gratification.

Consensus means the parent's agreement with the general aims and methods of schooling, as distinct from other forms of education, and the encouragement of a willing attendance at school by their children. The aims of schooling are understood by the parent as the general development of their child's character, abilities and knowledge, those aims being achieved through systematic instruction given by a person recognized by the state as fit to give that instruction.

Non-consensus means that there is no such agreement or compliance either to the process of schooling, or to the methods of instruction that take place there. It is assumed that most school teachers are at, or towards, the consensus end of the continuum, and that they are committed to formal schooling as being the best method by which children gain an education. It may be assumed that those educationalists and parents who favoured the 'free school' movement, based on a 'dialogue with others and an exploration of oneself and one's relationships' (Pitts, 1988, p. 71), as a radical alternative are at the non-consensus end, being committed to education but against 'the oppressive structures of formal schooling' (Pitts, 1988, p. 71) as the method by which it is attained. There are many positions in between depending on the view taken of, for example, compliance under the law, teaching methods and styles, the school as a social or academic institution and the competence of teachers. It is likely that most school staff have such a continuum in mind, even if they do not express it, by which they make judgements about other people's readiness to be involved in the process of schooling. When parents register their child at school they may be regarded by the staff as having agreed a contract which implies acceptance of this, taken for granted, consensus.

The gratification continuum refers to the added value that a person considers can be obtained from schooling. Immediate gratification is intended to describe someone for whom the demands of everyday living cannot be postponed. It describes the parent who consistently requires the presence of their child at home for minding other children, for company, or to provide care for them, rather than the child going to school. It describes the child who prefers to be employed illegally during school time, or seeks excitement or entertainment during school time. At this end of the continuum the benefits of schooling, whether it be exam results or work preparation, or social interaction with schoolmates, are of less value than meeting a pressing social or economic need (Whitney, 1994, p. 20). The value placed on schooling is low, or non-existent, in comparison with other pressures or needs. School for them is a waste of time.

At the other end of the continuum individuals are prepared to defer meeting immediate wants or needs in order to be sufficiently successful in schooling to achieve a long-term goal. Such a goal may be to have a good school-leaving report, or Compact report, or record of achievement, that helps in finding a job, or further training for a job; or exam results that lead to higher education which in turn leads to entrance to the professions. For some people aiming to become doctors or lawyers the goal can be many years ahead. Deferment extends dependence on others, may be the product of a

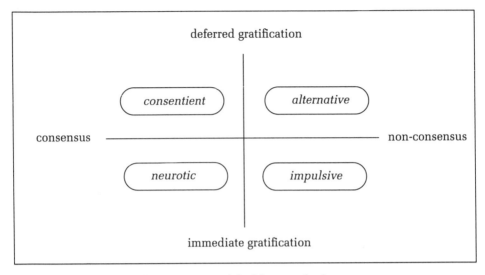

Figure 1.1 A model of frames of reference

family tradition, and usually requires the co-operation of wage-earners within the family.

The model, and the four quadrants that it gives rise to, is illustrated in Figure 1.1. The four quadrants may be understood in the following ways. The consentient group may be considered as representing the 'silent majority' for whom for one reason or another school represents the right place to be, and who required no legislation to compel them to send their children to school. Parents expect and encourage willing attendance and will act quickly to deal with any form of truancy. In the discussion on the development of compulsory education these were the parents who already sent their children to school and for whom the payment of fees was, and in some cases still is, considered worthwhile. The impulsive group represents what could be seen as the opposite extreme. School and what it stands for are not important and getting what you need to survive is paramount. This group may encompass some of the poor of previous times and elements of the underclass of today. Their behaviour might be seen by them as the only logical response to the conditions under which they live. They may be so heavily into an alternative economy and lifestyle that school is meaningless, or they may be rebelling against all forms of authority of which school is but one. As school increasingly fails to confer employment on some working-class children, so more may join this group.

> It is ... increasingly difficult for the ordinary kids to see why they should continue bothering to 'make an effort' in school if it is no longer the basis for personal survival in the labour market.
>
> (Brown, 1987, p. 175)

The alternative group may be largely unknown to schools. They are able to make an argued rejection of schooling, as made by the 'free school' move-

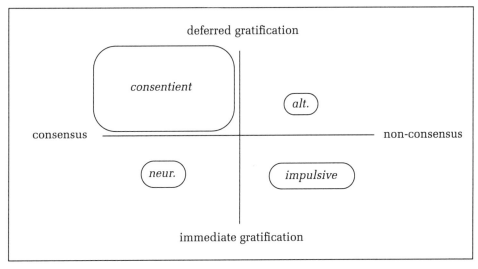

Figure 1.2 Proportions in model of frames of reference

ment, or as has been made by some school drop-outs, or as may be made by parents who want to use the 'otherwise' option in the legislation. There is no rejection of the need to learn and no rejection of a child's need for a period of dependency within which to accomplish learning, but school is not the place to do it. Some children who reject school for these reasons could be placed in a safe work environment allowing an 'apprenticeship' form of learning as an alternative to demanding attendance at school.

The neurotic group is of considerable interest to the educational psychologist and the psychiatric social worker. This group is likely to contain the depressed parents of rebellious adolescents who need support to help them find the energy to get their child to do what they will say they believe is right. It is also likely to contain the timid and phobic children, who cannot face the demands of school but respond well to individual teaching (see Chapter 4).

The four quadrants produced by the intersection of the continua shown in Figure 1.1 are not intended to indicate the relative proportions of the child population within each section. In terms of proportion the model may well look more like that produced in Figure 1.2.

In general terms much of the effort of educationalists may be understood as increasing the size of the consentient group at the expense of the other three groups. The concerns of the politicians may be understood as reducing the size of the impulsive group both as an end in itself and as part of the drive to reduce deviancy and crime among young people.

Notes

1 Subsequently further amendments were introduced in the *Education (Pupil Registration) Regulations 1995.*
2 Subsequently repealed and re-enacted with minor amendments in the Education Act 1996.
3 GEST was renamed the Standards Fund and the budget for improving attendance and behaviour increased for 1998/9 to £21m.

## CHAPTER 2

Unauthorized Absence and Criminality

For Satan finds some mischief still for idle hands to do.

(J. Kelly, *A Complete Collection of Scottish Proverbs*, 1721)

The Conservative government set the context for education in the 1990s with the Education Reform Act 1988. Flynn (1990, p. 56) says that the result has been a shift from professionalism to managerialism which removes autonomy from teachers and education authorities and sets up mechanisms through which central government can exercise greater direct control over what is taught; setting the scene for 'recipe' management (Reynolds, 1996) or what Gunter (1997) calls 'management-by-ringbinder'. It is clear that the school is seen as a powerful agent influencing the lives of future citizens. Successive governments can be expected to build on the 1988 Act by taking greater controls to ensure that schools conform to a prescribed curriculum based on a common set of values (Carlen *et al.*, 1992, p. 58).

> ... the ethos of any school should include a clear vision of the values within it, and those of the community outside. Those values include respect for people and property; honesty and consideration for others; trust, fairness and politeness.
>
> (DfE, 1992, section 1.30)

> [children] ... need to appreciate and understand the moral code ... to develop ... responsibility, determination, care and generosity, which will enable them to become citizens of a successful democratic society.
>
> (DfEE, 1997, section 1.5)

Mary Warnock suggested that political involvement in education is a proper development of democracy: 'We ought to welcome the overt politicising of education – provided we are ourselves, all of us, prepared to accept political responsibility' (Warnock, 1976, p. 355). The last Conservative government intervened on our behalf. It required schools to teach the National Curriculum, to have acts of collective Christian worship, and sought to develop the 'general style and atmosphere of the school itself' (DfE, 1992, section 1.32). It wanted, and the present Labour government also wants, parents to take the responsibility by becoming involved in the life of the school (DfE, 1992, section 1.33 and DfEE, 1997, section 1.20).

In the white paper *Choice and Diversity* the Conservative government acknowledged the power of the school as an important socializing agent. Unauthorized absence from school is seen both to limit the school's effectiveness and to lead to delinquency:

> Regular attendance at school and taking advantage of a good education within a strong moral, spiritual and cultural context, are not only essential to becoming well qualified and to growing up well balanced, they are also one of the best deterrents against criminality. A good school is a bulwark against those pressures which undermine individual and community values. Mere attendance at school is not going to stop a boy, or more rarely a girl, becoming a criminal, but it is certainly one of those things which, like parental guidance and influence of contemporaries, is likely to help. Ask any police officer or probation worker, and he or she will tell you that the slide of a boy into criminality often has a depressingly familiar pattern. It starts with hanging around street corners, drifting into shop-lifting and stealing bicycles, 'progresses' to petty burglary, perhaps becoming involved with drugs, and then moves on to stealing cars or criminal damage. Before long, the journey from street corner to prison cell is complete; the boy is an habitual criminal, and a significant part of his young life may then be spent behind bars. This cycle of criminality is too often triggered by being truant from school.
>
> (DfE, 1992, 1.27)

A similar, but somewhat less zealous, statement was made by the Labour government in its white paper *Excellence in Schools* (DfEE, 1997, section 6.17). Politicians' belief in the proverb with which this chapter opened is evident; but is there research evidence to support their belief in a causal link between truancy and crime?

This chapter explores the evidence both for and against the views expressed in the white papers. It reviews evidence on the amount of attendance at schools, the amount of absence from them, and the reasons for that absence. It considers the amount of truancy that actually takes place and whether any generalizations can be made about which pupils are absent, when they are absent and for how long. Data from longitudinal studies of the criminal careers of young offenders are considered, along with a review of the influence schools have on protecting young people from criminality. The chapter ends with a discussion on the relationship of unauthorized absence to criminality, arguing that because there appears to be an association between them the one does not necessarily cause the other (Graham and Bowling, 1995, p. 42).

How much attendance?

Establishing the amount of attendance has proved problematic. Up until 1989 HMI were reporting that 'accurate measures of attendance are difficult to obtain' and that what was obtained was often unreliable and inaccurate (DES, 1989a, pp. 4–5).

The government appeared to deal with the unreliability of attendance data in relation to all English schools by first amending the *Pupils' Registration Regulations, 1956* by the *Education (Pupil's Attendance Records) Regulations 1991*, subsequently issuing the Education (Schools Information (Wales)) Regulations 1994, SI 1994/2330, and the Education (Schools Information (England)) Regulations 1996, SI 1996/2588. The intention was that reliable statistical information be collected and published (SI 1994/2330, section 7 and schedule 2, section 15; and SI 1996/2588, section 10 and schedule 2, section 24). Tables on the rates of unauthorized absence were first produced by the DfE in November 1993 based on information supplied by schools in England (excluding private schools). Tables on absence, as well as unauthorized absence, were first produced in 1994.

It remains an open question as to whether these new data are accurate and therefore useful. Certainly there was evidence from my study that despite the introduction of computer-based administration the data recorded were as unreliable and inconsistent as they had previously been. Two examples serve to illustrate the point: first, some schools did not know of, or record, absence following registration; second, there was confusion about whether absence from the school site on school-agreed business should be recorded as absence (Collins, 1996). HMI had reported both these matters as difficulties in 1989 (DES, 1989a).

The difference in data collection methods before and after 1994 makes for some difficulties. Surveys and inspections prior to 1994 often used a census system which relied upon each school counting pupils present during a specified time. This can be seen in the ILEA survey of 1987 which calculated absence on the basis of a census taken on 13 May 1987. HMI data already referred to were based on two sample weeks of 1988. These approaches suffer from the problem that the census period can be held by the school not to be typical of general attendance levels and therefore misleading, and they do not set the school's performance in the context of other schools in the area. The data need explanation and commentary to be useful.

After 1994 data record half-days lost (by inference half-days achieved) expressed as a percentage of all possible attendances. These data are produced by the school and, subject to the inconsistencies of recording, are a reasonably accurate record of absence. However, without a commentary from the school it is not possible to determine a pattern to non-attendance, nor the number of pupils who absent themselves from lessons following registration, and the data still fail to set the school's performance into the local context.

There is evidence from data collected prior to and after 1993 that whatever the basis for the figures they conceal wide differences of attendance achieved by schools of similar type both within and between LEAs. Despite this difference a 90 per cent rule of thumb was adopted as the inspection baseline for adequate performance (OFSTED, 1993, p. 25). OFSTED (1995d, HS B12) require information from the head teacher on the percentage of half-days missed through absence. The annual report from HMCIS makes comments on the number of secondary schools that do not reach the 90 per cent target (one-third during the 1995/6 academic year) (OFSTED, 1997).

The origin of the 90 per cent may well predate 1994 and come from Reynolds *et al.* who summarize findings from many studies and conclude that they 'all ... present a remarkably consistent picture – a general absence rate in all British secondary schools of about 10 per cent ...' (Reynolds *et al.*, 1987, p. 42). This combined with similar results produced by HMI seems to have given rise to the base-line. However, given the wide range of attendance rates any norm derived from research should be used with caution. Schools may find that more useful management information is obtained by analysis of their attendance performance year-on-year, and by comparison with schools with similar intakes.

The discussion now turns from considering the general rates of attendance to trying to determine whether there are any generalizations that can be made about patterns of absence. At this stage in the discussion it is necessary to separate absence in general from unauthorized absence in particular. This is not easy to achieve since some of the material reviewed makes statements about general levels of absence from studies that have unauthorized absence as their focus. Furthermore, many reports give very little idea as to whether there are large numbers of pupils absent occasionally, or a small number of pupils absent frequently (DES, 1989a, p. 4; Whitney, 1994, p. 50).

The effect of social class on attendance

Although poor attendance can be more of a problem in non-selective city schools (NACEWO, 1974, p. 7), Reynolds *et al.* point out '... rates of truancy are most strongly related to social class and academic ability rather than to the type of school' (Reynolds *et al.*, 1987, p. 43). There is evidence that this finding in relation to unauthorized absence is also true of absence in general. In his analysis of studies in the 1960s and 70s Galloway finds that pupils classified as coming from the working class (where fathers were unskilled or semi-skilled) were four times more likely to be absent than those coming from the upper class, and that 'within any one social class, absentees are more likely to come from the more disadvantaged homes' (Galloway, 1985, p. 12). Similar findings are reported by Terry (1975, p. 7) and by Billington (1979, p. 2), quoting some of the same sources as Galloway. More recently in a report to the DfE O'Keeffe suggests that the 'poverty factor' is still related to 'high absence levels from school' (O'Keeffe, 1994, p. 85). Carlen *et al.* (1992, p. 66) say that many studies identify the 'deprived-neglectful family' as one of the causes of non-attendance, the characteristics of such families being poverty, overcrowding, unskilled employment of the householder, and criminality within the family. Within this type of family it is difficult to be certain of the cause of absence; it could be greater susceptibility to illness, or a manifestation of the 'impulsive' attitude to education. Whatever the cause it is worth noting that it is much the same class group that presented attendance problems in the late 1880s, and was one of the main targets for the introduction of compulsory schooling (see Chapter 1).

The effect of ability on attendance

Pupil ability also seems to be associated with absence. HMI state that:

> Research has not been able to illumine whether poor attendance precedes or follows low attainment, but it does show that pupils placed in lower ability groups, and not entered for public examinations, have a much higher absentee rate than those for whom school is more successful in academic terms.
>
> (DES, 1989a, p. 44)

Evidence to support the HMI statement in relation to ability and examinations can be found in Rutter *et al.* (1979, p. 175); in relation to streaming by ability in Fogelman and Richardson (1974, p. 9), and Galloway (1985, p. 4); with regard to statistically significant individual differences between 'truants' and others on verbal, numerical and perceptual tests, in Billington (1979, p. 3). Rutter *et al.* studied the progress of a cohort of children through 20 London secondary schools between 1970 and 1975. They summarize their findings in relation to class and ability thus:

> Pupils of below average intellectual ability or from families of low occupational status were the ones most likely to show poor attendance records.
>
> (Rutter *et al.*, 1979, p. 72)

The effect of age on attendance

Rutter *et al.* showed that there was a relationship between school attendance and age group. Figure 2.1 shows the percentage of attendance achieved at twelve secondary schools by first-, third- and fifth-year children for a sample two-week period (a census), during the academic year 1975/76.

This figure is notable for a number of reasons. First it shows the existence of a range of attendance rates between schools of similar type. Secondly it shows attendance rates well below the 90 per cent level for the weeks in question. Thirdly it shows that within all twelve schools absence rates rise as the school-leaving age approaches, and that despite similarities between schools the rise is greater in some than others. Fourthly it shows that some schools have greater success in achieving more consistent levels of attendance than others. Finally, it shows that first-year absence rates are not always predictive of fifth-year rates. In relation to age groups these findings tend to confirm those of NACEWO (1974, p. 8), who report that '... irregular attendances increased in each secondary age group'.

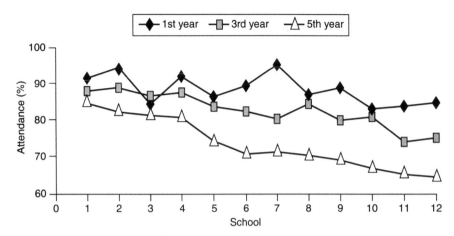

Figure 2.1 Per cent attendance achieved

The effect of gender on attendance

There is some evidence to suggest that the rates of absence of girls may be greater than of boys. Spooner, the head teacher of a Leeds comprehensive school, reviewed 'absence figures in a large city', and found that:

> The absence rate was greater in 'down-town' localities, it increased as pupils grew older, it was greater among girls, it increased dramatically on Fridays, it grew as term went on and it was markedly greater among below average pupils. On Fridays, towards the end of term, in down-town girls' schools, it was likely, therefore, to be dramatic and demoralising.
>
> (Spooner, 1979, p. 104)

Spooner's suggestion that absence may be greater among girls is supported in a review of literature by Carlen *et al.*:

> In terms of gender, Reid and Kendal (1982) note that, at both primary and secondary levels, girls are more frequently absent than boys although 'illegitimate' absence rates are virtually the same for both. These higher legitimate absences for girls (if accurate) may be explained in terms of different gender roles, especially the expectation that young women will fulfil domestic commitments, along with the lower social value placed on the education of females.
>
> (Carlen *et al.*, 1992, p. 65)

The question of the reasons for absence will be taken up later in this chapter. It is important to note here that girls may outnumber boys in relation to authorized absence and that as many boys as girls have absence that is unauthorized (a finding supported by O'Keeffe, 1994, p. 89).

The effect of 'endings' on attendance

Absence from school may increase as 'endings' approach. Galloway reports:

> Jackson's (1978) study was of interest in demonstrating in the fourth year of a large comprehensive school, a cumulative tendency for attendance to deteriorate towards the end of the day, the week, the term and the year ... all the differences were statistically significant.
>
> (Galloway, 1985, p. 13)

From evidence so far presented the finding in relation to the year is not surprising. Jackson's findings lend support to Spooner's view of greater absence at the end of the week.

These findings suggest that pupil motivation appears to be a significant factor in attendance. During my research I asked head teachers if any changes had been made to the curriculum or timetable to increase the motivation of year groups (as distinct from individual motivators or reward systems). The majority of schools had not made changes, citing the need to deliver the National Curriculum as presenting restrictions on such change. However, one head teacher reported removing the last lesson on a Friday afternoon for the whole school to encourage attendance on Fridays, a change that had limited success. Additionally for those children in year 11 who were ending their school career with no 'targets for life' staff had been trying to produce some enthusiasm for learning using subjects that did not stem from the curriculum. This had been successful in developing enthusiasm in some pupils, but there was no evidence as to whether it had improved attendance.

Summary

So far it seems safe to assume that there will be a wide range of attendance rates between schools. To apply a norm of 90 per cent to all schools may be unhelpful, particularly to schools serving deprived areas and with intakes of generally low ability and low examination success. It may be wiser for these schools to set their own targets. In considering the patterns, non-attendance will be highest among working-class children and among those with average to low ability. Among these pupils, rates of attendance will fall towards the end of the week and the end of the term, and will decrease dramatically in the final year of schooling. More girls than boys will be absent.

Having attempted to identify who might be absent, attention now turns to considering why pupils are absent.

Reasons for absence

A major survey was conducted by NACEWO on attendance during one week in October 1973 which sought, among other things, to discover the reasons for absence. Four counties and twelve cities took part, involving a total of 27,270 school-aged children. Of these 15,599 were of secondary age.

Table 2.1 has been produced from a reworking of the data in relation to

Table 2.1 NACEWO survey 1973

category	male %	female %	total %
illness	67.16	68.95	68.10
accident	4.98	2.93	3.91
family neglect	5.73	7.63	6.72
school refusal	1.25	2.06	1.68
holiday	6.03	4.20	5.07
other causes	6.30	8.70	7.56
subtotal	91.45	94.47	93.04
lateness	2.18	1.68	1.91
truancy	6.37	3.85	5.05
subtotal	8.55	5.53	6.96
total	100.00	100.00	100.00

(after NACEWO, 1974, p. 14)

secondary school children. The categories of illness, accident, family neglect, school refusal, holiday and other causes have been combined into a subtotal to give a figure for what would now be called authorized absence. The categories of lateness and truancy have been combined to give a figure for unauthorized absence.

Before considering the data in Table 2.1 some explanation of the two categories is required. Illness and accident are self-explanatory and are legitimate reasons for absence. Family neglect was a term used in the survey to cover reasons for non-attendance such as not having shoes, no bus money, no uniform, family breakdown, and so forth: reasons which then, and now, cause debate as to whether absence is justified or not. School refusal only included those pupils undergoing treatment and their absence was justified as a result. The 'other causes' category was used sparingly but not detailed; it has been assumed that it did not include any unauthorized absence. These categories have been combined on the assumption that the reasons for non-attendance were legitimate, or beyond the control of the pupil. Lateness was defined as more than 15 minutes late, and truancy as absence without parental knowledge or permission and therefore without the school's permission.

Of the 15,599 pupils on the registers of the secondary schools, 3,807 (24.4 per cent) were absent at some time during the sample week. These 3,807 pupils accounted for 12,464 absences in total, an average of 3.27 absences per pupil for the week. From the comments made about the excellent attendance at some of the secondary schools (NACEWO, 1974, p. 21) the average attendance rates conceal considerable variation between schools. Clearly illness accounted for the greatest proportion of absence. If illness is combined with accident and family neglect they account for over three-quarters of all absence. By combining the remaining categories in that subsection it appears that of all absences just over 90 per cent were authorized.

The figures in the table support the evidence presented above that there are more girls than boys absent with 'good' reason. Within this combined category it seems as though boys are more likely to have accidents than girls, but girls are more likely to be affected by family difficulties which keep them off school (reflecting later findings reported by Carlen *et al.* quoted above).

The figures put the amount of truancy at approximately 7 per cent of the total of all absences, with boys truanting more than girls in a ratio of about 3:2.

How much absence is unauthorized?

The study by NACEWO gives the main reasons for absence and gives an idea of the proportions of absentees that are likely to be absent for those reasons. It also shows that between 3.5 per cent and 7 per cent of that absence is unauthorized (NACEWO, 1974, p. 38), but the study falls short of providing information on the performance of individual schools, year groups, or ability groups. There is confirmation of the NACEWO survey findings in more recent studies summarized in Carlen *et al.*:

> The most frequently quoted figure for unauthorised absences derives from a one-day survey of all secondary schools in England and Wales (DES 1975). This survey reported that 9.9 per cent of all pupils were absent on that day, and that 2.2 per cent of all pupils were absent without good cause. Thus 2 per cent has subsequently been regarded as the national truancy rate (Carroll 1977), although some consider that to be an under estimate (for example, the National Association of Chief Education Welfare Officers' own survey in October 1973 revealed a truancy rate of between 3.5 and 7 per cent (NACEWO 1975, *sic*)). More recently, *(1988)* figures have supported the NACEWO estimate, with a three-year study by Her Majesty's Inspectors suggesting that 7.5 per cent of pupils are missing from class each day. . . . evidence emerging from the Youth Cohort Study at Sheffield University . . . supports the studies cited above in finding that 6 per cent of fifth form pupils were serious truants (i.e. absent for days or weeks at a time), and a further 10 per cent were selective truants (i.e. absent for particular days or lessons).
>
> (Carlen *et al.*, 1992, pp. 64–5)

The results of the Youth Cohort study cited by Carlen *et al.* above are worth closer examination. Between 1985 and 1988 the Sheffield team analysed questionnaire responses from young people who had recently left schools in England and Wales. A representative sample of school-leavers, 20,000 in each year, were surveyed in the year following their leaving compulsory schooling, and asked to complete a questionnaire relating to their last year in school. One of the questions was 'Did you play truant in your fifth year at school?' Respondents were given five options (Gray and Jesson, 1990, p. 3) by which to classify their own view of their attendance. These were:

- for weeks at a time
- for several days at a time
- for particular days or lessons
- for the odd day or lesson
- never.

The first two options were combined into a single category which was termed 'serious' truancy, and the second two options were combined and termed 'selective' truancy, with selective truancy including post-registration truancy. Over the survey period 40,000 responses were received covering 2,300 secondary schools. In addition to the findings reported by Carlen *et al.*, the team found that (pp. 4, 13–14):

- Ten per cent of all fifth-year pupils engaged in 'selective' truancy.
- About one in five secondary schools face a situation where more than 10 per cent of their fifth-year pupils are reporting being involved in 'serious' truancy.
- In about one in twelve secondary schools more than 20 per cent of the fifth-year pupils reported 'serious' levels of truancy.
- About one in four inner city secondary schools had 10 per cent or more of their fifth-year pupils reporting 'serious' levels of truancy.
- About one in eight inner city secondary schools had over 20 per cent of their fifth-year pupils reporting serious truancy.
- 'Serious' truants were especially likely to secure few if any qualifications in public examinations. Seven out of ten inner city youngsters who admitted to serious truancy obtained no exam passes whatsoever.
- The levels of truancy reported by males and females were very similar.

These findings tend to support the findings of other research considered previously. It is clear that some schools experience very high levels of 'serious' truancy. The report indicates that 44 inner city schools, about 13 per cent of the inner city total, are likely to have more than 20 per cent of their fifth year absent for much of the time. Some 140 of the other schools, about 7 per cent of the total, are likely to experience the same rates of 'serious' truancy (Gray and Jesson, 1990, fig. 3). Applying the Youth Cohort Study finding that 6 per cent of fifth-year pupils are 'serious' truants to the 300,000 leavers who left English schools in 1988/9 then it appears that about 18,000 could have been so classed (well short of the 500,000 alleged to be regularly missing school at that time in the *Guardian* article quoted in Chapter 1; school-leaving information from the Central Statistical Office, 1991, p. 139).

The findings from the Youth Cohort Study in relation to serious truancy are supported by O'Keeffe (1994, p. 31, table 2). Although definitions and data collection methods differed, O'Keeffe found that 5.6 per cent of Year 11 pupils truanted more than twice per week, very similar to the YCS 6 per cent. The two studies differ considerably in relation to selective truancy: O'Keeffe found that 30.4 per cent truanted at some time in their final year of compulsory schooling compared with 10 per cent of the YCS sample.

The YCS report shows that serious truants obtained limited or no success in public examinations; such limited success predicts future failure. Hibbert *et al.* (1990) in their analysis of data from the National Child Development Study found that there was an association with low qualifications and 'subsequent difficulties in the labour market' (p. 35). In a later analysis of NCDS data Fogelman concluded:

> What is clear is that the former truant is not someone who has simply outgrown school and is ready to settle successfully into adult life. On the contrary, there are sad continuities between their disadvantaged status at school and in society subsequently. Furthermore their disadvantages and difficulties are greater than would be predicted from their social background.
>
> (Fogelman, 1996, p. 94)

The evidence so far reviewed clearly indicates that successive governments are right to be concerned about the problem of absence, even if the amount of it is not clearly known. They are also right to be concerned about unauthorized absence, regardless of any supposed anti-social consequences. There are many young people leaving school earlier than the legal leaving date, who leave with no qualifications, and for whom job insecurity and unemployment are more likely. They appear not to have had much, if any, 'value added' as a result of their school careers. The question remains as to whether these young people are drawn into crime either during compulsory schooling or in the years following. The evidence on this is now considered.

Criminality and unauthorized absence

Records of the rates of unauthorized absence have not been kept with sufficient accuracy over a long enough period to know for certain whether rates are stable or increasing. However there is some evidence that rates of absence may be stable (Galloway, 1985), or possibly rising (Carlen *et al.*, 1992; O'Keeffe, 1994). No study so far reported has indicated that the rates of absence, or the rates of unauthorized absence, are falling. If there were a causal link between unauthorized absence and criminality then it might be supposed changes in one would be mirrored by changes in the other.

Figure 2.2 overleaf shows rates of offending by young people aged between 10 and 20 for the years 1971, 1981 and 1991.

This shows that the rates for all school-aged children were higher in 1981 than in 1991 (the slightly higher rate for females being more than offset by the reduction in males). Crime committed by this group appears to have fallen in the last 10 years, while there is no evidence that this is mirrored by

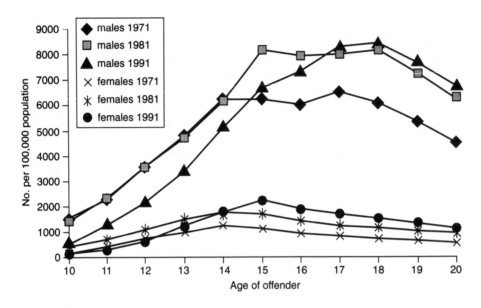

Figure 2.2 Offenders found guilty or cautioned

decreased rates of unauthorized absence. The data presented in Figure 2.2 require careful consideration for their usefulness in determining any link. First, the information given in the table is produced from consistent court data, whereas the information on unauthorized absence may be inconsistently recorded. Second, the information in Figure 2.2 overestimates the number of offenders because 'A person found guilty of, or cautioned, on two or more separate occasions during the year will be counted more than once' (*Criminal Statistics*, 1991, p. 87). Third, the table reports the number of young people who have been caught. Since the clear-up rate of notifiable offences is 33 per cent of all offences in England (Central Statistical Office, 1991, p. 128), nothing is officially known of the other 67 per cent (a method of overcoming this difficulty is considered later). Fourth, the increased use of unrecorded informal warnings by police means that there is a widening gap between official records and unofficially 'known' offenders (Farrington, 1992, p. 123), which makes it increasingly difficult to judge trends over time. This informal process 'would help to partly explain the substantial fall in the number of juveniles found guilty or cautioned' (*Criminal Statistics*, 1991, p. 88), but there can be no measure of the effect of this within the official statistics. The table is helpful in that it presents information on 'the worst offenders and the worst offences' and can be used for making comparisons over time (Farrington, 1992, p. 125).

The 1991 data in Figure 2.2 show that male offending rates increase after the ending of compulsory schooling and peak at age 18. Males between the ages of 17 and 20 'have the highest rate of known offences at 7676 per 100,000 population' (*Criminal Statistics*, 1991, p. 87). These high levels of offending occur as compulsory education finishes and the males move into the wider world. Female offending rates climb gradually throughout schooling, peak at age 15 and then gradually decline. Their offending pattern is very different from males, suggesting different behaviours and/or different societal reaction to those behaviours. The ratio of female to male offenders at age 15 is 1:3.2. It will be recalled that the ratio of unauthorized absence has been found to be two females to every three males. Thus the female offending ratio at 15 is half the (general) unauthorized absence ratio. Given the very different offending ages for females and their different pattern of reasons for unauthorized absence there is some evidence that different factors are at work and that understanding the link between offending and unauthorized absence requires a separate analysis for each gender (Rutter *et al.*, 1979, p. 77; Graham and Bowling, 1995, p. 48). The Conservative government made a comment about gender difference in relation to numbers only (DfE, 1992, section 1.27, quoted above), but assumes a link between offending and unauthorized absence for both genders. However, the genders are more similar in relation to truancy than they are in relation to offending, a finding which suggests that if a causal link exists it is likely to be more true for males than females.

Table 2.2 gives a clear indication of the offending behaviour of the genders. This table shows that theft and handling stolen goods is one group of offences with a high rate of commission by both genders. Within the 10–20 age group 75 per cent of all female offenders and 52 per cent of all male offenders commit offences falling into this category (*Criminal Statistics*, 1991, p. 104).

Another group of offences common to both is violence against the person; 10 per cent of both male and female offenders within the 10–20 age group are involved. The table shows that males are more often involved in burglary and drug-related offences than females.

A comment has already been made in relation to the unsatisfactory nature of the official records and statistics (such as those used in the table above), in that they do not provide an accurate account of the prevalence of offending by young people. To overcome some of the difficulties researchers have combined official criminal records with evidence from self-report studies. Farrington states:

> The most important alternative method of measuring delinquency is the use of the self report survey, in which juveniles are asked to say whether they have committed certain acts during a specified period such as the last year. The main problem with self report surveys is that juveniles may conceal or exaggerate their delinquencies or fail to remember them. More trivial acts (such as stealing small amounts of money from home) tend to be over-represented in such surveys. Also, the most delinquent juveniles may be missed from the sample interviewed, because they are in the most transient living arrangements, incarcerated, the most difficult to find, the most uncooperative, or the most likely to be missing from school. The advantages and disadvantages of official records and self reports are to some extent complementary. In general, official records include the worst offenders and the worst offences, while

Table 2.2 Offenders by gender

indictable offences	males by age			females by age		
	10 and under 14	14 and under 17	17 and under 21	10 and under 14	14 and under 17	17 and under 21
violence against the person	1.7	6.9	12.8	0.5	2.2	1.6
sexual offences	0.3	1.1	1.3	0.0	0.0	0.0
burglary	4.6	11.2	18.6	0.3	0.8	0.7
robbery	0.3	0.9	1.6	0.0	0.2	0.1
theft and handling	14.8	30.7	44.1	5.4	12.8	12.6
fraud and forgery	0.2	0.8	4.1	0.1	0.3	1.4
criminal damage	1.1	2.0	3.3	0.1	0.2	0.3
drug offences	0.1	2.6	13.6	0.0	0.4	1.1
other (ex. motoring)	0.2	1.7	9.2	0.0	0.1	0.8
motoring	0.0	0.3	2.5	–	0.0	0.1
total indictable offences	23.3	58.2	111.1	6.5	17.0	18.7
summary offences	5.9	21.4	61.2	0.5	2.8	10.1

(number of offenders in thousands) (adapted from *Criminal Statistics*, 1991, p. 104)

self reports include more of the normal range of delinquent activity. Self reports have the advantage of including undetected offences, but the disadvantages of concealment and forgetting. The key issue is whether the same results are obtained with both methods.

(Farrington, 1992, pp. 124–5)

Farrington (p. 127), in comparing the findings from both forms of enquiry, suggests that in relation to serious offending both agree on the prevalence of offending. The self-report studies show that nearly all the young people who admit committing serious offences (called 'official delinquents') have been arrested at some time; however, 'official delinquents' report that they have committed far more offences than those for which they were arrested. Very likely, then, the perpetrators of serious crimes not cleared up are largely the same as those officially cautioned or found guilty. This means that findings in relation to the characteristics of official delinquents may be held to be accurate for them all. This relationship does not hold for less serious offences: official records appear to underestimate both the number of offenders and the number of offences. Farrington states:

As many as 89 per cent of boys admitted at least one offence between 10 and 14, and 67 per cent between 15 and 18; but the corresponding proportions convicted were 11 per cent and 20 per cent respectively. Other self-report studies indicate that the majority of boys (Willcock 1974; Belson 1976) and even girls (Campbell 1981) have committed at least one minor delinquency, although only a small minority have committed serious acts such as burglary.

(Farrington, 1992, p. 127)

Minor and infrequent offending appears to be commonplace among adolescent boys, and possibly most common during compulsory school age. Those that commit the more serious offences are fewer in number and are most likely to get caught at some time during their delinquent career. However, those that commit the less serious offences are much more numerous and much less likely to get caught. As an example of this Farrington reports that in one of his studies the number of shoplifting offences was probably underestimated by official records by a factor of 100, and the number of offenders convicted was very small at between 2 and 3 per cent (Farrington, 1992, p. 127).

Farrington and West in their 'Cambridge Study in Delinquent Development' followed the development of 411 working-class London males born in 1953 from age 8 to age 32, seeking to discover factors that produced delinquency, or protected against it. In so doing they produced information on the link between unauthorized absence and criminality. This study has been replicated in different parts of the world producing similar findings (Farrington, 1992, p. 124). Farrington was able to show that those children who were classed as impulsive and troublesome at primary school by their teachers and their classmates tended to become both official and self-reported delinquents. At secondary school they were aggressive, liars and bullies, by age 18 they were anti-social, heavy drinkers, using drugs, sexually promiscuous, as well as offending. Rates of convictions and rates of self-reported crime declined after age 20. The findings of the 24 years of study are summarized by Farrington as follows:

> The typical delinquent – a male property offender – tends to be born in a low income, large-sized family and to have criminal parents. When he is young, his parents supervise him rather poorly, use harsh or erratic child-rearing techniques, and are likely to be in conflict and to separate. At school, he tends to have low intelligence and low attainment, is troublesome, hyperactive and impulsive, and often truants.
>
> (Farrington, 1992, p. 155)

Farrington also found that the boys rated as most troublesome at primary school tended to go on to secondary schools that had the highest rates of official delinquency. Conversely, boys rated least troublesome at primary age went on to schools with low delinquency rates. The variation between schools' official rates of delinquency was considerable, ranging from 21 court appearances per hundred children to 0.3 per hundred. Farrington states:

> ... it was clear that most of the variation between schools in their delinquency rates could be explained by differences in their intake of troublesome boys. The secondary schools themselves had only a very small effect on the boy's offending.
>
> (Farrington, 1992, p. 138)

The study found that frequent unauthorized absence (for 12- to 14-year-olds) was a highly significant predictor of both official and self-reported delinquency. Furthermore, unauthorized absentees were nearly six times more likely to become officially delinquent than their peers, the highest ratio found within the study (Farrington, 1992, p. 129, table 6.1(e)).

Rutter *et al.* (1979) in their study of 12 matched London secondary schools sought information on the effects that different schools had on their pupils. In so doing they provided interesting information on absence and delinquency. The research combined information from a confidential self-report questionnaire completed by pupils with observations made of them by teachers and researchers, and with their official records of delinquency. The pupil questionnaire provided information on matters such as missing lessons, absconding and 'truanting'. Observations provided information on pupil behaviour in relation to such things as violence, fights, lateness, and disruption of the class. Data collected on the 1974 cohort of children were compared with official data on their delinquency collected in 1977 when the pupils had reached 18 (their peak age for offending). Rutter *et al.* report (p. 93) that for boys 'there were substantial correlations between ... delinquency and attendance' (r = 0.77) when comparing the rank order of the 12 schools. In other words, schools with high delinquency rates had high absence rates. In summarizing the conclusions of their whole study, the following points about delinquency are made:

> ... secondary schools in inner London differ markedly in the behaviour and attainment shown by their pupils. This was evident in the children's behaviour whilst at school ... the regularity of their attendance, the proportions staying on at school beyond the legally enforced period, their success in public examinations, and their delinquency rates.
>   ... schools which did better than average in terms of the children's behaviour in school tended also to do better than average in terms of examination success and delinquency.
>   ... academic balance in the intakes to schools was particularly important ... delinquency rates were higher in those with a heavy preponderance of the least able.
>
> (Rutter *et al.*, 1979, pp. 178–9)

These findings suggest that when comparing schools that have somewhat similar catchment areas those with a higher intake of low-ability pupils are more likely to have high unauthorized absence rates and high delinquency rates. Thus both Farrington and Rutter agree that intake variables such as troublesomeness and low ability 'predict' criminality and unauthorized absence. At the time of the research intake variables were beyond the power of the schools to control as a result of ILEA policy (Rutter *et al.*, 1979, p. 154).

The above findings seem to suggest that the schools themselves may not have a very significant influence on children's criminal behaviour, or their unauthorized absence. However, some writers think that there is evidence that what goes on within the schools has an effect on offending when out of school. In his review of six studies on the effects of schools, undertaken between 1966 and 1977, Mortimore concludes:

... in terms of behaviour outside the school, it seems that such schools are able to protect their pupils from participation in delinquent acts, even when the pupils live in an area of high risk.

(Mortimore, 1977, p. 66)

HMI in their summary of research findings in relation to attendance at school make a similar claim for the beneficial effects of schools:

Some schools may have intakes that are more likely to have high rates of absenteeism than others. Yet even given similar catchment areas, levels of socio-economic disadvantage and nature of intake, there is a marked variation in attendance rates between individual schools. ... The conclusion drawn is that what schools do, and the quality of the education they offer, does make a difference.

(DES, 1989a, p. 44)

Graham, in his review of research, tends to support the HMI's findings. He suggests that there is some evidence of a link between unauthorized absence, disruption in school and the development of a delinquent career:

Research on attendance and behaviour in school and a propensity to delinquency is less conclusive, although it would appear that truancy and disruption are not only related to academic failure (and through this to delinquency) but may also constitute an important element in the development of delinquent careers in their own right. The findings of research suggest that schools quite clearly have an *independent* influence on these three outcomes, although the *extent* to which they do so has still not been conclusively resolved.

Through their capacity to motivate, to integrate and to offer each pupil a sense of achievement irrespective of ability, schools would seem to be able to prevent some of their pupils being drawn into the juvenile justice system. The converse is also true. There are processes in school which, albeit inadvertently, categorise certain pupils as deviant, inadequates and failures, and this in turn increases the risk of such pupils drifting into delinquent activities and ultimately delinquent careers.

(Graham, 1988, p. 47)

Although it may appear that some schools protect pupils from offending and being caught and some may not there is little evidence of the overall effects of either type of school. It is reasonable to argue that schools may have some effect on the margins, possibly being successful with pupils who may be at some risk of 'drifting' into offending or anti-social actions. But those most at risk of developing a criminal career do not drift, they grow up in families where the combination of 'adverse factors' (Graham and Bowling, 1995, p. 47) overwhelms the school's influence. In a review of a wide range of studies the National Association for the Care and Resettlement of Offenders report:

The findings of the principal research studies indicate that the factors most significantly related to an increased risk of criminality are:

* economic deprivation
* poor parental supervision
* parental neglect
* harsh or erratic discipline
* parental conflict

- long-term separation from a biological parent
- having a parent with a criminal record.

(NACRO, 1997, p. 3)

It has already been noted in this chapter that it is just these children who are most likely to have poor attendance records and unauthorized absence. The NACRO report goes on to say that one major study, the National Survey of Health and Development, found that 'a lack of parental interest in children's education was correlated with future delinquency'. The issue of engaging parental interest is taken up again in Chapters 5, 6 and 7.

Summary

Despite data collection difficulties it seems that there is evidence of a wide range of attendance rates between schools, and a wide range of unauthorized absence rates. Research indicates that there is also a wide range of delinquency rates between schools, and that schools with high rates of unauthorized absence are likely to have high rates of criminality. There is evidence that one likely cause of these variations is the social background and ability of children admitted to the school.

Evidence indicates that the majority of school-aged children have committed some 'petty' criminal acts. A few commit more serious crime more frequently, and are more likely to be caught. There is evidence to suspect that a large proportion of children have been unauthorized absentees at some time, and about 6 per cent of pupils are absent without good reason for long periods. There is some evidence that the children who commit serious crimes are also persistent unauthorized absentees. These children tend to come from economically deprived families: their parents are unskilled, neglectful, in conflict or separated, and other members of the family will have criminal records. The children are likely to be of low ability and have a history of troublesomeness at school. There is some evidence that what goes on within the school may not be able to compensate for these deficits.

For males, unauthorized absence and criminality increase during the period of secondary schooling, and the rate of offending continues to rise beyond the ending of compulsory education. For females unauthorized absence also increases, but offending reduces a little during the last year at school. These variations between genders may conceal variations in motives. Because of the low rates of offending by young females it seems reasonable to assume that most of the generalizations about criminality relate to young males.

There is no evidence from the research that a good school is a deterrent to crimes classed as serious. In relation to less serious crime research suggests that a good school can protect some pupils from becoming delinquent. There is also some evidence that a good school can stop some pupils becoming unauthorized absentees. Research is less clear about who is protected and by what process. The Conservative government suggested that the slide into criminality was started by a pupil being an unauthorized absentee. The assumption appears to be that there is some causal link; that the idle hands of the truant turn too often to crime. The research evidence reviewed suggests that there is a link, but this is because both have a common cause. Low-ability young people from poor social circumstances are more likely to be unauthorized absentees and be, or become, known criminals. There is little evidence that, on their own, lengthy periods of unauthorized absence are predictive of habitual criminality.

Schools can have a positive effect by protecting some pupils from trouble. The more troublesome the pupil is the less the school can do. Schools can also fail to protect pupils and some may make difficult situations worse. Chapter 4 will consider what schools can do to improve their protective performance in relation to unauthorized absence. Before this, however, consideration needs to be given to the legal context of unauthorized absence. Pupils, parents, teachers, schools and the LEA all operate within the constraints and opportunities of the law, and these have a considerable effect upon what can be done; these issues are considered in the next chapter.

## CHAPTER 3

The Management of the Legal Obligation to Attend

> The pressure of some thirty amending acts has eroded the foundations of the 1944 Act, which could scarcely have been expected to survive the addition of a penthouse, the Education Reform Act 1988 . . . more extensive than the foundations themselves, which crumbled under the added weight of an even heavier burden, the Education Act 1993.
>
> (Liell *et al.*, 1997, p. A3)

This chapter reviews the legal duties which LEAs and schools have to perform in relation to attendance and how they both carry these out when seeking to enforce attendance. These duties have their origin in the Education Act, 1944, itself massively amended, and which, as predicted above, finally collapsed taking the 1993 Act with it. From that collapse came the Education Act 1996. That new Act brought together all elements of legislation remaining in force with only minor drafting amendments; consequently it was not debated and had the agreement of all major political parties (Hansard, 1996, p. 657).

This chapter is divided into three sections. The first section considers the relevant duties of the LEA (or the Funding Agency where one exists), including a brief introduction to the duty to enforce attendance. The second section considers the relevant duties laid on the school. The third section considers in detail the requirements laid on the LEA by statute and regulation when carrying out its enforcement function.

Section 1: Duties of the LEA (or Funding Agency)

The following duties relate directly, or indirectly, to absence and unauthorized absence.

Duty to provide schools

Under section 14 of the Education Act 1996 it is the responsibility of an Education Authority to 'secure' sufficient schools to meet the needs of the area served by the LEA, so that parents can discharge their duty to have their child of compulsory school age educated. This should not be taken to mean that the LEA must educate children in accordance with parents' wishes by meeting every demand that might be made. The schools 'secured' by the LEA must 'prepare the child for life in a modern civilised society' and 'enable the child to achieve his full potential' (Liell *et al.*, 1997, p. B2050). A parent who believes that a local authority is in breach of its duty should complain to the Secretary of State under the provisions of section 497 of the Education Act 1996 (p. B2067).

The LEA may fulfil its duty by either establishing schools itself, or by maintaining schools established by others (Education Act 1996, section 18). These schools must be sufficient in number (section 14(2)) to cater for the children of the area, and must be able to develop the particular and varied abilities and aptitudes of the individual pupil. This duty includes the provision of schools catering for children with special educational needs. Parents have the right to expect the LEA to provide sufficient schools, offering appropriate teaching methods, so that they can state a preference for the school that they consider best meets the needs of their child (section 14(3)). However, the LEA 'is not bound to provide education in accordance with parental preference if it would prejudice efficient education or the efficient use of resources' (Clarke *et al.*, 1993, p. F4).

Under the Education Act 1996 these duties can be carried out by the Funding Agency acting in collaboration with the LEA (section 27(1)(a)), or by the Funding Agency alone (section 27(1)(b)).

Duty to enforce attendance

It is the LEA's duty to ensure that the parent complies with his duty under section 7 of the 1996 Act. 'Proceedings for school attendance offences may be brought only by an LEA' (Liell *et al.*, 1997, p. A15). This duty is not extended to the Funding Agency. It follows that the enforcement of attendance is the sole responsibility of the LEA in relation to all the schools in its area (private, grant maintained, independent, or whatever), whether or not the Funding Authority has control of the schools, school provision and meeting parental preference. The process of enforcing school attendance is discussed in detail later.

Duty to make arrangements for admissions and for appeals

The LEA has the duty to make arrangements so that parents can express their preference as to the school their child is to attend (Education Act 1996, section 411). Under the provisions of the *Updated Parent's Charter* (DfE, 1994b, pp. 9 and 10) parents have a right to state the school they prefer their child to attend, and their child has a 'right to a place in the school you want unless all the places at the school have been given to pupils who have a stronger claim to a place in that school'. In considering applications for school places the LEA cannot favour children living within its area as against children living outside its area (*R.* v. *Bromley London Borough Council*, ex-parte *C* (1991)).

Where the LEA and the Funding Agency share responsibility, or where the Funding Agency operates alone, then the Education Act 1996 (section 430) provides for the Secretary of State to approve schemes agreed between schools 'for the purpose of co-ordinating arrangements for admitting pupils to the schools concerned'.

These duties are described because it is possible that parents who fail to get their choice of school could withhold their child from attendance pending appeal, thus breaking a pattern of regular attendance. Also it is possible that exercising the right of choice, and the right of appeal, can be used as a ploy to delay prosecution for non-attendance. In either case if the parents' action in withdrawing their child is held by the LEA or the courts to be unreasonable they may be found to be in breach of their duty to educate their child. But the grounds for their choice, and for any appeal, need not be reasonable. The court has ruled that the LEA must consider a parent's application for admission even if the LEA does not approve of the reasons given. The parent's reasons can be bad or unlawful, but the LEA must consider them (*R.* v. *Cleveland Council*, ex-parte *Commission for Racial Equality*, Macpherson, J., 18 October 1991, 91 LGR 139).

In cases where parents do not have a child placed in the school of their choice, and unreasonably withhold the child from registering with a convenient school, the LEA may specify a school at which the child must attend under the provisions of section 438(2), or section 441(2), of the Education Act 1996.

> This ... is intended to ensure that there is a means of resolving the increasingly frequent cases where children are held away from school by their parents because they cannot obtain a place at a school which they want.
>
> (Morris *et al.*, 1993, p. 76)

Parents do not appear to have the right to appeal against the LEA's specification of a school. However, the school named by the LEA to accept the pupil has that right under section 439 (7) of the Education Act 1996 to seek 'direction' from the Secretary of State which is in effect a form of appeal, but the process is likely to be 'cumbersome and protracted' (Morris *et al.*, 1993, p. 77).

Duty to publish information as to schools and admission arrangements

> LEAs have a duty to publish detailed information about their policies, and information must also be published about individual schools. It should be made available free to parents and prospective parents. Regulations set out a detailed list of the categories of information that must be provided by the schools. There are further

duties to provide information on the curriculum and syllabuses. Heads must ensure that the LEA's and school governors' policies on the school curriculum are available.

(Education Rights Handbook, 1987, p. 31)

The LEA's duty to publish information on policy stems from section 29(5) of the Education Act 1996, and on admissions from section 414 of that Act.

The governors of grant maintained schools are required to provide annual reports that are available free to those who enquire at the school (schedule 23, para 7 of the Education Act 1996). The information so published will provide some of the information on which parents will exercise their right to choose a school; see the *Updated Parent's Charter* (DfE, 1994b, pp. 3–8). It is included here for two reasons. First, it is fundamental to the process of choice described. Second, from November 1993 and each year thereafter, parents were able to obtain information on the rates of unauthorized absence experienced by the school their child attends. Parents may also request information on the attendance rates of all the schools to which they may consider sending their child. This additional information, not previously made widely available, is intended to help parental choice. Such information can help in stating the initial preference for a school, or when exercising their right to move their child from one school to another. Information on the rates of unauthorized absence might influence some parents to remove their child from a school if they consider the rates to be too high.

Duty to provide transport

In order that parents are not prevented from exercising their duty to educate, the LEA must make arrangements for the provision of free, supervised, 'non-stressful' transport as is considered necessary (Education Act 1996, section 509).

Duties in respect of special educational needs of pupils

The LEA, or the Funding Agency, has the duty to see that educational provision is made for pupils who have special educational needs (Education Act 1996, section 321) in accordance with the Code of Practice issued by the Secretary of State (Education Act 1996, section 313). The Education Act 1996 requires that the LEA retains its responsibility for keeping its own provision under review in consultation with the Funding Agency, if appropriate (section 315). Both the LEA and the Funding Agency may provide education in ordinary schools where this is possible (section 316). The LEA, but not the Funding Agency, may arrange for special education otherwise than in school if it appears appropriate (section 319). The Education Act 1996 requires LEAs to provide the mechanism for identifying, assessing and maintaining statements of the special educational needs of all of the children in its area (sections 321, 323, 324), for dealing with appeals (sections

325 and 326), and for reviewing statements (section 328). The LEA will retain these duties even if all the schools in its area are the responsibility of the Funding Agency.

The arrangements for special educational needs are relevant for two reasons. First, in Chapter 2 it was shown that non-attendance by children of low ability enrolled at ordinary schools was high. Second, since the introduction of the provisions for special education in 1981 'attention has tended to focus on the 2 per cent of the school population who have statements and the statutory procedures that follow this' (DES circular 22/89 (as amended) quoted in Liell and Saunders, 1993, p. E1203). However, mainstream schools, and the LEA, are responsible for providing for the special educational needs of children for whom no statement has been made. 'Schools should publish information for parents indicating their special support provision for children with SEN, but with no statements' (Liell and Saunders, 1993, p. E1203). Evidence presented in Chapter 2 suggests that these children may have high rates of unauthorized absence, and a need for special provision. This issue is taken up again in Chapter 4.

Duty to make special arrangements for education otherwise

Under the provisions of the Education Act 1996 (section 19), LEAs have a duty to make special arrangements for education to be provided otherwise than at a mainstream school if a child can not attend school for reasons of illness, exclusion, or otherwise. This special provision is called a 'Pupil Referral Unit' and is a school in its own right. This duty is specific to the LEA and cannot be laid on the Funding Agency.

This duty makes it possible for all parents whose children face exceptional circumstances to discharge their duty under section 7 of the Education Act 1996. The introduction of these units is of interest to this study since they may well be used to provide education for pupils who do not attend school regularly. Further consideration is given to these units in Chapter 4.

LEAs' duties in relation to work

There are two quite distinct duties for the LEA within this category. The first is a general duty 'to arrange work experience for pupils in the last year of their compulsory attendance at school' (Education Act 1997, section 560). Such a duty is considered here only in so far as it relates to the relevance of the final year curriculum to pupils who are unlikely to achieve academically, and among whom there are increasing levels of unauthorized absence.

The second duty is to regulate the employment of children of compulsory school age. The LEA has the power to impose restrictions on pupils under the Education Act 1996, section 559, and its own bye-laws. The 1996 Act allows the LEA to judge whether the employment of a child who is a registered pupil is detrimental to their education, and to prohibit that employment if so judged. Children under 13 cannot be legally employed either part or full time (Children and Young Persons Act, 1933, section 18(1)). Children have to be licensed by the LEA to take part in public performance (Children and Young Persons Act 1969, section 37). The importance of the issue of enforcing attendance and thereby removing the earning power of some children was considered in Chapter 1.

Section 2: Duties of the school

The law lays the following duties on schools in relation to the regulation of attendance and the identification of absence and unauthorized absence.

Admissions registers

The boards of governors of county, voluntary and grant maintained schools and managers of other schools are required to keep an admissions register and (except for schools in which all pupils are boarders) an attendance register under the provisions of the Education (Pupil Registration) Regulations 1995. The contents of the admissions register and the way that it is to be kept are laid down in regulation 6. The admissions register is the source of information as to whether a child is registered at the school. Regulation 9 lays down the grounds on which a child's name is to be deleted from the register. These grounds include obvious reasons such as a move to another school or area, or death, or on ceasing to be of compulsory school age. Reasons of greater significance to the concerns of this book are:

- any changes to the requirements of a school attendance order which result in a move to another school or alternative education provision (regulation 9(1)(a))
- following notification by the parent that the pupil is receiving education otherwise than at school (regulation 9(1)(c)); following removal of the name from the register the school must notify the LEA (regulation 13(3))
- when a pupil who has been given leave of absence for a holiday fails to return to school within 10 school days following that holiday and the school is satisfied that the absence is not due to illness or other unavoidable cause (regulation 9(1)(e))
- that the school medical officer has certified that the pupil 'is unlikely to be in a fit state of health to attend school before becoming legally exempt from the obligation to attend' (regulation 9(1)(f))
- that the pupil has been continuously absent for more than four weeks, and neither the school nor the LEA have been able to locate the pupil (regulation 9(1)(g))
- that the pupil has been permanently excluded from the school (regulation 9(1)(k)).

Attendance registers

The school's duties in relation to maintaining the attendance register are as follows:

> There shall be recorded in the Attendance Register at the commencement of each morning and afternoon session the following particulars:
> (a) the presence or absence of every pupil whose name is entered in and not deleted from the Admissions Register; and
> (b) in the case of any such pupil of compulsory school age who is absent, a statement whether or not his absence is authorised in accordance with paragraph (3).
>
> (Education (Pupil Registration) Regulations 1995, section 7)

Paragraph 3 gives the reasons for authorizing absence as:

- having leave of absence given by the school
- sickness, or other unavoidable cause
- keeping a religious festival
- the school is not within walking distance and the LEA has failed to make suitable transport arrangements
- the pupil is attending another school at which they are registered.

Paragraph (4) of the regulations makes it clear how the attendance register should be completed in situations of uncertainty as to the reason for absence:

> Where the reason for a pupil's absence cannot be established at the commencement of a session, that absence shall be recorded as unauthorised until the person with responsibility for completing the register has ascertained that the absence was authorised and has amended the register accordingly.
>
> (Liell *et al.*, 1997, p. D5963)

These two paragraphs require the person completing the register to determine whether or not the absence is authorized, either at the time of taking the register or as soon after as possible. Thus the school has the final responsibility for deciding how to classify the absence and recording that decision in the register.

Duty to determine legal absence

The acceptable reasons for not attending school which make the absence authorized are given above. The regulations do not state what action the person completing the register is to take in deciding whether the absence is authorized or unauthorized, but some advice is given in DES circular 11/91 which leaves the final decision to the common sense of the school management.

In relation to absence 'for sickness or other unavoidable cause' it appears to be the parent's duty to inform the school of the reasons, but it is the school that judges the validity of those reasons (DfE, 1994, p. 4).

Annual holiday in term-time may be requested by the parent and granted by the school (generally two weeks in any year except under exceptional circumstances (Education (Pupil Registration) Regulations 1995, regulation 8, paragraph (4)). Leave of this sort is discretionary and the decision to grant it is entirely the responsibility of the school. Leave can also be given by the school in order for the pupil to attend employment for work experience, or take part in approved public performance (regulation 8(2)).

The foregoing reasons for absence are legally sanctioned; other reasons, such as leave prior to public examinations or absence following the death of a relative, are examples where 'schools might reasonably exercise discretion' (circular 11/91, paragraph 24). The temporary closure of the school by the LEA for good reasons resulting in the absence of the pupil is a further form of authorized absence (*Meade* v. *London Borough of Haringey*, 2 All ER 1016, 1979).

Duty to inform the LEA of absence

The school has a duty under the Education (Pupil Registration) Regulations 1995, regulation 13 to provide information to the LEA on any pupil 'who fails to attend regularly or who has been absent from school for a continuous period of not less than ten school days', giving the cause of absence if known.

Duty to keep records

The school must keep the admission and attendance records in ink (regulation 14) or computer printout (regulation 16(5)), and bind them in a single volume for each year and keep them for three years (regulation 16(4)). Schools may maintain their admission register and their attendance register on computer (regulation 16(1)).

Duty to publish information

Schools have a duty to publish information on unauthorized absence occurring in the preceding three terms in their prospectuses and annual reports (Education (School Information) Regulations 1981, as amended, and Education (School Curriculum and Related Information) Regulations 1989, as amended).

Comment

From the points so far considered it appears that the LEA will retain its current responsibilities for dealing with attendance matters, regardless of who has management responsibility for the schools in the area. It is very likely that the LEA's responsibilities will be undertaken by their Education Welfare Departments. As more and more schools become grant maintained and become the responsibility of the Funding Agency, so good collaboration between the Agency and the LEA will have to be established. For example, grant maintained schools will have to keep the LEA informed on pupils' absence, but it will be for the LEA to enforce their attendance through attendance orders or court action. One way of dealing with non-attendance could be for such pupils to enter an LEA referral unit. In these circumstances the LEA could be seen as having to make provision for the grant maintained school's failures. In order for the system to work well, high levels of co-operation will be required.

Attention now turns to the enforcement of attendance by the LEA.

Section 3: The LEA's enforcement of school attendance[1]

The decision-making process of enforcement of school attendance by the LEA is outlined in Figure 3.1. The figure has been compiled from various sources and is laid out in the form of a decision flow-chart representing the framework within which legal decisions have to be made. The processes described are complex and changing and subject to alteration as new regulations are issued; the figure includes changes resulting from the passing of the Education Act 1996, much of which was implemented on 1 November 1996. Each of the numbered boxes that appear in Figure 3.1 are discussed in turn below, starting with box 1. For ease of reference the sentence that appears in each box is repeated as the section heading.

1   Is the child of compulsory school age?

The Education Act 1996, section 8, makes education compulsory for all children from their fifth birthday to the age of sixteen. Determining the actual date at which compulsory education ceases depends upon when the sixteenth birthday falls in relation to the school-leaving date; section 8(3) specified the relationship between the birthday and the school-leaving date but did not specify the school-leaving date: that remained to be determined by regulation. Subsequently the Education (School Leaving Date) Order 1997 provided that regulation and set the leaving date as the last Friday in June for 1998 and onward. Therefore a pupil ceases to be of compulsory school age if he or she becomes sixteen on that Friday, or in the period from then to the beginning of the next school year. If the birthday falls at any other time then they remain at school until the next leaving date; it follows that some pupils will cease to be of compulsory school age at 16 years and nine months.

It is self-evident that if a child is not of compulsory school age then enforcement of attendance is not possible.

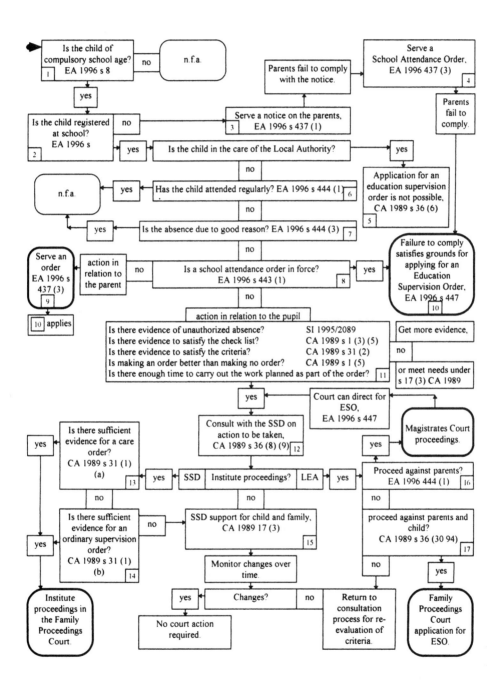

Figure 3.1 The enforcement of school attendance

2   *Is the child registered at school?*

A parent does not have to register their child with a school, nor is there any requirement laid on the parent to notify the LEA of their child's existence, or of their reaching compulsory school age. If the parent does not register the child then the LEA has the power to enquire of the parent what provision is being made, and the parent will have to prove, to the satisfaction of the LEA, that the child is receiving suitable full-time education by some other means. Most parents send their children to school.

> For nearly all parents the only practicable method of complying with their duty to cause their children to receive education as required by (*law*) is to cause them to be registered as a pupil at a school which provides suitable education.
>   (Clarke, Hall and Morrison, 1993, p. F/2)

If a child is not registered at a school, and in the opinion of the LEA is not receiving suitable education by any other means, then the LEA has the power to begin the process of enforcement. In so doing the LEA would be prudent to enquire into the reasons for the parent's actions, but all the law requires at this stage is that 'it appears' that the parent is failing in their duty (Education Act 1996, section 437(1)). The first stage of enforcement is for the LEA to . . .

3   *. . . Serve a notice on the parents*

This requires the parents to satisfy the LEA that their child is being educated. If the parents fail to comply with the notice, then the LEA may serve a school attendance order.

4   *Serve a school attendance order*

If the parents fail to comply with the notice, or if their reasons are considered insufficient, then the LEA can serve a school attendance order on the parent specifying a school that the child must attend (section 437(3)). That order is an administrative order which does not require court action. The Education Act 1996 allows parents some choice of school in this process (sections 438 for a child without a statement of special educational needs and 441 for a child with such a statement). Failure to comply with the school attendance order satisfies some of the grounds for the making of an education supervision order under the Children Act 1989, section 36(1). When hearing a case brought under section 36 of the Children Act the Family Proceedings Court must ensure that the circumstances of the case also satisfy sections 1 and 31 of the Children Act before making an order. Failure to comply with the school attendance order is not the only consideration before the Family Proceedings Court when it hears the case (see 11, below).

5   Application for an education supervision order is not possible

This is the case if the child is in the care of the local authority (Children Act 1989, section 36(6)); however, 'Children in care ... have exactly the same rights to education as other children' (*Education Rights Handbook*, 1987, p. 43), so it follows that all other action described here to enforce attendance can be taken, including the making of an school attendance order and its enforcement in the Magistrates Court. Children in care have the additional right to be consulted about their education (Child Care Act 1980, section 18). A child who is subject to a supervision order made as a result of criminal proceedings can also be subject to an education supervision order; however, in such circumstances the supervision order made as a result of criminal proceedings cannot contain an education requirement (Clark, Hall and Morrison, 1993, p. F/9).

6   Has the child attended regularly?

If a child is a registered pupil at a school (other than a boarder at a boarding school) then the parent has the duty to make sure that the attendance is regular (Education Act 1996, section 444). The law assumes that the pupil will attend on all 380 half-day sessions on which attendance is required and at the time prescribed by the LEA or school. There are special arrangements for the children of a parent 'engaged in trade or business of such a nature as to require him to travel from place to place' (Education Act 1996, section 444(6)(a)). In such cases, if the child has attended as regularly as possible and has made at least 200 half-day attendances then that is sufficient to satisfy the parent's section 7 duty (Education Act 1996, section 444(6)(b)(c)).

7   Is the absence due to good reason?

School records should indicate the reasons for absence including all authorized absences and who authorized them. The authorization of absence is by school staff, not the parent. Absence returns must be made by the school to the LEA regularly and should specify the cause(s) of absence (the Education (Pupil Registration) Regulations 1995, regulation 13). The process of enforcement by the LEA can break down at this stage if the primary evidence is flawed. The categorization of absence is explained in *School Attendance Policy and Practice on Categorisation of Absence* (DfE, 1994).

8   Is a school attendance order in force?

As described in 4 above, a school attendance order may have been in force because the parent did not register their child with a school. It is also possible for an order to be served for unauthorized absence. In either case failure to comply can result in court action in relation to the parent separately (in the Magistrates Court), or the parent and the child together (in the Family Proceedings Court). As noted above, the serving of a school attendance order is not as a result of any court process, nor of any specified enquiry by the LEA. However, since failure to comply with the order may result in court action the evidence on which the LEA issues an order may at some stage have to withstand a test in either the criminal or civil court, and should therefore be based on appropriate admissible evidence.

9   Serve an order

If a school attendance order is not in force then the LEA may decide that one is required. Before serving an order the LEA must serve a preliminary notice in writing on the parent 'requiring him to satisfy them … that the child is receiving … education'. Failure to comply with the notice will result in the serving of an attendance order which will name one or more schools that the child should attend. Attendance orders remain in force 'for so long as the child is of compulsory school age', unless revoked by the LEA or, in subsequent proceedings, the parent is found not guilty by the Magistrates Court, or the Family Proceedings Court decides it cannot make an education supervision order (section 437(4)).

10   Failure to comply

The failure to comply with a school attendance order is an offence under the Education Act 1996, section 443, in that the parent is not satisfying their legal duty under section 7 of that Act and has failed to comply with the school attendance order. Under these circumstances the LEA may apply, or a court may direct the LEA to apply, for an education supervision order. Under certain circumstances described in 11 below the LEA need not comply with the court's direction.

11   Action in relation to the pupil

Any action taken in respect of the child's unauthorized absence from school that relates primarily to the child will be brought under the provisions of the Children Act 1989 and usually heard by the Family Proceedings Court. The court is part of the civil jurisdiction, with court procedures and rules of evidence appropriate to civil proceedings. The evidence presented to the court must show that the child is of compulsory school age, registered at a school, and that as a result of unauthorized absence from that school 'is not receiving efficient full-time education suitable to his age, ability and aptitude and any special educational needs he may have' (Children Act 1989, section 36(1)(3) and (4)). Evidence regarding the amount of unauthorized absence comes from the attendance register and evidence as to the effects of that absence comes from reports supplied by the school and, at the request of the court, any officer of the local authority, or probation officer (Children Act 1989, section(7)). The law does not specify the amount of a pupil's unauthorized absence before court action can be taken.

When considering whether to begin proceedings the LEA must consider the other tasks that the court will have before it. When hearing the case the Family Proceedings Court must have regard to the Children Act 1989, section 1(3) and (5). In effect this means that the court will consider all the important aspects of the child's life as well as school, the amount of any harm being suffered as a result of both non-attendance and other circumstances, the ability of parents or carers to meet all the child's needs, and the wishes of the child. Obtaining knowledge of the child and the family circumstances will be based on information supplied by the child and the family and will require their co-operation to some extent.

The court will also have to have evidence that making an order would be better than making no order at all (Children Act 1989, section 1(5)). The LEA will be required to show that an education supervision order is necessary to ensure that the child receives efficient full-time education. Therefore the court must be given some evidence of what has already been attempted to achieve attendance, and a plan of what will be done under the order that will achieve attendance (see 17, below).

The LEA will also need to consider whether there is sufficient evidence to present to the court that will allow the court to be satisfied that the criteria of the Children Act 1989, section 31(2) will be met. Although this section relates to care orders and supervision orders in general, it is those issues that are relevant to education supervision orders that are considered here. This section only allows the court to make an education supervision order if it believes that the child is suffering, or is likely to suffer, significant harm, and that harm is as a result of the child not receiving the care a reasonable parent would be expected to give. The LEA must have reasonable evidence on these matters before taking action, and must have some prospect of being able to achieve some change that will benefit the child.

It follows from the above that there must be time, after the making of any order, for the order to have effect, and the LEA will have to consider this time factor before taking proceedings against the child. It is evident from the requirements of the court that taking action against the child is a form of 'treatment' of the child, dependent upon the family and the child's co-operation, and not a form of punishment. There was an element of punishment present within the provisions of section 1(2)(e) of the Children and Young Persons Act 1969 which allowed for a child placed under supervision for unauthorized absence and who continued that absence to be taken into care by the local authority. That part of the Act was repealed by Schedule 15 of the Children Act 1989. Supervision orders under section 36 of the Children Act are not a direct substitute for the previous provision and are not intended as punishment.

12   Consult with the SSD

Once the LEA is satisfied that it has the required evidence and can make a reasonable case for the need for and likely success of an order, then the Children Act 1989, section 36(8) requires the LEA to consult the Social Services Department for the area in which the child lives.

> Generally consultation will in fact be with a professional officer of the social services department authorised to act as an agent of the Social Services Committee under the usual arrangements for the exercise of delegated authority. Delay can be detrimental to the child's education. Consultation should therefore be completed as quickly as practicable. The outcome should be confirmed in writing, and should indicate whether or not the social services department are involved with the child and/or the family, and if there are any known reasons why an education supervision order would not be appropriate. Whilst it is a requirement to consult, it does not necessarily follow that an agreement will be reached in all circumstances. Where the social services department are already involved they may require the assistance of the local education authority, who are under a duty to comply with the request in accordance with section 27 of the Act, subject to the conditions set out in that section.
>
> (*Children Act 1989, Guidance and Regulations*, vol. 7, p. 23)

Section 27 provides for the co-operation between authorities, or persons, likely to have an interest in the child so long as that co-operation does not 'unduly prejudice the discharge of any of their functions' (Children Act 1989, section 27(1)).

13   Is there sufficient evidence for a care order?

Following the process of consultation the Social Services Department may decide that there are grounds for applying to the court for a care order. The grounds are set out in section 31(2) of the Children Act 1989 and are 'that the child is suffering or is likely to suffer significant harm which is attributable to a lack of reasonable parental care' (Clarke, Hall and Morrison, 1993, p. F/9). Persistent failure to attend school that is attributable to poor parenting has been held to result in significant harm. If this were believed to be the case the SSD can apply for a child assessment order (section 43), or make an application for a care order (section 31). 'Harm' is defined in such a way as to include the impairment of development, i.e. physical, intellectual, emotional, and social or behavioural development (*O.* v. *Berkshire County Council* [1992] 1 FCR 489). The Social Services Department must have proposals which show that any application is part of a 'carefully planned process' that will promote the welfare of the child (*Children Act 1989, Guidance and Regulations*, vol. 1, p. 20). The court will want information that a care order will result in the child receiving appropriate care that will promote development, and that it cannot be done by making a supervision order.

14   Is there sufficient evidence for an ordinary supervision order?

Either the Social Services Department or the court may decide that the evidence produced requires that some intervention is needed but not the making of a care order. Judgements of this sort are not based on clear criteria, depending in part on the report made by the guardian *ad litem* who will 'make enquiries, establish the child's and others' views, investigate the applicant's plans and prepare a report and recommendations for the court' (*Children Act 1989, Guidance and Regulations*, vol. 1, p. 27). In effect any application to the court may result in any of the disposals available to the court, unlike decisions in criminal proceedings.

15   SSD support for child and family

If the Social Services Department believe that they can meet the needs of the child without application to the court, they are empowered by section 17 and part 1 of schedule 2 of the Children Act 1989, to provide services for the child or the family to that end. Any court proceedings will require evidence of what action has been taken prior to the application to safeguard and promote the child's welfare under this provision (*Children Act 1989, Guidance and Regulations*, vol. 1, p. 20). If provision is made under this section then progress will be monitored over time, including the child's attendance at school and protection from significant harm, and if there is no improvement then court action may result.

16   Proceed against the parents?

Following consultation with the Social Services Department the LEA may decide to take proceedings itself. The decision whether or not to proceed against the parents at this stage will have resulted from these consultations. The process will be as described in 9 above, but the reasons may be different. For example the Social Services Department may already be involved with the family and want action taken against the parents to reinforce some of their work. Or, in a contrasting example, neither the LEA or the SSD may be certain of their evidence for civil proceedings and may decide to offer the case to the magistrates, under criminal proceedings, with a view to the magistrates referring the case for an education supervision order to the Family Proceedings Court.

17   Proceed against parents and child?

The LEA, having consulted, may decide to proceed for an education supervision order. Such proceedings do not require investigation by a guardian *ad litem*, but the LEA must supply a report which relates to the checklist (see 11 above), and includes the following (adapted from the *Children Act 1989, Guidance and Regulations*, vol. 7, p. 24):

(a) the record of attendance over the previous twelve weeks, and in general
(b) the child's background, and educational (including any special) needs
(c) assessment of the reasons for poor attendance
(d) work already undertaken and the need for an order, and
(e) an outline of the intended intervention, and its aims, including how the intervention will improve attendance.

> The report should be prepared in full consultation with both the child and the family. If they disagree with the assessment of the causes of the poor attendance, this should be indicated in the report to the court. The child's welfare is the court's paramount consideration and the report should include relevant information so that the child's needs can be properly assessed together with details of the 'checklist' of circumstances and an opinion as to whether an order is itself prejudicial to the child's interests (section 1). It may also be helpful for the court to be supplied with a report from the child's school assessing educational progress.
>
> (*Children Act 1989, Guidance and Regulations*, vol. 7, p. 25)

Once an order is made it is the responsibility of the LEA to appoint a supervising officer (*Children Act 1989, Guidance and Regulations*, vol. 7, p. 24, para 3.13).

Comment

The framework sets out the major elements of the enforcement process. There are likely to be variations in application between LEAs, and local idiosyncratic applications of the law. What is evident is that the legal process in relation to education supervision orders is complex, time-consuming, possibly expensive and has an uncertain outcome. This may account for the very small number of education supervision orders made. Assuming that the number of serious truants leaving school remains constant at about 18,000 (see Chapter 2), the 314 education supervision orders made in 1994 represent only 1.7 per cent of that total. Action against parents in the Magistrates Court, which is somewhat more straightforward, resulted in 3,688 prosecutions in 1994 (20.5 per cent of the parents of that total) (prosecution data from Hansard, 1997, column 113).

Putting the law into action

Having considered Figure 3.1, attention now turns to the responsibilities schools and LEAs have in implementing the law. These responsibilities are taken from the Education (Pupils' Attendance Records) Regulations 1991 (DES, 1991) and amount to statements of what the government considers good practice. The responsibilities are considered in this chapter since they have a basis in law. Some of the same issues will be returned to in the next chapter.

The schools' responsibilities

So far as the schools are concerned DES circular 11/91 proposes action in three areas: (1) providing information for the public; (2) improving the relevance of education; and (3) responding effectively to any form of unauthorized absence. These issues are taken in turn below.

1 Providing information for the public

Information must be provided by schools on unauthorized absence and published in their school prospectuses and annual reports. The government's intention is that:

> Publication of data on attendance should form part of the process of accountability of individual schools to parents and the wider community.
>
> (DES, 1991, para 19)

Additionally, a pupil's attendance was an element added to their National Record of Achievement from 1992. It is obviously important for the schools to keep accurate data on attendance, and on non-attendance determined as unauthorized, in order to be able to complete these public documents properly. Guidance to schools on the categorization of absence was issued by the DfE in May 1994 in order to help schools deal with 'attendance questions' (DfE, 1994, para 3) 'which are known to cause difficulty for schools' (para 67). It seems very likely that the guidance was intended to bring some conformity to classification so that comparison between schools can be made. From 1993 onward summary information has been collected annually from schools by a contractor on behalf of the DfE/DfEE for publication in national school performance tables.

In addition to the national tables schools are required to publish their own data on unauthorized absence. These should be produced as two percentage figures per term for each year group. The first calculation produces a percentage of sessions missed through unauthorized absence, the second produces a percentage of pupils missing one or more sessions due to unauthorized absence (Education (School Curriculum and Related Information) Regulations 1989, regulation 3). The information published by the DfEE will be an average for each year group over the whole school year. The information, whether for the term or the year, indicates the total amount of unauthorized absence the school experiences as a result of the first calculation, and how confined the problem is as a result of the second. Each school must publish this information early in the autumn term of each year, or if later, at least six weeks before the closing date for admissions.

2 *Improving the relevance of education*

In relation to improving education the government considers that 'the current programme of educational reforms, in particular the National Curriculum, will help to improve school attendance rates' (DES, 1991, para 15). The expectation is that more pupils will be better motivated and so more will attend regularly and willingly. All schools need the education reforms that are being introduced 'to be buttressed by further regulations and guidance on attendance' (para 17). Those schools where unauthorized absence remains a problem will benefit most from the stronger regulations.

3 *Responding effectively to any form of unauthorized absence*

It is within the above context that the circular re-emphasizes the importance of effective systems of control and management in the school. The circular states:

> Schools need to give a high priority to attendance and ensure that this commitment is underpinned by effective management systems. The school should convey a clear message to pupils and parents that regular attendance is vital and that unauthorised absence will not be tolerated. All teachers should be appraised of the importance attached to attendance and to dealing appropriately with such matters as lateness and post-registration truancy. The school's senior management should in particular ensure that new and supply teachers are aware of the school's attendance policy and practice.
>
> (DES, 1991, para 36)

The circular suggests that every school should give high priority to the process of registration, have a policy for dealing with lateness, and institute a system of random spot checks throughout the day in order to deter pupils from registering and then not appearing in class. Schools should use their discretion to grant leave sparingly. When unauthorized absence is first noted the parent should be contacted by the school and, if that produces no change, the school should seek the help of an Education Welfare Officer.

Appendix 2 of circular 11/91 gives detailed guidance on the design and marking of attendance registers; this and the guidance given in part 2 of *School Attendance: Policy and Practice on Categorisation of Absence* (DfE, 1994) provide explanations for the categories of absence. Both are an attempt to standardize the completing of registers across England and Wales. Both documents were updated by the Education (Pupil Registration) Regulations 1995, which require that unexplained absence should be recorded as unauthorized until discovered otherwise.

Appendix 2 of circular 11/91 proposes a way of marking the register with symbols to distinguish different forms of absence which schools might consider using. It identifies many of the legal and commonsense reasons for authorized absence. However, it fails to suggest a symbol for absence due to lack of provision of transport (a reason for non-attendance recognized by primary legislation as lawful) or a symbol to indicate absence due to closure of the school (also lawful). The DfE guidance (DfE, 1994) fails to resolve these issues.

There was evidence from my research that, notwithstanding the existence of circulars and guidance in operation at the time, decisions by staff as to the reasons for absence, and how to record them, remained idiosyncratic to the teacher or the school. Generally teachers had little time or inclination to devote resources to finding out the reason for absence of a pupil whose attendance was generally good. Much more effort was put into investigation and treatment of a pupil who had been discovered to be a 'selective' truant. A detailed consideration of the findings is presented in Chapter 5.

Putting the law into action: the LEA's responsibilities

The LEA's duty in relation to the provision of schools and the responsibility to enforce attendance has already been considered. Most LEAs arrange that many of these functions are carried out by a section of the Education Department called the Education Welfare Service, or Education Social Work Service. Chapter 1 described the origins of that service, and Chapter 4 gives information on the work of the present-day services. The government, in circular 11/91, suggests the following tasks for these services:

> 1   The principal function of the Education Welfare Service (EWS) is to help parents and LEAs meet their statutory obligations on school attendance. The EWS is the attendance enforcement arm of most LEAs. Its officers are able to bring to the assistance of schools a wide range of skills. Through their home visiting, they may be especially well placed to assess a non-attender's problems in the wider family context. Schools should develop an effective working relationship with Education Welfare Officers (EWOs) based on a clearly delineated division of labour.
> 2   The EWS should always give the highest priority to securing satisfactory rates of school attendance. The service needs to deploy its resources so as to meet that objective and to be ready to call in other specialists when appropriate.
>
> (DES, 1991)

There are no government directives as to how the services should be organized, or staffed, or what qualifications the staff should have. Although the services remain a mandatory exception (SI 1995/178 para 3(e)), with their costs being taken from the General Schools' Budget prior to resource allocation to schools, the amount spent on the services depends upon local, not DfEE, decision. HMI stated 'Different LEAs have very different policies for the deployment and priorities of their EWS' (DES, 1989a, p. 30) and OFSTED reported that the type of work and workload 'varied considerably in scope and size between LEAs' (OFSTED, 1995, p. 1). Services are therefore likely to reflect local need and local practices, stemming in part from determination of priorities by local elected members. The degree to which the service is involved with enforcement will vary from LEA to LEA, and the advice in DES, 1991, or DfE, 1994, may not be followed. The result is that there is no national standard of service provision. As schools admit pupils from wider catchment areas they will be faced with the need to develop effective working relationships with EWOs from different LEAs, each with their own way of working.

DES 1991 does not make mention of the possible involvement of the EWS in work related to the Children Act 1989, particularly as it relates to section 36 (discussed above). In many but not all cases the staff undertaking the work will be EWOs. The situation is described in the *Children Act 1989, Guidance and Regulations*, vol. 7:

> 3.13   The Act does not prescribe the most appropriate supervising officer. This may be an education welfare officer or an education social worker who may already be known to the child and the family, and who is in a good position to deal with any educational issues which arise in such cases. . . . If local education authorities use an education welfare officer as a supervising officer . . . they should consider whether the officer is suitably qualified, by training or experience, and can command the confidence of the court. A professional social work qualification as recognised by the Central Council for Education and Training in Social Work would provide one indication that the supervising officer possesses the necessary skills and knowledge. Local education authorities should ensure that they provide capable supervising officers.
>
> (*Children Act 1989, Guidance and Regulations*, vol. 7, p. 24)

The circular indicates an enforcement role for the EWS, which includes the prosecution of parents under criminal law if their children are absent from school without authority. As was described above, action taken under the Children Act is within the civil jurisdiction, and is intended to help the child and the parent(s) by an agreed and collaborative 'treatment'. These two roles are not in conflict with each other, but they do have the potential for misunderstanding by the school. The school might reasonably expect an education supervision order to be part of an enforcement process. That is not what the Family Proceedings Court intends when making the order: the prime focus is on helping the child. Non-compliance with an education supervision order results in a request for investigation by the Social Services Department to 'consider whether it is appropriate for them to take action to secure the welfare of the child' (*Children Act 1989, Guidance and Regulations*, vol. 7, p. 27). That investigation can lead to a decision for no further action, in which case the LEA may apply for the discharge of the education supervision order (Children Act, schedule 3, para 17(1)). The circumstances described above may not appear to be enforcement to the school involved.

A further source of misunderstanding can come from the focus of work undertaken by the supervising officer. It is possible that the 'treatment' plan put to the court and agreed with the parents and the child does not have improving attendance as its most immediate priority. Family and personal difficulties may have to be resolved before attendance improves. During these early stages there may be no improvement in attendance, perhaps not what the school hoped for and something that does nothing to improve its statistical returns.

This chapter has considered the response to absence from a legal perspective during a time of legislative change; however, these changes may have been more administrative than fundamental. The general intention of previous legislation in relation to absence appears to have been consolidated and reinforced, not radically altered.

Recent legislation has also had an effect on the ways in which schools are managed, allowing more discretion to governors and senior staff. This could provide an opportunity for schools to think again about how they can stimulate and motivate their pupils. As will be shown in the next chapter, some suggestions have been made that could help to reduce some schools' levels of unauthorized absence by making the school more stimulating on the one hand, and more responsive to individual needs on the other.

Note

1   Section three appeared in amended form as 'Enforcement of school attendance: a critical path analysis', *Education Management and Administration*, vol. 24, Jan. 1996, London, Sage.

## CHAPTER 4

Approaches to Dealing with Unauthorized Absence

In this year also (1898) a list of the ten most regular attenders during the year was issued. Managers reminded parents that regularity might be called the fourth 'R' and that unnecessary irregularity proved a real hindrance to the teachers. Robert Allen had made the record number of attendances – 401 out of a possible 408.
(excerpt from *Clifton-on-Dunsmore, a Warwickshire Village in the 19th Century*, p. 12, Clifton-on-Dunsmore Local History Group)

The purpose of this chapter is to review source material on how schools and other agencies might approach the problem of dealing with attendance and unauthorized absence, and what might motivate pupils to maintain or improve attendance.

The chapter is divided into three main sections. The first section considers the ways in which schools can be managed so as to reduce the rate of occurrence of unauthorized absence, and the actions that the school can take to deal with unauthorized absence when it does occur. This section uses the report and recommendations of the Committee of Enquiry into Discipline in Schools (DES, 1989) as the main focus for discussion, augmented where necessary by evidence from research.

The second section focuses on those outside services that help schools deal with more persistent cases of non-attendance. In these cases schools have neither the resources nor, as was shown in Chapter 3, the legal powers with which to act. The provision that is reviewed includes the Education Welfare Service, the Education Psychology Service, and Child Guidance and Psychiatric Services.

The third section considers the work of the Social Services Departments in relation to behaviour problems in school and unauthorized absence from school, including reference to the difficulties of co-operation between schools and social workers that have become evident.

Section 1: In-school factors

The Committee of Enquiry into Discipline in Schools, under the Chairman-
ship of Lord Elton, was set up in 1988. It included unauthorized absence
from school and unauthorized absence from classes while in school within its
terms of reference since both

> ... are forms of misbehaviour which are damaging to the pupils involved because
> they hinder their educational progress. They also fall within our terms of reference
> because they affect the progress of other pupils and the atmosphere of the school as
> a whole.
>
> (DES, 1989, p. 165)

The committee made extensive enquiries into all types of misbehaviour and
commissioned research into aspects of discipline, but it did not commission
research into attendance. Even so, the committee's report, published in
1989, states that:

> Many of those submitting evidence to us suggested that standards of behaviour have
> deteriorated in recent years. Our evidence does not show similar perceptions of an
> attendance crisis. ... [The] evidence from individual LEAs and HMI indicates that
> attendance levels have remained fairly stable for at least the last five years, and
> probably for much longer ....
>
> (DES, 1989, p. 165)

Clearly the committee believed that attendance and behaviour in school
were aspects of the same phenomenon, despite having evidence that a
deterioration in one was not matched by a deterioration in the other.
However, as was shown in Chapter 2 there is insufficient evidence to know
whether or not attendance is deteriorating. It is also clear that at that time
the government believed there was a crisis, and that improving attendance
remains a political priority. It is therefore 'fortunate' that many of the
recommendations made to government in the committee's report are relevant to attendance. In many respects Elton sees good discipline and
attendance as having common causes, and indiscipline and absence common solutions. Clearly the committee did not draw on evidence produced in
1988 that 'school effects upon attendance are significantly different from
those upon other outcome variables', such as behaviour (Reynolds, 1996, p.
43, quoting Mortimore *et al.*, *British Junior School Project*, 1988). The committee's view of the origin of good discipline, and by implication good
attendance, was in the contribution they both made to the school's 'atmosphere':

> Visiting different schools left us with the strong impression that the attitude and
> motivation of their head teachers and staff were decisive influences on their
> atmosphere .... Heads manage schools in different ways. Teachers use different
> classroom styles. Schools have different discipline codes and different timetables.
> Research shows that differences in the ways in which schools are run are associated
> with different standards of work, behaviour and attendance among their pupils.

> Rutter suggests that the school atmosphere, which is produced by all these routines
> or processes working together, also has an effect on pupils' behaviour which is
> stronger than the sum of the individual processes.
>
> (DES, 1989, p. 89)

The committee suggests that the routines and processes that contribute to the school's atmosphere are a combination of all the major features of the school:

> These include the quality of its leadership, classroom management, behaviour
> policy, curriculum, pastoral care, buildings and physical environment, organisation
> and timetable and relationships with parents.
>
> (DES, 1989, p. 90)

Since these features contribute significantly to 'atmosphere', each is considered separately below. However, I have given special emphasis to their effect on attendance and absence, and drawn on additional evidence.

Leadership

The quality of management leadership within the school appears to be crucial to its successful operation. The committee suggests that effective leadership of schools has its basis in the ability of the head teacher to combine successfully her or his own personality and management style with activities which provide the school with 'a sense of direction', and 'a sense of security'. Good leadership produces an effective and co-operative team of senior managers, and successful team functioning is 'crucial to a school's success in promoting good behaviour'. Attendance is one among many matters on which the team should focus. They should

> recognise the potentially unsettling effects of any absence, particularly of unjustified
> absence, on the atmosphere of the school, and on pupils' behaviour. They should
> also recognise that the quality of a school's atmosphere and curriculum is an
> important factor in encouraging regular attendance.
>
> (DES, 1989, pp. 166–7)

This statement does not find its way into the committee's recommendations, standing simply as an assertion of good practice based on HMI evidence. Research into effective leadership and management has been undertaken since the committee reported, for example by the Schools Management Task Force Working Party, reported in *Effective Management in Schools* (Bolam *et al.*, 1993). That research confirms many of the elements of good practice considered by the committee. The findings emphasized the inter-relationship of effective management style, good working relationships, positive ethos and clear structures on students' performance and behaviour, including attendance (Bolam *et al.*, 1993, p. 123). What is missing from both reports is evidence of actions that have improved attendance.

Peters and Austin (1985), in describing successful managers' passion for excellence, provide examples from education. They describe the actions of a highly successful American high school head teacher with a passion about attendance which contributed to a sense of direction for the school:

> Mastruzzi is obsessed. His particular fetish is attendance, and it is regularly and visibly demonstrated. As in the private sector, he could be criticized for not having a subtle and sophisticated system for measuring the quality of his service. But ... the energy focused on a single factor makes it a credible indicator of the success of the school's endeavors. ... [He] has a hand-done attendance count given to him once a day, within a couple of hours of the opening of the school. ... His fetish with attendance figures reflects the dual concern for image and essence. High attendance rates are critically important, says Mastruzzi, 'because unless kids come to school they won't learn'. However, he is equally concerned about the appearance of high attendance scores. He believes they are a quick indicator of a school's goodness, a visible and measurable sign.
>
> (Peters and Austin, 1985, p. 399)

Mastruzzi provided the energy at Kennedy High and was supported by his senior staff. Attendance was used as a measure of the success of the school and its management, high attendance scores becoming a matter of public celebration in the school and with parents.

Peters and Austin describe research which shows that head teachers were instrumental in producing change within their schools (p. 397). Research reviewed by Graham supports this view and makes the point that heads cannot produce change unaided:

> where teachers, preferably working in teams, are fully involved in the decision-making process, and expectations are kept at a realistic level, change is easier to introduce and sustain.
>
> (Graham, 1988, p. 49)

The evidence so far considered seems to suggests that any change introduced by managers and staff which is aimed at producing a better atmosphere will have some beneficial effect on standards and therefore on attendance, and that attendance can become a performance indicator of the success of a school. The existence of this link remains firmly entrenched in the mind of government (see for example the white paper *Excellence in Schools*, DfEE, 1997), although the evidence reviewed in Chapter 2 suggests that schools cannot always compensate for individual and family deficits.

Although all of the schools involved in my research sought to improve atmosphere, none reported making attempts to improve atmosphere solely, or primarily, in order to improve attendance. However, one-third of the schools reported introducing some form of individual or group incentive or reward scheme for good or improving attendance, and senior staff believed these schemes to be effective in further improving attendance levels. The effect of these schemes on atmosphere was not tested either by myself or the schools.

The example from America suggests that levels of attendance can be used as a measure of the general quality of service supplied. My research showed that two-thirds of the schools used attendance information in reports for governors. One head teacher made a comment typical of that two-thirds:

> We are required to put it into the prospectus and into the annual Governors' report. I report to the Governors at every meeting on matters relating to pupil welfare. The Governors have not used the data in my time here to target resources. If non attendance were to increase I would advise them that it was something the Governors should know about, and it would be addressed by them by giving it back to the management of the school.

The use of the information in this way allows the school to make comparisons over time, and presumably declining attendance would result in a change in resource allocation. However, the majority of schools appeared to be reluctant to inform parents of changes to attendance, or on action taken to improve attendance, and to compare performance with other schools. Schools did not make the data available as a significant performance indicator, perhaps because many schools are aware that attendance and truancy are, if anything, only weak indicators of performance (Morrison, 1992; Reynolds, 1996).

Classroom management

The Elton committee emphasizes the need for teachers to be trained in 'ways of motivating and managing groups of pupils' by developing the skills of effective classroom management (DES, 1989, p. 12, para 7). These skills include:

> the ability to relate to young people, to encourage them in good behaviour and learning, and to deal calmly but firmly with inappropriate or disruptive behaviour.
> (DES, 1989, p. 67)

The committee appears to be referring to two separate functions of the teacher. The first is that of tutor and model of good behaviour, which is considered in the section below on pastoral care. The second function is that of teacher as pedagogue and it is this function that is considered now.

The committee's report describes the behaviour of the poor teacher who, lacking good classroom control, creates a 'negative' atmosphere with frequent reprimands, threats and sarcasm (p. 68). The report suggests that such a teacher produces disaffection that expresses itself in disruption; the presumption appears to be that this will do nothing to encourage regular attendance, although this is not stated, and the report provides no clear evidence of a direct causal relationship between the performance of a poor teacher and the onset, or maintenance, of unauthorized absence. It is interesting to note that of the forty persistent unauthorized absentees interviewed by Carlen et al. (1992, appendix 1), only two pupils reported difficulties with their teacher as being a factor in the start of their careers as truants. Graham, in his survey of research, says that 'there are very few studies that set out to establish a relationship between disruptive behaviour and teaching methods', but there is a widespread acceptance 'that such methods are influential' (Graham, 1988, p. 28). Tackling the poor performance of teachers is a priority for government and is linked with poor behaviour in the classroom (DfEE, 1997); the link with poor levels of attendance is implicit.

The Elton committee's report does not make the distinction between individual teacher performance and whole school performance when considering solutions to unauthorized absence. Unauthorized absence is seen as an element of whole school discipline to be dealt with through improved regulation and controls (see recommendations 99, 100, and 101, p. 167) and not by improved pedagogic performance. While it is possible to argue that the quality of classroom management may contribute to the atmosphere generated in the school, there is very little evidence of its effect on attendance.

Behaviour policy

The Elton committee made a distinction between having a general behaviour policy, which many schools they visited did not have, and having rules for pupils, which most did have. The committee emphasized the need for a good behaviour policy since it provides guidance for all the school, the staff, pupils, governors and parents; it is not just for pupils. A good policy sets out the expectations of behaviour of all those involved with the school, providing a rationale for the school rules and describing how the rules are developed, changed and applied (DES, 1989, pp. 97–8). The report recommended that the policy should be published; that rules are consistent with the policy and that they should be applied fairly and without humiliation; and that there should be rewards as well as punishment. It made no recommendations concerning the need for a school policy on attendance, and therefore made no recommendations on what rules are required to support such a policy. The examples of behaviour policies given in appendix F of the report (pp. 283–92) do not mention attendance at all. However, the report does make the following two recommendations concerning action by staff in relation to attendance:

> We recommend that senior school staff carry out frequent random checks on individual lessons.
> We recommend that governors should obtain regular reports on attendance, including internal truancy, with a view to encouraging and supporting action by the school.
>
> (DES, 1989, p. 167)

It seems reasonable that the school's behaviour policy and its rules should take account of the way that the school intends to deal with attendance matters, particularly given the importance attached by Elton to the inter-relationship between attendance and discipline.

The main elements to be considered when developing a policy and rules relating to attendance are given below.

Legal rights and duties   It has already been shown in Chapter 3 that schools and parents share the legal responsibilities in respect of school attendance. A restatement of the legal obligations on both would set the context of the policy and its rules within the legal framework. The policy should include the expectation set on all pupils that full attendance is the norm, and that only the school can authorize absence. The reasons for absence recognized by law may need to be made clear for all, and included in the rules (DfEE, 1995).

Monitoring attendance   The policy should state the legal requirements on the school to keep an attendance register, and how this will be done. The rules should state how the register can be inspected and how and when it is to be taken. In secondary schools the policy should include the role and function of the form tutor and the tutor group. The policy may include specific comments on the uses of any electronic registration system. The rules will need to specify what action will follow from late registration and absence following registration. Rules on authorizing absence will be needed, and the ways in which staff of the school will follow up absence if unauthorized (DfE, 1994). The school may decide that letters to parents on both attendance and absence are needed to keep parents informed (DES, 1989a, para 49) and that home/school attendance agreements might be used when poor attendance or unauthorized absence becomes a problem. Its policy on involvement with LEA 'truancy sweeps' may also be included if thought appropriate.

Rewards   The school's behaviour policy may include a scheme for rewarding good behaviour if the Elton committee's recommendations have been implemented. Any such scheme could include rewards for high levels of attendance, given either to individuals or groups. All rewards that are given should be carefully considered in relation to their perceived value through a process of negotiation with pupils (Graham, 1988, p. 33).

Sanctions   There are likely to be two levels of sanction in operation: those used by the school and those applied by the LEA. Sanctions applied by the school for incidents of unauthorized absence should conform to the general policy applied to all poor behaviour. However, a special policy for applying sanctions to non-attenders will be needed since punishments when applied to this group can be self-defeating by increasing the incidence of absence (Reid, 1989, p. 126). The LEA's policy on prosecution should be stated. The expectations laid on the school by the law to provide reports to the Education Committee and the courts on absence and related issues should also be clear, along with the process by which such reports are prepared and discussed with pupils and parents (DfE, 1992a, p. 7).

Help   The policy should indicate the role the school will take in providing help to both pupils and parent when attendance becomes a problem. Rules in this case may not be necessary, but there may be some document that gives guidance on the services provided by the school and by other agencies, and how to contact them. There is evidence from Graham that where high levels of skilled help are available to pupils some improvement in behaviour within the school is likely and pupils have a reduced chance of becoming delinquent (Graham, 1988, p. 37).

Returning to school   A need for a policy 'for receiving back frequent absentees' is suggested by the Elton committee (DES, 1989, p. 167), this should provide guidance to teachers on helping the pupil catch up and on the provision of additional work (DES, 1989a, para 45; OFSTED, 1995b, p. 6).

Information   The policy should make it clear that the school is required to publish information on attendance rates to parents, to governors, and to the DfEE. It may be that the governors, or managers, will want to set attendance targets for the year ahead, together with their proposals for supporting action to attain the targets.

A review of behaviour and attendance policies was undertaken as part of my research. Of the twenty secondary schools involved all had school rules relating to attendance, six had behaviour policies, none had published attendance policies (Collins, 1996a, p. 125). OFSTED reports that having attendance and behaviour policies was the 'exception rather than the rule' (OFSTED, 1995b). It is likely that all schools will be required to have a behaviour policy (DfEE, 1997, p. 55). The effects of not having an attendance policy, or not making it widely known, are taken up again in Chapter 5.

Curriculum

The Conservative government hoped that education reforms would reduce absence.

> The Secretary of State expects that the current programme of educational reforms, in particular the National Curriculum, will help improve school attendance rates. By making education more relevant to modern needs, better geared to the needs of particular groups of pupils and giving a greater role to parents, the reforms should improve opportunity and motivation for all pupils and thereby reduce levels of unauthorised absence.
>
> (DES, 1991, para 15)

The National Curriculum, established by the Education Reform Act 1988, had not been in operation long enough to provide the Elton committee with any evidence of success in reducing misbehaviour or unauthorized absence. It will obviously be some years before the full effects can be known. The evidence of continuing significant rates of unauthorized absence was considered in Chapter 2. Stoll, in a summary of O'Keeffe's findings, reports:

> The reasons for truanting are diverse and complex. The one, however, which was given more than any other is dissatisfaction with the curriculum. The desire to miss lessons is the most powerful motive for truancy especially in the case of post registration truancy. Even more worrying, perhaps, are the lessons truants say they like to miss ... top of the list are the two basic subjects, Maths and English.
>
> (Stoll, 1994, p. 11)

This finding suggests that the reforms may not yet be having the effects the Conservative government wanted. This may be due to some of the early difficulties associated with the introduction of the reforms:

> In reality, the emphasis placed in the National Curriculum on the universal delivery of core and foundation subjects, phased assessment and statutory testing at key stages and ages has not received universal acclaim among teachers, parents and pupils and remains a continuing and unresolved source of conflict.
>
> (Carlen et al., 1992, p. 162)

It may take time for the reforms to be accepted, but in the meantime significant numbers of pupils appear to be absent without legal cause and missing elements of the National Curriculum.

The National Curriculum has the potential to produce particular difficulties in relation to pupils of low ability or attainment. The Elton committee considered that the problem was likely to be most acute in relation to Years 10 and 11, which were considered to be the most difficult group to teach. The committee's report is at some pains to find ways of motivating this group and recommends that the main elements of the National Curriculum should be adapted to meet their needs through the provision of an 'alternative curriculum':

> This often means studying a more limited range of subjects than other pupils. It may also mean more active learning involving practical and problem-solving methods and project work.
>
> (DES, 1989, p. 105)

The report hoped that such provision would improve their attendance at school, and improve their behaviour when in school:

> Since lower achieving fourth and fifth year pupils in secondary schools have the highest rates of absence, we believe that the kind of 'alternative curriculum' approaches designed for this group which we refer to in chapter four may be particularly important in encouraging their attendance.
>
> (DES, 1989, p. 167)

The committee made other recommendations aimed at improving motivation in this group. In essence these were for the school to find ways of praising non-academic achievement, to try to place children in different class groups according to ability, to make sure that low-ability groups received their fair share of good teachers, and to use more 'off-site' learning opportunities.

Missing from the committee's analysis of this group was the negative role played by some low-achieving pupils who become a focus for 'modes of resistance' against the authority of the school (Carlen *et al.*, 1992, p. 156), and as trouble-makers. Evidence from research by Brown suggests that pupils identified both by the school and by other pupils as needing remedial teaching (known as 'rems') may be the focus for trouble within the school.

> The rem within the informal culture of the school ... is not used simply to refer to the pupil's perceived innate abilities, but to their failure or unwillingness to at least try to make something of themselves. ... [The] term rem was almost exclusively reserved for a group of boys adopting a male anti-school subculture.
>
> (Brown, 1987, p. 70)

This group 'deploy the symbolic and stylistic elements of the working class street corner culture in the context of the school' (p. 75) and have 'no regular attendance at school or lessons, indeed are banned from many lessons, finding refuge in certain parts of the school where they are beyond regular staff supervision' (p. 73). It may be that this group cannot be motivated to make something of the schooling on offer. Certainly Brown makes no suggestions for 'in school' action. Perhaps all the school can do is to protect other pupils from the worst effects of the group through a generally agreed and firmly applied behaviour policy as a method of damage limitation.

In my research I enquired whether the schools had taken steps to motivate low-ability pupils in Years 10 and 11 by adapting the National Curriculum, and sought to discover whether such adaptation has resulted in improved attendance. Many of the schools had made some changes within the constraints of the National Curriculum. One deputy head teacher reported attempts common to many:

> We don't have the freedom to set our own curriculum as we did in the past. Certainly part of the general expectation of achievement is to create policies in all faculties so that differentiated work is available within a mixed ability context. Changes can be made to the groupings a child is with, we adjust groups in order to get the best chemistry.

In one school action had been applied to Years 10 and 11 to improve motivation:

> A week before half term was our work experience week, but only half of year ten were out on work experience. Rather than the rest of the pupils having a very disrupted curriculum we created a special curriculum for that week which is about study skills, career choices, and so on. The feedback from the kids was really good. They valued that and got a lot out of it. We have learnt a lot from this as a school. There are lots

of opportunities in Years 10 and 11 for us to take different styles of learning. I sometimes think that it must be the most boring thing in the world to be a year 11 pupil because you go from one sitting lesson to another sitting lesson, potentially. One of the things I want year heads to do is a pupil trail to see what it is like to be a pupil in their year group. That's going to get the messages across to the staff for more variety. Apart from anything else it recognizes that children have different types of competencies and capabilities and you have to play to those.

In all of the schools involved in my study changes had been made for the general benefit of groups of pupils. None of the schools reported assessing whether the changes they had made resulted directly or indirectly in improved attendance for those groups, or whether there had been any effects on levels of unauthorized absence. This lack of analysis was also reported by OFSTED (OFSTED, 1995b, p. 5).

Pastoral care

The Elton committee's report emphasizes that one of the strengths of the British secondary education system is the way in which teaching staff combine the functions of discipline, welfare and pedagogy into an integrated approach to pastoral care, through the mechanism of the tutor group (DES, 1989, pp. 111–12). The committee recommends that this 'integrated' system should continue to be the basis for pastoral care and that schools 'should identify clear aims for the use of tutorial time, and that these aims should include reinforcing the school's behaviour policy' (DES, 1989, p. 113). The report considers that a well-thought-out programme of work for the tutor group will be of benefit to the pupils, providing an opportunity for the tutor to get to know the children individually, and can be used as a way of getting information on the pupil's evaluation of the school (DES, 1989, p. 113).

However, what Elton recommended need not result in an integrated approach. It appears that the form tutor is being recommended to deliver a programme of work which will be additional to the academic curriculum through which it will be possible to get to know the pupils as individuals, discover their views of school, and deal with issues of discipline. This approach appears to ignore the opportunities available to the class teacher to undertake these functions as part of the normal curriculum. Elton did recognize that the class teacher will be responsible for dealing with behaviour problems when they first arise, supported when required by the form tutor (DES, 1989, p. 112), but recommends a process which makes both form tutor and class teacher responsible for the control of pupils, but only the form tutor responsible for their care. The report does not quote any evidence, or research, to support these recommendations, only reporting evidence of the call for better organization of the tutor group: 'HMI comment that there are still too many schools not making good use of tutorial time' (DES, 1989, p. 112).

Evidence from research suggests that the need for a pastoral care system is usually well understood, but that it is sometimes not delivered with the needs of the child coming first. Best *et al.*, in reviewing the results of five years of research into the pastoral care system at one school, say:

> Whatever the level of commitment to the personal welfare of individual children, . . . teachers, when interviewed and observed, behaved as though this was of less significance than the problems of . . . the school as an organisation.
>
> (Best *et al.*, 1983, p. 255)

Galloway, in his review of research, suggests that many schools have not resolved the organizational or functional difficulties of the system. He states that the organization of the pastoral care system is often hierarchical:

> Typically, assistant head teachers responsible for boys' and girls' welfare are answerable to the head. Year tutors, or less commonly heads of house, are answerable to the assistant heads. In their turn, year tutors co-ordinate the work of form tutors. Head teachers would generally agree that the form tutor is the basic unit of pastoral care.
>
> (Galloway, 1985, p. 148)

While this arrangement does make it possible for tutor contact to be made with all pupils, it requires that all the roles within the system are clearly understood and consistently used; unfortunately, this is not always the case (Galloway, 1985, p. 149). Galloway states that although the form tutors may be seen by the heads as the basic unit of the system, this was not how they saw themselves. Many form tutors considered that their time with the group was too short to do anything more than take the register and pass on messages; they did not see it as their responsibility to deal with problems, many believing that these were the tasks of those higher in the hierarchy; and they certainly had little time to get to know the children as individuals. Galloway points out that it is the teacher in the role of pedagogue who gets to know the pupil best and that it is not wise to separate the pastoral function from teaching. He states that 'the best form of pastoral care lies in a carefully planned and well taught curriculum' (p. 150). Galloway's review of the research seems to indicate that the class teacher ought to be seen as the basic unit in the pastoral system, not the form tutor. It also appears that some schools do not allow enough time for form tutors to develop activities for their tutor group, so for some there will be little opportunity to undertake the work recommended to the Elton committee by HMI.

There is some evidence to show that if form tutors and class teachers can act collaboratively then they can have a beneficial effect. Galloway is able to show that in four of the schools he studied for his own research 'pastoral care had contributed to exceptionally low rates of problem behaviour' (p. 152). He states that in these schools:

> Form tutors were expected to know the pupils in their tutor group. They were also expected to be involved in discussions about the management of any pupil who was presenting problems. This meant that if another teacher was having attendance or discipline problems from a child, the first person with whom to discuss these was the

> form tutor. It also meant that the senior staff had to direct their colleagues to the
> form tutor if they were approached directly. In an emergency, of course, senior staff
> could, and did, act unilaterally. Because serious incidents seldom occurred they did
> not threaten the general principle that matters be discussed initially with the pupil's
> form tutor.
>
> (Galloway, 1985, p. 153)

Galloway does not report how it was that the form tutor got to know the
pupils in the tutor group, but it does not appear to have been through a
'structured programme of activities' as suggested by the Elton committee,
and may have been through the more fleeting contact he describes.
Research seems to suggest that an effective system of pastoral care is one in
which the form tutor supports the pedagogic work of the class teacher rather
than producing alternatives. Thus tutor and teacher combine together to
demonstrate the integration of care and control.

Tattum suggests that the successful integration of care and control is not
often achieved in schools. This is because pastoral staff are most often
overtaken by the immediate need for crisis management and are unable to
develop the more positive, and caring, aspects of the pastoral policy (Tattum, 1989, p. 150). The system, however organized, will be most severely
tested by disruptive pupils. 'Disruptive pupils have, more than any other
group, highlighted the inconsistencies in a system that professes concern but
concentrates on control' (Tattum, 1989, p. 151). Reporting research by
others, Tattum suggests that many pastoral tutors appear to spend 'a dis-
proportionate amount of time coping with a few difficult pupils', and have
little time for 'working towards a more constructive caring role' (p. 150). He
goes on to say that in his work with disruptive pupils he has found they
believe that their pastoral tutors did not care for them either as persons or as
pupils being 'harsh, censorious and punitive ... [and] not caring about their
progress and achievement in class' (p. 150). Clearly pastoral tutors are more
at risk of being perceived as controlling by those they have to control, but it
appears that some may not able to demonstrate an element of care at the
same time.

The difficulties that teachers may have in combining care and control are
not confined to them alone. McLaughlin (1989), in considering the way
schools may respond to disaffection, reports a typology developed by Heron
in 1975 in which transactions, termed interventions, between people in all
organizations are divided into 'authoritative' and 'facilitative'. These two
divisions are broken down into subsets shown in Table 4.1.

The authoritative interventions clearly demonstrate control, and the
facilitative ones care. McLaughlin considers that the framework can be used
to analyse transactions within the school (pp. 231–2), in order to determine
what action should be taken to deal with disaffection (p. 240). He says:

> This framework can be a starting point for examining interventions with individuals
> and groups. It emphasises the need to have a repertoire of responses and to tie them
> to an assessment of each particular situation. Heron (1975) makes the general point

Table 4.1 Common interventions in organizations

Authoritative

1 *Prescriptive* This includes giving advice, being judgemental, critical, evaluative. A prescriptive intervention seeks to direct behaviour.

2 *Informative* This involves being didactic, instructing, interpreting. The aim is to impart new knowledge and information.

3 *Confronting* This involves being challenging and giving direct feedback. This intervention aims to challenge a restrictive attitude, belief or behaviour.

Facilitative

4 *Cathartic* This is to do with the release of emotion and tension.

5 *Catalytic* Here the intervention is reflective and encourages problem-solving or aims to elicit information. It seeks to enable learning and self-direction and self-discovery.

6 *Supportive* This is concerned with being approved, confirming and validating. The aim is to affirm the value of the other.

(McLaughlin, 1989, p. 232)

that, in his experience, practitioners in our society show a greater deficit in the skilful use of facilitative interventions than in the use of authoritative ones.

(McLaughlin, 1989, p. 232)

If teachers behave in similar ways to other practitioners, which McLaughlin considers to be the case, then there appears to be a need for them to improve their facilitative, caring, skills. The need for individual teachers and pastoral care staff to develop the caring part of their work by understanding and using basic counselling skills was recommended in the Elton committee's report. These skills are described as 'listening to young people and encouraging them to talk about their hopes and concerns' (pp. 114–15), which is a somewhat limited interpretation of counselling. The use of counselling skills in the classroom is regarded by Tattum as an essential element of effective pastoral care. He suggests that these skills are based on the teacher attitude of 'unconditional positive regard', which means that teachers:

[do] not . . . become saints overnight but that, believing firmly in the essential worth of each pupil, they avoid cynical and denigrating remarks and persist in a pupil-centred rather than a subject-centred response to their problem.

(Tattum, 1989 (quoting Bolger, 1986), p. 153)

In taking this approach teachers may be faced with the need to deal with any conflict between their pupil-centred counselling approach and the subject-centred approach of the National Curriculum. As Tattum suggests (above) this conflict is likely to be greatest when dealing with discipline issues.

The Elton committee says that counselling skills are particularly required by senior pastoral care staff (DES, 1989, p. 144), who, as Galloway pointed out, are more likely to be seeing individual pupils in relation to serious incidents of indiscipline. They too will have the task of resolving any conflicts between the wish to understand through caring, and the school's need to retain control. Given their position in the hierarchy some may feel constrained into controlling (authoritative) rather than caring (facilitative) behaviour.

There are two other elements of the facilitative approach worth considering. The first is to recognize the pupils' ability to carry responsibilities in the school (facilitative, subset catalytic). The second is in developing a reward system for good behaviour (facilitative, subset supportive). Both may be seen as opportunities to encourage the personal development of the pupil, a common goal for the pastoral and academic systems in the school.

The Elton committee reported research evidence that indicated that improved pupil behaviour was associated with pupils' carrying responsibilities appropriate to their age (DES, 1989, p. 142). The report states:

> We recommend that schools should create opportunities for pupils of all ages to take on appropriate responsibilities, and that they should recognise pupils' non-academic performance.
>
> (DES, 1989, p. 15, para 23)

The committee suggests that it is appropriate for pupils' responsibilities to include 'active participation in managing the school community' through involvement in school councils (p. 143), developing the school behaviour policy (p. 144), and training pupils as mediators to help resolve disputes that occur within the school (p. 144). There appears to be no research indicating an association between devolved responsibility and improved attendance.

The importance of giving rewards or providing incentives for non-academic achievement has been recognized for some time. In a review of literature on the subject, Tattum reports:

> Although there are some differences of the perceptions in the research finding there is also considerable agreement about the efficacy of a reward system as an approach to improving pupils' behaviour. Sufficient evidence also exists to guide and encourage those schools who wish to tackle the problem of indiscipline in a positive and constructive way. Rewards also combine the pastoral and academic systems both structurally and in the process by which they are operated. Furthermore, the quality of teacher–pupil relationships should be less fractious and the overall ethos of the school conducive to effective learning.
>
> (Tattum, 1989, p. 157)

The Elton committee sees rewards as entries in the pupil's record of achievement which will specifically include comment on attendance and punctuality (DES, 1989, p. 145). Tattum lists a number of more immediate rewards that are commonly used in schools where high standards of behaviour are known to exist (Tattum, 1989, p. 155). The list may be summarized as follows:

- immediate verbal praise to pupils, either privately or publicly
- written praise to pupils, through merit records, points, or certificates
- any of the above given by a senior member of staff

- public presentation of prizes
- school reports praising good behaviour
- special letters to parents commending good behaviour.

During my research I sought evidence from pastoral staff of the effects of a reward system to motivate pupils to attend. Schools had established a variety of systems, ranging from entries in the individual pupils' Compact record to school-wide systems. An example of a school-wide approach was given by one director of pastoral care:

> I intend to introduce 'traffic lights' to the school. If a kid is in the red zone they are below 80 per cent on attendance, and they will be hit pretty hard on targeting. If they are in the amber zone they have got to be watched because they could go either way. On the green zone, 90 per cent plus, we would consider them pretty safe. If a child transfers from one zone to another upwards, say from red to amber, they would get a reward. Initially it will be a key ring, if they get 100 per cent attendance they will get a mug with the school crest on. And each half term we will raffle off a stereo system. Every child who gets 100 per cent attendance for a week would get a raffle ticket that goes into the draw. Anything that we can do to get the children to be more positive towards the school, and not see it as a prison, we will try.

Learmonth in his analysis of projects funded by the Truancy and Disaffected Pupils GEST scheme reports on the successful introduction of a reward scheme in a Leeds school. This included certificates for attendance, annual reports home, £5 reward vouchers for 100 per cent attendance for a year, commendations and points systems for good and improving attendance, tutor group certificates and public displays of year group attendance levels (Learmonth, 1995, p. 83). That school monitored attendance over time, using it as a performance indicator of the measures adopted, and reporting improved attendance. The 'traffic lights' project intended to undertake a similar evaluation and report the outcome to the governors.

Building and physical environment

The Elton committee reports that, in their view, there is an association between the appearance of the school and the behaviour (and by implication attendance) of the pupils (DES, 1989, p. 115). The Elton committee's recommendations can be divided into two categories: the first relates to the way the existing environment is managed and is considered below; the second is the way in which buildings may be designed, or redesigned, to provide a more easily managed environment (this aspect is outside the scope of this book).

The management of the existing environment can be divided into aspects relating to control and aspects relating to care. In relation to control the Elton committee suggested the following:

- Deliberate damage and graffiti should be dealt with as quickly as possible. The school's behaviour policy should make it clear that

Deliberate damage 'will result in appropriate punishment' (para 117.1).

- It should be made everyone's responsibility to keep the school free of litter (para 117.2).
- Consideration should be given to circulation control in corridors and the need for teachers to have a clear view of pupils in their charge (paras 120–1 and 131).
- Lunch-time supervision should be well managed by properly trained staff (para 137).

In relation to care the Elton committee suggested the following:

- The building should be well decorated and the equipment and grounds well maintained, thus demonstrating care and concern for pupils through care for the plant (para 114–15).
- Movement within the building should be quietened by the use of carpets and other noise-reducing features (para 125).
- Displays of work should be commonplace in the school, with the aim of creating 'an attractive environment, increasing pupils' self-esteem and fostering a sense of ownership of the premises' (para 117.3).

All schools involved in my research appeared to be safe and well supervised. Many of them were undergoing additional building, or adaptation, and displays of work were commonplace. None of the schools had noise-reducing features in the corridors. None of the schools had set out to test what the effect on attendance would be of the changes that were being made. None of the GEST projects evaluated by Learmonth (1995) had used additional finance to improve the environment.

Organization and timetable   The Elton committee considered that it is not possible to be prescriptive about the way that different schools organize their timetables (DES, 1989, p. 119). However, the report considers that there are some ways of organizing the timetable that are associated with behaviour problems and should be avoided. Of particular concern are timetables that:

- require a great deal of movement between classrooms (p. 119)
- do not allow for the time taken to move from one place to the next (p. 120)
- do not allow a mix of activities (p. 120)
- do not take into consideration the level of experience of the teacher in relation to the needs of the class (p. 120)
- do not take account of the views of the teachers on how they should be organized (p. 120).

The Elton committee recommended that the timetable should be constructed to avoid these difficulties as much as possible, and that when known difficulties are likely to occur they are tackled rather than ignored. There was a strong recommendation that locking pupils out of the school, or out of the toilets, as a way of dealing with a known difficulty in relation to supervision, was not continued (p. 122).

During my research I collected data from head teachers on whether changes had been made to the timetable or curriculum as a way of dealing with unauthorized absence. Sixteen heads reported that no changes had been made for that purpose. Of the other four head teachers, one reported setting up special vocational courses for pupils who were 'out-growing the school', another had removed the last lesson on Friday afternoon from the timetable, another had experimented with doing away with the registration period (an experiment that had failed: the school reverted to the previous system), and the fourth had collected all the worst unauthorized absentees into one form group so that all the other form groups in the school were able to compete for attendance prizes on a more equal basis.

Most of the schools had not made any changes to deal specifically with post-registration absence. Those that had reported making changes had made them for the benefit of all pupils. For example, one school had shortened the school day by reducing the lunch break period; this had the side effect of reducing the number of pupils going off site at lunch-time, and was thought to have reduced afternoon absence.

Relationships with parents

The Elton committee saw the schooling process as a co-operative partnership with parents (DES, 1989, p. 133), notwithstanding the fact that the need for the partnership is based on a legal duty. The report emphasizes the need for the school to develop good relationships with all parents, keeping them well informed on all matters (not just when things have gone wrong), welcoming them into school, helping them to be clear about their rights and responsibilities and about school rules (p. 14). The report recommends 'breaking down barriers between home and school' and the careful and well-managed development of PTAs that can be used by all the parents (p. 138). The report suggests that some schools are unwilling to engage with parents because 'teachers' picture of parents is generally very negative' (p. 133). Recent evidence suggests that parents expect to be informed and involved (OECD, 1995, p. 115) and that the government sees collaborative links with parents as a way of improving the education of children and their parents (DfEE, 1997, p. 53).

The Elton committee made few suggestions as to how good communication can be established. However, Woods (1989, p. 191) suggests that there are three principles that are prerequisites to developing a good partnership with parents. These can be summarized as follows:

- respect for individuals and individual difference

- openness, including open access to information
- equality of power.

Woods goes on to suggest that parents need a 'guide to their rights and responsibilities and on how they can help in the education of their child' (p. 197). He also suggests that, for example, schools could arrange regular scheduled parents' evenings (p. 192), or class meetings in which parents of children in a class meet collectively with the class teacher (p. 193), or visits by teachers to the parents' homes (p. 194), as ways of improving co-operation. These and other activities obviously require commitment from all concerned and an allocation of resources which may not always be forthcoming. Research undertaken on behalf of the DES concluded that policy changes were needed if work with parents was to be developed:

> This research has demonstrated the need for a time allocation for work with parents to be available across the age range, and for practical and motivating support to be available. Work with parents needs to become a key element in the school system, incorporated into the changes brought about by the National Curriculum, acknowledged by senior staff and seen as a worthwhile use of time. Schools are working in a climate of dramatic change and need to respond to a variety of initiatives. To ensure progress, work with parents must either be built into practice (which would require policy directives) or specifically resourced.
>
> (Jowett and Baginsky, 1991, p. 144)

The success in establishing effective communication established between parents and schools in matters related to unauthorized absence was one of the main concerns of my research. The findings are presented in later chapters. Suffice to say that there was some evidence of negativity towards the parents of unauthorized absentees, but not as widespread as suggested by Elton. There was evidence of the need for staff to develop their skills in dealing with parents who made themselves, as well as their children, absent. Many staff believed they could break into this cycle of avoidance if they had more time to give to the parents.

Having considered the major features within the school that contribute to its 'atmosphere', and how 'atmosphere' may affect pupil motivation to come to school and make the best use of their time there, attention now turns to those services supplied by LEAs which are intended to deal with the more persistent cases of non-attendance.

Section 2: Services to schools

The Education Welfare Service

The origins of this service were described in Chapter 1, where it was shown that local decisions based on bye-laws were the main determinants of how the services were organized in the early years of compulsory schooling. The more modern context of the services was described in Chapter 3, where it was

Table 4.2 EWS services to schools

- Specific detailed casework in identifying and following up pupils whose attendance was beginning to cause concern
- Working with primary and secondary staff to facilitate transfer and visiting 'new' children's homes to introduce the school
- Assisting parents to obtain scarce nursery placements for those children who were likely to find difficulty in settling at school
- The establishment of regular multidisciplinary meetings to promote preventive action from agencies helping the schools
- Acting as a mediator, co-ordinator or the 'named person' for assessment, appeals and review of children who were the subject of special educational needs statements
- Helping schools to arrange alternative forms of education for persistent non-attenders, including home tuition
- Running groups for potential long-term absentees, and for their parents
- Acting as a source of information and a mediator for children excluded from school
- The development of a consultancy service to staff on child abuse and active involvement in the procedures related to such abuse
- Involvement in preventive programmes on drug and especially solvent abuse
- Involvement in other inter-agency work, mostly as an intermediary, and on occasions personally supervising pupils on court orders

(DES, 1989a, pp. 31–2)

---

suggested that most local education authorities fulfil their legal duties in relation to attendance through their Education Welfare Service. However, in that chapter it was shown that in the absence of any government directives the organization of the service remained to be determined, as in the past, by local decision, that there is no national standard of service provision, and that it is for schools to discover what type and quality of service are available to them locally. Each LEA also has its own policy in relation to the qualifications of those employed within the service (Johnson, 1980, p. 134; Galloway, 1985, p. 88; OFSTED, 1995, p. 3), and the majority have no relevant training in teaching, social work, or other related professions (DES, 1984, p. 29; NASWE, 1990, pp. 1–2; Halford, 1991, para 6; OFSTED, 1995, p. 9). HMI, in their study of eight Education Welfare Services, found considerable variation between the services supplied by, and within, LEAs (DES, 1984, p. 3); however, by 1989 HMI found it possible to determine the most common services available to schools, albeit 'some of them were established on the personal initiative of an EWO as a response to perceived need' (DES, 1989a, p. 31). The most common services available to schools, pupils and parents are given in Table 4.2.

This list of services was produced as a result of a number of surveys and inspections undertaken by HMI over an unknown period prior to 1989. The list is largely but not completely supported by information obtained by Halford during his 1991 postal survey of the Education Welfare Services of 107 of the 117 LEAs in England and Wales. Halford found that services were

Table 4.3 Sample range of intervention by EWS with regard to child welfare

n = 107	frequently or often	seldom	not at all
1 home visiting to interview parents and children	107 100%	0	0
2 offering counselling to children in schools	104 97.2%	3 2.8%	0
3 organizing case conferences and meetings to discuss school attendance problems	98 91.5%	8 7.5%	1 1%
4 working collaboratively with teachers on pupils' problems	97 90.6%	10 9.4%	0
5 interviewing parents and children at office	85 79.4%	19 17.8%	3 2.8%
6 active collaboration with other agencies in work with pupils and their families	85 79.4%	21 19.6%	1 1%
7 providing welfare rights advice to parents and pupils	69 64.5%	36 33.6%	2 1.9%
8 providing group work or counselling to parents and children	53 49.5%	42 39.2%	12 11.3%
9 setting up group ventures for pupils during school holidays	42 39.2%	32 29.9%	33 30.9%
10 involvement with police in truancy patrols	6 5.6%	21 19.6%	80 74.8%

(adapted from Halford, 1991, para 14)

not involved in two of the tasks mentioned by HMI. Services did not report spending time helping pupils during the primary to secondary transfer, nor did any report being involved in seeking nursery provision. Halford obtained some information on the interventions used by Education Welfare Services when they undertook their tasks, something that HMI did not do, and these are summarized in Table 4.3. The interventions were categorized by respondents on a four-point scale (very frequent, often, seldom, not at all). In Table 4.3 the categories 'very frequent' and 'often' have been combined for the sake of clarity, and the table has been produced to give a rank order of the frequency of response in relation to that combined category.

Some of the more commonly employed interventions can be said to require considerable levels of skill if they are to be practised successfully. Counselling and group work skills are needed for interventions 2, 8 and 9, and managerial skills are needed for effective inter-agency work required by interventions 3 and 6. These skills are sufficiently similar to those employed by social workers in other agencies for a minority of EWOs to have changed their title to 'education social workers to reflect ... the range of their skills and tasks' (DES, 1989a, p. 30). In the majority of Education Welfare Services it has already been noted that the skill levels are very variable and that many EWOs may not have been trained to sufficient levels to provide complex interventions. Therefore, no list of service provision should be used as an indication of what is actually available to an individual school. In order to help schools know what is available, Education Welfare Services have been encouraged to describe the services that they offer to all the schools in their area in terms of policy statements and good practice guides (DES, 1989a, p. 32), or to make service level agreements with individual schools which provide clear statements of what will be provided (Collins, 1993, p. 24; OFSTED, 1995, p. 10).

When a school uses the services of an Education Welfare Officer, or an Education Social Worker, then he or she may have to cross the organization's 'boundaries of care' which exist to help protect the school as an institution from the outside world (Johnson, 1980, p. 89). In order for the EWO/ESW to carry out the tasks described above the school has to be prepared to allow for at least four different forms of exchange:

- First, the school may have to provide information on pupils identified as 'at risk' by the pastoral system 'so that preventive action can be taken' (DES, 1989, p. 183).
- Second, the school must have sufficient confidence in the EWO to allow that person to represent the school to parents and outside agencies.
- Third, the EWO needs direct access to class and form tutors, and vice versa, something that HMI found to be unusual (DES, 1989a, p. 33).
- Fourth, the EWO may need to have direct contact with pupils, without that contact being mediated by school staff (OFSTED, 1995, p. 10).

In these circumstances it is not surprising that HMI, in describing best practice, indicated that a well-developed relationship between EWO and school should be based on a good flow of information, mutual trust, clear tasks and procedures, and a formal joint evaluation of the interventions used (DES, 1989a, pp. 33–4). Where these circumstances exist HMI report that 'the effect on attendance rates is most significant' (p. 32).

My research sought to discover whether schools were furnished with clear policy statements and practice guides by the Education Welfare or Education Social Work service that serves them. In all but one school the respondents knew of no such statements. Only one school had negotiated a service level agreement and that was as a result of dissatisfaction with the service provided. The majority of the schools had established an effective exchange of information with their Education Welfare Officer. Many reported that the service they received varied depending on the officer's personality and experience, a finding also reported by OFSTED in their inspection of Education Welfare Services (OFSTED, 1995, p. 10).

The Educational Psychology Service

Just as the Education Welfare Services vary in organization size and task, so do Educational Psychological Services. Galloway, reporting on his study of unauthorized absence in Sheffield, states:

> All local authorities employ educational psychologists. The number of psychologists in any l.e.a. depends not only on the size but also on the generosity and/or priorities of the Education Committee. In Sheffield there has since 1974 been a ratio of one educational psychologist to every 8,000 children of school age. A few l.e.a.s are more generously staffed. Several still expect their psychologists to provide a useful service with a ratio of one to 12,000.
>
> (Galloway, 1985, p. 77)

In relation to task, Galloway reports that educational psychologists spend a large part of their time involved with identifying and assessing children with special educational needs (p. 77). Other tasks include 'identifying problems in school organisation or teaching method' and 'in-service education for teachers' (p. 77). Pik adds to the tasks by including help given to teachers in handling disruptive classroom behaviour (Pik, 1987, pp. 164–5). Some educational psychologists provide individual treatment for unauthorized absentees assessed as needing help to overcome 'school refusal' (Galloway, 1985, p. 79; Carroll, 1996, p. 233). School refusal is a term used to describe an anxiety state existing within the child that results in them being so fearful of attending school that they do not go. Galloway says that this group of pupils accounts for 'probably less than 1 per cent' of all unauthorized absentees, and that referrals for individual psychological treatment of unauthorized absentees vary according to the rates of attendance experienced by schools. In schools with high rates of attendance there is a tendency for higher rates of referral of absentees to educational psychologists. In schools with high rates of unauthorized absence referrals are low (p. 76). Galloway considers that this may indicate different attitudes by referring teachers as to what constitutes normal and abnormal behaviour in the school.

It is clear from the above that educational psychologists, in dealing with unauthorized absence, are most likely to deal with a few individual pupils referred to them suffering from an anxiety state, and who come from the 'neurotic' group (see Chapter 1). The rates of successful treatment in these cases is reported by Galloway as excellent provided:

> (a) the child is pre-adolescent; (b) the child is referred very soon after the problem has started; (c) there are no long-term social problems or particularly complex relationship problems in the family.
>
> (Galloway, 1985, p. 84)

The Educational Psychological Service may have involvement with low-ability pupils who are 'at risk' of being unauthorized absentees as a result of dealing with their special educational needs. The service is involved with the preparation of statements of special educational need (DES, 1989, recommendation 84, p. 152), and such statements can be made for pupils whose difficult and disruptive behaviour in school is the product of emotional and behavioural difficulties (p. 150). Further, the Elton committee suggested that the Educational Psychological Service should have a role to play in the provision of remedial education for disruptive pupils for whom special needs statements are not made (recommendation 85, p. 152). As has been stated previously the Elton committee considered that disruptive pupils can become unauthorized absentees, or cause others to become unauthorized absentees. Therefore, although the committee does not make any recommendations for action by the service in relation to unauthorized absence, there is a role in assessing and providing for special needs that might have an indirect effect on the incidence of unauthorized absence.

Evidence gathered during my research showed that the Educational Psychological Services would only become involved with unauthorized absence if it was associated with other behavioural difficulties. All schools reported that the service was almost completely devoted to dealing with special needs and there was a decreasing amount of time for anything else. As a result there were very few referrals to the service and involvement was limited to offering advice at informal meetings.

The Child Guidance Service

Galloway reports that the Child Guidance Service is normally composed of:

> a social worker, usually seconded from the local social services department, a child psychiatrist employed by the local area health authority and an educational psychologist.
>
> (Galloway, 1985, p. 78)

Galloway reports that referrals are usually made by 'teachers, parents and doctors' (p. 78), and Johnson reports that most services will not accept referrals without parental agreement (Johnson, 1980, p. 158). Galloway says that 'poor school attenders form a fairly small minority of children referred . . . varying from one per cent . . . to eight per cent' (Galloway, 1985, p. 78). Child Guidance teams usually deal with the assessment and treatment of disturbed children and their families (Johnson, 1980, p. 152), where the families are 'motivated to help themselves' (p. 160). Galloway reports only limited success of treatments employed by Child Guidance teams. This may be because treatments tend to be isolated from the child's social environment because schools are not always willing to be involved, and because the teams themselves have made themselves too remote from the school (Galloway, 1985, p. 87).

None of the respondents questioned for my research used the Child Guidance Service to deal with pupils whose primary problem was unauthorized absence.

Pupil Referral Units

Pupil Referral Units are schools established and governed by LEAs under the Education Act 1996, section 19 to provide education for children of compulsory school age who for various reasons cannot attend ordinary school. PRUs take pupils who have a history of 'intermittent schooling and fragmented educational history' which includes attendance problems (OFSTED, 1995a, p. 8). Schedule 1 of the Education Act 1996 regulates the operation of the units. It requires the delivery of a broad and balanced curriculum (section 6(2)), but it does not require them to deliver the National Curriculum. PRUs were brought into being by the Education Act 1993, the basis for their development being the wide range of 'off-site' provision already provided to cater for those pupils withdrawn from mainstream schooling prior to the 1993 Act. Galloway, commenting on the growth in the number of withdrawal units in the 1980s, says:

> Some have been established by the l.e.a. to cater for pupils from several schools. Others have been set up by individual schools, to cater for their own pupils. The initial aims of both on-site and off-site units sound eminently reasonable. A few have catered specifically for poor attenders. A large number have catered principally for disruptive pupils, many of whom have had a record of absenteeism. They generally aim to admit pupils who cannot cope with pressures in the school's mainstream or who cannot be tolerated in the mainstream, hoping that after a period in the unit they will return to the mainstream, attending regularly, without disrupting classes.
>
> (Galloway, 1985, p. 161)

Graham suggests that 'on-site' provision is generally more successful in reintegrating pupils than 'off-site' provision (Graham, 1988, p. 39). However, he reports that 'on-site' units may well have the effect of labelling individuals and increasing their chances of being stigmatized, isolated and excluded from the main school (p. 40).

In relation to 'off-site' units, the precursors of PRUs, Graham reports that they:

> enable pupils to make a clear break with their school, enabling a fresh start. With their favourable teacher/pupil ratios, flexible curricula and resources for intensive counselling, they allow teachers considerable freedom to develop new and exciting educational techniques and opportunities, which may provide benefits for staff and pupils alike.
>
> (Graham, 1988, p. 40)

Graham reports that the disadvantages of these units are amplifications of the same disadvantages as the 'on-site' units, with the additional difficulty of the curriculum being so different from the mainstream as to make reintegration a great deal more difficult (pp. 40–1).

OFSTED, in a largely critical report on inspections of twelve 'off-site' PRUs set up under the Education Act 1993, commented on low pupil attainment, low expectations, poor support from LEAs, limited success in reintegration and some very high rates of unauthorized absence (OFSTED, 1995c). Despite Graham's optimism quoted above the current reality for pupils is that inclusion in a PRU usually means exclusion from mainstream education altogether. Getting a seriously disruptive and sometimes truanting pupil into a PRU may help a school to provide more effective schooling for other pupils. Getting a serious truant into a PRU may improve the school's statistics but do little for the pupil.

On a more positive note, Graham reports the development of peripatetic 'school support teams' as a potentially more successful approach to dealing with difficult pupils that has the advantage of keeping pupils in mainstream schooling. He states:

> School support teams consist of a group of specialist teachers, sometimes supported by a social worker or education welfare officer, with substantial experience in, and/ or qualifications for dealing with, difficult pupils. The team responds to requests for assistance with disruptive pupils from a number of schools by offering their expertise, advice and support to both teachers and pupils.
>
> (Graham, 1988, p. 43)

Graham reports that these teams show 'encouraging signs of constituting a more effective form of intervention, both from the pupil's and the school's point of view'. These teams avoid the difficulties associated with units which withdraw pupils from the mainstream, and have the potential to help young and inexperienced teachers deal with discipline and control problems (p. 49).

During the data collection for my research no pupil referral units were available to the schools for serious truancy alone. A few schools used special off-site units for difficult children, some of whom had attendance problems. One pastoral care manager reported that the school had use of a separate unit for EBD children that included children with attendance problems.

Only two respondents reported the use of special support personnel (both on-site), in relation to dealing with unauthorized absentees. One such provision was described thus:

> We have one woman who comes in on a regular basis, and helps to work out routines for disaffected pupils. She will spend time in class watching what goes on, seeing what the mechanics of the lesson are, what the chemistry in the lesson is. She will suggest strategies for improving the situation, and will make suggestions in terms of either staff or pupils monitoring progress. She will also deal with non-attenders. I am very enthusiastic about this service. She is very good, as an ex-teacher she understands the hands-on of the classroom. She is willing to spend a lot of time going between school and home if necessary, which eases our burden quite a lot.

Having considered those services that might help to deal with unauthorized absence, our attention now turns to the work of the Social Services Departments and some of the problems of professional co-operation between teachers and social workers.

Section 3: Schools and social work

Social Service Departments can have dealings with pupils through four distinctly different forms of contact. These are:

- Protective. Referrals from police, NSPCC or others, or direct referral from the school, or their EWO, for help with children thought to be at risk of, or suffering, significant harm. As a result of the judgement in *Re O.* mentioned in Chapter 3 (see p. 54) unauthorized absence in itself can amount to significant harm and the school can refer on that ground alone. The investigations are carried out under the provisions of the Children Act 1989, section 47(1)(b) and *inter alia* will enquire into behaviour in school and attendance at school (Children Act 1989, section 47(5)).
- Corrective. Referrals from the Local Education Authority as a result of a child's persistent failure to comply with directions given under an education supervision order (Children Act 1989, schedule 3, para 19). Such referrals will result in investigations similar to those mentioned above.
- Preventive. Departments have a special duty to help promote the welfare of children in families thought to be at risk of breakdown or court appearance (Children Act 1989, section 17(1)). This preventive work includes working to encourage children not to commit criminal offences (Children Act 1989, schedule 2, para 7).
- Restorative. Departments take over parental responsibility while the child is in their care, either by placement in residential care or in foster care. One of the biggest groups of pupils who are looked after in this way are those with learning disabilities (DoH, 1993). Many children in care have a history of absence from school and their education needs are often ignored. 'More attention is given to immediate social work concerns such as care, relationships and contact with parents' (Sone, 1995, p. 16; OFSTED, 1995a, p. 3).

From the above it can be seen that social workers are likely to come into contact with teachers and other school staff either to investigate a pupil's circumstances or in a caring or quasi-parental role. Some, but by no means all, of these contacts will focus on a pupil's school behaviour and attendance. There is evidence that the interactions between social workers and teachers on issues related to a pupil's behaviour and attendance are sometimes not as helpful and co-operative as they could be. Galloway (1985) reports that a difficulty exists in relation to the acceptance by teachers of all 'outsiders', including social workers:

> The ethos of each professional group makes active co-operation very difficult indeed. Teachers are sensitive to implicit criticism from outsiders. For their part

outsiders feel vulnerable when visiting schools. They cope with this feeling of vulnerability either by accepting the staff room ethos, becoming kind of adopted honorary members, or by withdrawing into a quite separate professional group, for example of social worker colleagues, in which teachers are the 'out group'.

(Galloway, 1985, p. 128)

Galloway develops his argument by presenting two case histories that illustrate the reasons for the teachers' feelings of vulnerability (pp. 128–31). Both cases involve unauthorized absence from school, one as a consequence of a deteriorating relationship between the pupil and his pastoral tutor, the other as a reaction by the pupil to the irrelevance of what the school had to offer to her immediate life experience. Galloway points out that both pupils, by their absence from school, are criticizing their teachers and their school. Furthermore these two pupils are representative of a much larger group of disaffected pupils within the school who have similar reasons for their absence. The involvement of social workers, who generally have no experience of teaching, will expose the pupils' criticism of the school and the levels of disaffection within the school to analysis by 'outsiders' who may be unsympathetic to the difficulties the teachers face.

The lack of co-operation between teachers and social workers may be further compounded by research evidence reported by Graham that there is no evidence that social workers 'have any positive effect on pupil behaviour' (Graham, 1988, p. 37). A further source of difficulty, reported by Johnson, relates to the different practice focus of teachers (as pedagogues) and social workers. She states that teachers usually meet their pupils' need for the knowledge that 'equips them for work or leisure and for citizenship generally' (Johnson, 1980, p. 15) by teaching them in groups (p. 6), within the norms of the school as an institution (p. 124). Social workers, on the other hand, seek to help individuals (their clients) make their own decisions based on the client's own wishes (p. 122), within the norms of society in general (p. 124). It is possible that teachers see themselves as instructors of groups operating within clearly defined institutional norms, while social workers may see themselves as facilitators of individuals operating within rather more loosely defined social norms. If the teachers' view of social workers is that they also do not have anything to offer by way of solution to the behavioural problems of pupils, it is not surprising that relationships are sometimes characterized by a lack of co-operation (OFSTED, 1995a, p. 3). Johnson points out that there are many ways of resolving these difficulties, but these have to be set up and managed in the knowledge of the differences. This is usually done through the pastoral care system of the school (p. 125).

My research sought to discover the involvement of social workers from the Social Services Department in dealing with individual cases of unauthorized absence. In the majority of cases contact with social workers was limited to protective issues. There was ample evidence of the pastoral staff welcoming social workers into the school and treating them as professional equals. A response typical of many was:

It depends on the reason for referral, if it's child protection they will be here in half an hour, if it's anything else it's days or weeks. I've never had a situation where they have never responded. They may have responded and chatted to us and said it is not applicable, but they have always responded in some way. We have a really good relationship with Social Services, I can phone them up and ask informally for advice when the need arises and they will advise. They will come to school, they have the use of rooms to see the students. It wasn't like that 10 years ago. The change was as a result of a particular individual who took over at the (local SSD) office. Also I have been on joint teacher and social worker courses. The Children Act meant that we had to work closely together and I am the nominated officer in the school. So I know the social workers now and they know me. It depends on personalities rather than policies, the same relationship has not developed between schools and another office of the SSD.

Effective working relationships seem to have been dependent on the development of professional respect, trust and the easy flow of information.

Conclusions

This chapter has reviewed evidence from the report of the Elton committee and from research that suggests that what happens in school can have an effect on behaviour within school. What happens within each school contributes to its own 'atmosphere', and one of the most important elements affecting atmosphere appears to be the quality of the leadership provided by the head and the senior management team. They are one of the most significant change agents within the school and any changes that are to be made to those features of the school that contribute to its 'atmosphere' appear to require senior management action. A relationship between 'atmosphere' and levels of attendance is believed to exist, but remains unproved by research.

A significant feature of the school that will affect behaviour is the development and use of a behavioural policy. That policy should include attendance. Evidence suggests that the policy and its rules should be agreed by, and have the active support of, the school management, staff, pupils and parents. The policy and its rules should be consistently applied by all. However, pastoral care tutors are likely to be the most involved with its application. The pastoral care tutors need to find ways of combining care and control so that their actions appear to pupils to be fair, both in relation to the formal rules of the school and any informal codes of conduct.

The curriculum, and the manner of its delivery through competent teachers operating a well-thought-out timetable, also affect the 'atmosphere', with special consideration to be given to the needs of low achievers, especially those in Years 10 and 11. It seems very likely that the troublesome behaviour and poor attendance of that group could so overwhelm the resources of the pastoral system that it becomes involved almost exclusively with control issues. If the pastoral system becomes overwhelmed then there may be less energy to spend on seeking support from outside. Parents are an important source of outside help, sometimes ignored and underused, and with whom schools may need to establish more productive relationships. Parents are not the only source of help that could be tapped. Other outside agencies are available to help the school, its pupils and their families. To make the best use of them the school may need to discover what levels of skill and services are available and how they can best be used. The school may also need to find ways of welcoming and encouraging outside help.

Because the head and senior management team are the major change agents within the school and because the pastoral care system carries the major responsibility for dealing with issues of troublesome behaviour and poor attendance they were the major contributors to the data collection for my research. Their contributions are analysed in the next chapter.

## CHAPTER 5

Analysis of Twenty Schools

The Department recognises that those most in need are frequently those least aware of the services that are provided and intends, through processes of consultation and partnership, to promote such awareness.
(Excerpt from Nottinghamshire Social Services Department Equalities Mission Statement of July 1994)

This chapter analyses information gathered from the twenty secondary schools included in the research sample and describes the method used to select four schools for more in-depth study. There are three main sections to this chapter. The first reviews selected aspects of all twenty schools' communication with parents, and others, over attendance matters. The second section considers aspects of the methods used by the schools to motivate pupils to attend. The third section proposes a typology by which some of the aspects of the two previous sections might be better understood and which influenced the selection of the four schools. The four schools, code numbers 3, 14, 15 and 18, appear in bold type within the tables in this chapter, and are analysed in depth in Chapter 6.

Section 1: Communication with parents and others

This section analyses how the schools established which pupil was absent and what action was taken as a result of absence. It then considers how much information on attendance matters is supplied to parents at the time of registration that both provides an explanation of the actions that will be taken and forms the basis of an 'agreement' with the parent on that action. Subsequently it examines what data are supplied to parents and governors on a regular, usually annual, basis that provide some explanation of the school's performance in relation to unauthorized absence. Finally it considers what information is supplied to parents on the help that is available from the Education Welfare Service to deal with unauthorized absence. Section one concludes with a summary of the major points considered.

Analysis of the schools' methods of recording and responding to absence

Information on recording attendance, and the immediate action taken to follow up non-attendance, was provided by pastoral care staff and by analysis of material published for parents. The findings in relation to the process are summarized in Table 5.1.

The table shows that eight of the schools were using computer-based systems of registration, eight were using the 'Oxford' manual registers, and four were in the process of changing from a manual system to a computer system. The introduction of computer software and hardware for the management of attendance records was new and in some schools had caused difficulty. An example of these difficulties was given by one upper school head.

> There have been a lot of problems with the system. From the tutors' point of view it is difficult to pick up from the present SIMS register the persistent truant, or absentees, on specific days. With the old register in front of you, you could pick up a pattern of absentees. To deal with that we've got the secretary giving us a spreadsheet. It is separate from the main register, and I'm not sure that the tutors use it as readily as maybe they should.
>
> I find it rather frustrating if by 10 o'clock I need to know that somebody is in, and if we come out of assembly very quickly and I've got all the registers there ready to take to be read, if I don't have the chance to quickly look down, and register in my mind who is in and who is out, I'm for ever ringing over to the secretary for information.
>
> We had a lot of problems about not having an overall picture. We had problems where it was being misread by the OMR, because staff weren't marking it clearly enough. Just recently we had a problem where two tutors had made a stupid error by putting the same number at the top of their sheets, one was read and when the other was read it undid the previous one. Minor things which we are told will be overcome as we get used to the system.
>
> I have a stand-alone PC here, which is updated every week by disk, there is no network as yet. So my information is a week old, for the current week I have to contact the secretary.
>
> (Upper School Head, School 9)

School staff reported that the accuracy of recording was dependent upon the vigilance and thoroughness of the those marking the register and updating it. The introduction of information technology had made no difference to this aspect of registration. Both forms of registration required the tutor to decide whether absence was authorized or not, an issue that will be discussed later in this chapter. Eighteen of the schools took the register both morning and afternoon. The two that only took a form register in the morning took class registers in the afternoon because the schools were on split sites; in both cases this was done to reduce pupil movement between sites.

Nine schools had established systems for dealing with post-registration truancy. This was done by taking class registers manually, with absence slips sent to the form tutor. Seven schools reported difficulty, either because the

Table 5.1 Analysis of the process of recording and responding to absence

Topic	method		checks			follow-up			action		r	comment
School	c	m	am	pm	prt	1	3	>	fm.t	yr.h		
10	✓	✓	✓	✓	✓		✓		✗	✓	hi	poor attenders targeted
17	✓	✗	✓	✓	✓		✓		✓	✓	hi	poor attenders targeted
15	✗	✓	✓	✓	✗			✓	✗	✓	hi	poor attenders targeted
13	✓	✗	✓	✓	✓		✓		✓	✓	m	action by yr.h if persistent
5	✓	✗	✓	✓		✓				✓	m	pm reg. at end of school day
20	✗	✓	✓	✓	✓		✓		✓		m	poor attenders targeted
6	✗	✓	✓	✓	✗		✓		✗	✓	m	
8	✓	✗	✓	✓	✓	✓	✓		✓	✓	m	action by yr.h if persistent
2	✗	✓	✓	✓		✓	✓		✓	✓	m	using an 'at risk' register
18	✗	✓	✓	✓	✗		✓		✓		lo	
3	✓	✓	✓	✓	✓	✓	✓		✓	✓	lo	poor attenders targeted
4	✗	✓	✓	✓			✓		✓		lo	poor attenders targeted
1	✓	✗	✓	✓	✓		✓		✓	✓	lo	
7	✓	✗	✓	✓	✗		✓			✓	lo	limited time for follow-up
12	✓	✓	✓	✓			✓		✓		lo	
16	✗	✓	✓	✓	✓		✓		✓		lo	
11	✓	✗	✓	✓	✗		✓			✓	lo	poor attenders targeted
19	✓	✓	✓	✗	✓		✓			✓	lo	pm class record of attendance
9	✓	✗	✓	✓	✗		✓			✓	lo	
14	✗	✓	✓	✗	✗		✓		✓	✓	lo	pm class record of attendance

Notes:
Explanation of **topics**:
method of keeping the register: **c** = use of computer equipment, **m** = use of manual registers
checks made on attendance: **am** = morning registration, **pm** = afternoon registration, **prt** = procedure for dealing with post-registration 'truancy'
follow-up, the normal period of delay before following up absence: **1** = one day, **3** = three days, **>** = more than four days
action, the person who normally follows up absence by contacting the parents: **fm.t** = form teacher, **yr.h** = year head or other senior manager
r presents the ranking position of the schools in relation to the percentage of pupils missing schooling – see text for explanation

Key:
✓ = topic operated, ✗ = topic definitely not operated

A blank indicates that an informal system or arrangement operates in some circumstances.

manual process was too time-consuming, or because the information exchange between class teachers and form tutor was too unreliable. The following example illustrates the difficulty.

Question   Do you have a problem with post-registration truancy?
Answer   Yes we do. Post-registration absence is a problem with some students, and I think that we don't know enough about it.
Question   What action has been taken to deal with post-registration absence?
Answer   The central thing is insisting on subject registers, followed up by an absence slip. The theory is that the slips will inform the tutor, who will be able to make a note of an absence against a presence. Then the tutor challenges the student. The tutor will talk to the student about it, and if serious the parents will be called in. The problem is the speed of that communication, which we have not cracked. It is difficult for the class teacher to arrive at the differentiation between someone who is not in their lesson and someone who is not in school.

(Upper School Head, School 18)

In the remaining four schools there were informal processes of information exchange, usually by word of mouth and usually about pupils with a history of post-registration truancy. None of the schools were using a computer-based system for class registration, but one school was investigating doing so.

Four schools had a policy of following up unexplained absences on the day that they occurred. In three of these this policy related to pupils with a known attendance problem. The one school that followed up all absences on the day that they occurred was only able to do so as a result of temporary GEST funding which provided money to pay for the additional administration staff and EWO time required.

The majority of schools had a policy of following up absences after the pupil had failed to show for three days. This was usually done by letter. Letters due to be sent to parents at this stage could well be held back if staff judged it to be inappropriate to send one. Staff might withhold the letter if there was no previous concern about the pupil's attendance, or if they had received information from other pupils, perhaps relatives, about the reasons for absence. A form tutor explained:

I don't always contact parents after three days. In this school there is normally a cousin, or brother, or sister, or a friend who lives nearby who will give you a reason. If I am suspicious I would get the head of year to phone. If I knew it was a kid who was never away unless it was genuine I would believe what I had been told by other kids. You know which kids try it on, you know which parents never send a note in until the end, you know which parents you can expect a phone call from on the first day.

(Form Tutor, School 8)

One school had a policy of following up unexplained absences after two weeks. This policy was associated with a semi-informal referral system of absentees to a full-time member of staff whose duties included a considerable amount of contact with parents through home visiting.

Three schools had established a policy which stopped form tutors making contact with parents over unexplained absences. The other schools either saw it as a primary duty of the form tutor, or a collaborative one with a year head or other senior member of staff.

It was common practice in all schools that as the number of unexplained absences increased, or as it became obvious that some absence might be unauthorized, or condoned by the parents, so senior pastoral care staff became more involved. This was in part due to form tutors having insufficient non-teaching time in the day to deal with the more difficult pupils and parents, and in part due to the serious view taken of the apparent breach of school rules and the law.

Table 5.1 has been arranged so that the schools are ranked, in descending order, in relation to the number of pupils missing teaching through unauthorized absence. A mean and standard deviation was calculated from published attendance data and the schools allocated to three groups (high, medium and low) based on multiples of the standard deviation. There is little evidence from this ranking to indicate the existence of differences of policy or action between schools that experience different rates of unauthorized absence. In the three schools that experienced the highest rates of unauthorized absence there is a definite policy to target poor attenders by responding to their absence more quickly. However, some schools in the medium or low categories have the same policy.

Analysis of prospectus information to parents

In Chapter 4 it was argued that a behaviour policy should include reference to how the school proposed to deal with absence and unauthorized absence, and some suggestions were made about what such a policy could contain. These suggestions are summarized in Table 5.2.

As part of the data collection for this study, information was gathered on the policies and rules of the 20 subject schools that were made known to parents before, or when they enrolled their child, rather than after enrolment. It was found that all 20 schools had rules and published them in their prospectus. Only six had a behaviour policy, and where these existed they were also published to parents. None of the schools had an attendance policy. The information published at the time of enrolment was analysed for its inclusion of matters relating to absence and unauthorized absence using the 25 points given in Table 5.2. The results of this analysis are given in Table 5.3.

Table 5.3 has been ranked in descending order based on the number of items included in the prospectus. The table clearly shows that some schools publish very little information in their prospectus to parents on matters relating to absence and unauthorized absence; however, no correlation was found to exist between the number of truants from a school and the amount of information it provided. Some schools with low rates of unauthorized absence publish considerable amounts of information, while others do not,

Table 5.2 Proposed elements of an attendance policy*

1.	**Legal rights and duties**
1.1	a statement of the legal obligations on schools and parents
1.2	that the parents and the school acting together can authorize absence
1.3	the lawful reasons for absence are made clear to all
2.	**Monitoring attendance**
2.1	the requirement to keep an attendance register
2.2	how this will be done
2.3	when it is has to be taken, and
2.4	that the register can be inspected
2.5	what action will follow from late registration and absence
2.6	the rules on authorizing absence, and
2.7	the ways unauthorized absence will be followed up
3.	**Rewards**
3.1	the school's scheme for rewarding high levels of attendance, and
3.2	whether rewards have been negotiated with pupils
4.	**Sanctions**
4.1	the sanctions applied by the school to incidents of unauthorized absence
4.2	the way these sanctions are applied so that they improve attendance
4.3	the LEA's policy on prosecution
4.4	the duty of the school to provide reports
4.5	how these are prepared, and discussed with pupils and parents
5.	**Help**
5.1	the help available from within the school to pupils and parents
5.2	the help available from other agencies
6.	**Returning to school**
6.1	a policy for receiving back frequent absentees
6.2	guidance to teachers on helping the pupil catch up, and
6.3	on the provision of additional work
7.	**Information**
7.1	the school's policy on publishing information on attendance rates
7.2	the attendance targets set for the year ahead
7.3	action to be taken to attain the targets

*See Chapter 4 for a discussion of these points.

and some schools with high rates publish considerable amounts while other do not. The variability of the amount of information published is of interest in the light of government regulations, and the Elton committee's recommendations. It is clear that some schools comply with few of the regulations or recommendations in relation to information in their prospectuses, and none of the schools in the sample complied with them all.

Only six schools routinely provided information to parents on their legal obligations in relation to attendance. This is surprising in that the legal obligation is the foundation of subsequent actions. The assumption appears to be that parents know their rights and obligations and do not need them

Table 5.3 Basic data analysis 1993/4 academic year; content of information to parents on absence and unauthorized absence

Topic	policy and rules		rights and duties			monitoring attendance							rewards		sanctions					help		returning to school			information			total
School	b.pl	rls	1.1	1.2	1.3	2.1	2.2	2.3	2.4	2.5	2.6	2.7	3.1	3.2	4.1	4.2	4.3	4.4	4.5	5.1	5.2	6.1	6.2	6.3	7.1	7.2	7.3	t
18		✓	✓	✓	✓	✓	✓	✓		✓	✓		✓	✓	✓					✓	✓				✓			**15**
10		✓		✓	✓	✓	✓	✓		✓	✓	✓	✓		✓					✓	✓				✓			14
3		✓		✓	✓	✓	✓	✓		✓	✓	✓	✓		✓					✓	✓				✓			**14**
4		✓	✓	✓	✓		✓	✓		✓	✓	✓	✓	✓	✓					✓								13
13		✓		✓	✓		✓	✓		✓	✓	✓	✓	✓	✓					✓	✓							13
1		✓		✓	✓			✓		✓	✓	✓	✓		✓					✓	✓				✓			12
5	✓	✓		✓	✓			✓		✓	✓		✓		✓					✓	✓				✓			12
12	✓	✓		✓	✓						✓		✓		✓					✓					✓			9
7		✓	✓	✓	✓							✓	✓		✓	✓				✓								9
16		✓		✓	✓		✓				✓				✓	✓												8
20		✓		✓			✓	✓							✓		✓				✓							8
6		✓		✓				✓				✓			✓					✓					✓			7
11	✓	✓		✓				✓												✓						✓		6
9	✓	✓													✓					✓						✓		5
2	✓	✓													✓					✓						✓		5
17		✓	✓	✓										✓						✓							✓	5
19		✓	✓												✓					✓							✓	5
8	✓	✓		✓																✓							✓	5
14		✓	✓																									**2**
15		✓																										**1**
Total	6	20	6	15	10	3	7	10	0	7	9	7	9	4	15	2	1	0	0	18	7	0	0	0	7	3	2	168

Notes:

- ✓ denotes a statement published to parents either in a prospectus, or in an accompanying document for 'new' parents.
- All statements made in the prospectus have been recorded whether they were legally correct or not.
- Issues are frequently discussed with individual parents or at PTA meetings; these were not included in this table.
- It should be noted that much more detailed information is available to teachers and other staff in the schools, either in a staff handbook or in notes to supply teachers.
- It is worth noting, for comparison, that all prospectuses from the subject schools included detailed instructions on the school uniform to be worn.

restated. This assumption may be wrong and is contrary to the guidance given in DfE, 1994, para 7.

Fifteen of the schools made some statement about the process for authorizing absence; in many prospectuses this information was potentially misleading through being incomplete. For example, schools gave the impression that a parental note was all that was required to justify the absence. The following prospectus statement, or something like it, was common:

> Pupils should attend regularly and punctually. When a pupil has been absent, a note must be brought explaining the absence and, when a pupil is absent for a period exceeding three days, parents are asked to contact the school by telephone or letter during the period of absence.
>
> (School 10)

A form tutor at the same school made it clear that the school actually does make the decision:

> *Question* How do you decide whether the absence is authorized or not?
> *Answer* From the notes. But also you get to know who is likely to be playing truant. You are making what might be an unfair judgement on a child when you say 'he is almost certainly taking time out from school'. I am more likely to respond quickly by calling in the EWO if that child has been identified as taking time out.
>
> (Form Tutor, School 10)

The above prospectus information was correct but it failed to state that it was the school that finally made the decision. It was clear from the teacher's comments that the school's decision was based on the previous attendance record of the pupil. Because in this case the prospectus information did not make it clear that it was the school that made the final decision, there was no need to provide parents with the criteria for decision-making. It follows that the school could not make it clear to them that the previous attendance history affected their decisions.

In column 1.3 of Table 5.3 there is evidence that only half the schools use the prospectus to tell parents the lawful reasons for absence. It is noticeable that in nine of these cases this is associated with the provision of information on who authorizes the absence. It seems logical that there should be such a link, but it is noticeable that in six other cases the schools commented on who authorized absence, but did not say what the legal reasons were. One school gave the legal reasons but nothing else, while the prospectuses of three schools made no statement on rights and duties at all.

Table 5.3 indicates, in section 2, that there was considerable variability in the information sent to parents on keeping the register. While it may be common knowledge that schools keep a register, only three of the schools said so and only seven said how it was kept. Half the sample schools said when registration occurred, and less than half indicated how absence or lateness would be followed up and what action would be taken if the absence was judged by the school to be unauthorized. None of the sample schools said that the register was open to inspection.

Nine of the schools gave information on the rewards available for good attendance (only four of these indicated that the rewards had been nego-tiated with the pupils), whereas fifteen schools told parents about the sanctions the school would impose if attendance were found to be unau-thorized. It can be seen from section 4 that it is unusual among the sample schools for them to tell parents why they impose sanctions and what action will be taken by them, or the LEA, if unauthorized absence is persistent. None of the schools told parents that they would supply reports to court, should matters proceed that far. All but two schools told parents how to get help from school staff if there were difficulties, but only seven schools gave any information about the help available from outside services like the Education Welfare Service, or Social Services. None of the schools told parents what action would be taken to help pupils who had been absent catch up with missed work. Seven schools indicated that they had a policy on the publication of attendance data, but it was not common for schools to indicate what action they were going to take to improve attendance.

Publication of data on unauthorized absence

Table 5.3 provides evidence of the information made available to parents in the prospectuses issued by the schools. In Chapter 3 it was shown that not only should general information on unauthorized absence be published but that the prospectus should also contain unauthorized absence data, and that the law requires the data to be made available to the governors and parents by way of an annual report. Table 5.4 opposite summarizes the evidence collected from the schools in relation to the data that they make available. The table has been ranked in descending order of the percentage of pupils missing one or more sessions. There is no obvious correlation between the rank order position occupied by the schools and the distribution of data made available. Schools with low levels of unauthorized absence, when compared with others in the sample, appear to make as much effort to meet the regulations as do schools with high levels. It is noticeable that the three schools with the worst unauthorized absence rates, 15, 17 and 10, do not publish the data to their parents.

Table 5.4 shows that many schools in the sample were ignoring the regulations. Only four published data on unauthorized absence in their prospectuses, although all twenty should be doing so. Just over half the schools made the data available routinely to their governors and their parents. Furthermore, some schools appear to give no data to parents or governors despite the fact that the data, generated and checked by them, are available from the DfEE and newspapers. Some members of staff com-mented, in their interviews, about the negative effect that the publication of the DfEE 'performance tables' had on them. A head teacher of a school that

Table 5.4 Data on unauthorized absence rates

Topic	in prospectus	to governors	to parents
School	data produced by the school		
15	✗	✓	✗
17	✗	✓	✗
10	✓	✗	✗
2	✗	✓	✓
8	✗	✓	✓
13	✗	✓	✓
20	✗	✓	✓
6	✗	✗	✗
5	✗	✓	✓
7	✗	✓	✗
4	✗	✓	✓
9	✗	✓	✗
3	✓	✓	✓
14	✗	✓	✓
1	✓	✗	✓
19	✗	✓	✗
18	✗	✗	✓
12	✗	✗	✗
11	✓	✗	✓
16	✗	✗	✓
Total	4	13	12

did include the raw data in the prospectus, but did not report on the data to parents or governors, reported:

> *Question* How are the data on unauthorized absence used?
> *Answer* For returns to the DfE. Also published in the school prospectus with reminders to parents to keep the school informed of the reasons for absence. The data are as honest and accurate as possible. They are used to keep track of students, individual performance is transferred to the Record of Achievement and Compact reference. The honesty of the records has lead to the school being low in the performance tables which has had the effect of lowering teachers' morale.
>
> (Head Teacher, School 10)

The opportunity for the head teacher to publish comments to parents and governors on the performance tables was lost in this case and because of the absence of an effective PTA in that school parents had no venue to seek clarification or explanation as a group.

Information on the role and functions of the EWS

The information provided to parents on the Education Welfare Service is summarized in Table 5.5. The schools are ranked in the same order as for Table 5.4. The information was taken from the schools' prospectuses, annual reports and other information leaflets issued to parents.

Table 5.5 Provision of information by schools to parents on the EWS

Topic	name of officer	how contacted		officer's functions described by school			
School		office	school	enforce-ment	attendance	support	s.l.a.
15							
17							
10			✓		✓	✓	
2							
8			✓		✓		
13							
20	✓		✓			✓	
6	✓						
5	✓		✓				
7							
4	✓	✓	✓		✓	✓	
9							
3			✓				
14	✓	✓					
1		✓	✓		✓	✓	
19			✓				
18		✓	✓		✓	✓	
12							
11					✓		
16							
Total	5	4	9	0	6	5	0

Notes:
Explanation of **topics:**
name of officer: information given by the school on the EWO/attendance officer involved with the school
how contacted: information provided on how parents should contact the EWO/attendance officer, either at their **office**, or through the **school**
officer's functions described by school: information provided by the school on the main tasks of the EWO
s.l.a.: service level agreement

The table shows that schools do not, in general, provide much information on the EWS. Ten schools indicate how to contact the Education Welfare Officer, the majority advising that such contact should be made through the school. It is not common for schools to describe the service that the EWO offers, and where they do it is in relation to attendance matters, such as following up absence; with an unspecified purpose; or offering support. None of the schools mentioned enforcement of the law as one of the service's tasks. None mentioned the amount of time made available to the school by the EWO, or the range of services the EWS could offer parents.

The absence of information does not mean that the service is ignored. Senior pastoral care staff said that they valued the work; however, the majority of schools did not inform their parents of a service available to them in documents that were intended to give parents basic information. This could limit the parents' independent use of the service, and their understanding of the service's relationship with the school.

Section summary: Communication with parents and others

All schools in the sample appeared to be fulfilling their legal obligations to take a register and investigate absences noted by that process. Eleven of the schools seemed to be struggling to deal effectively with post-registration truancy. It was common practice for the form tutor to follow up absences after three days, and for either the form tutor or a more senior member of staff to follow up more quickly pupils who have a known record of unauthorized absence or post-registration truancy. Immediate follow-up of all absentees was uncommon because of the expense; the sample schools did not have the resources to do so. The system that a school adopts to deal with absence and unauthorized absence was not necessarily related to the rates of absence experienced.

Many of the schools' prospectuses did not make parents thoroughly aware of their rights and duties, or school practices, in relation to attendance. Some schools may therefore be failing to make clear to parents the basis for their action in dealing with attendance and non-attendance at the time when parents are registering their children with the school, a situation which could set the scene for misunderstandings later. It seems that many of the schools did not regard the prospectus as an important way of setting an attendance agreement or 'contract' with parents. However, there appears to be no clear evidence that a failure to do so is associated with either high or low rates of attendance.

The lack of data in most of the prospectuses is surprising given the significance attached to the league tables. Some schools miss the chance to comment annually to parents on the data and provide them with an explanation of this aspect of the school's performance.

Few schools provide much information to parents on how to contact the Education Welfare Office direct or to explain the officers' role; none commented on their enforcement function. When this is coupled with the often limited information supplied to parents on the school's actions in relation to unauthorized absence it may increase the opportunities for misunderstandings. Those misunderstandings may only come to light as the parents experience the systems operating in relation to their child's non-attendance. Lack of basic information at registration may result in the parent not using available help early enough to deal with emerging problems, or, in contrasting situations, resenting or rejecting the interventions of the school or the Education Welfare Officer when enquiring into absence. The lack of information suggests that awareness levels may be low. This may present additional difficulties to those parents most in need of the services.

Section 2: Methods used to motivate pupils to attend

The first section of Chapter 4 reviewed the contribution certain significant 'in-school' factors had on attendance. In that section it was argued that these factors, if well and consistently applied, could motivate pupils to attend and continue to attend. This section offers an analysis of selected factors based on comments made by the staff of the twenty sample schools.

Comment was made in Chapter 4 on the sample schools' responses to three of these factors, namely leadership, curriculum and anti-school sub-culture, and further detailed comment will not be made. However, it is worth restating the comment made in Chapter 4 that none of the sample schools reported attempting to discover whether changes that they had made in relation to these three factors resulted in improved attendance or reduced unauthorized absence. It was also mentioned in Chapter 4 that very few of the sample schools had access to special units to which unauthorized absentees could be sent in order to re-establish motivation to attend. Further consideration of these units will not be made here.

The sample schools' responses in relation to the functioning of the pastoral care system, developing effective relationships with parents and the use made of Education Welfare Officers are analysed below.

The functioning of pastoral care

Interviews in relation to pastoral care matters were undertaken with senior members of the pastoral care staff and form tutors in each of the sample schools. Information on the operation of the pastoral care system was also gathered from available published material such as prospectuses, staff hand-books and policy documents. Not all schools had all these documents, and the documents collected varied in the amount of information provided on the operation of pastoral care. The analysis of pastoral care within the schools is presented in Table 5.6. The headings for the table are derived from the discussion of pastoral care in Chapter 4.

From the information on the time spent in form groups it seems that the afternoon session was generally not available for much more than calling the register. It also seems that although there was more time available on some mornings in most schools the form tutors do not have a set programme of work for their tutor group, as suggested by the Elton committee (DES, 1989, p. 113). The main focus of tutorial work was on school issues; examples were given of checking homework diaries, dealing with infringements of rules relating to school uniforms, completing records of achievement and gen-erally settling the pupils down.

The form tutors' style of working was judged from the number of caring or controlling words used in their responses. The descriptions of their roles showed many form tutors to be prescriptive, informative and confronting, and they would thus be judged authoritative (see Chapter 4). However, some form tutors described the lives of their pupils in ways that showed that they not only understood some of the difficulties faced, but were supportive and available to help the pupil solve the problem. In such cases they were classified as facilitative. An example of the facilitative style was provided by a form tutor in a school with a high rate of unauthorized absence.

> I have one girl in my class whose attendance is about 30 per cent. When she does come in I have to point out to her that her attendance is not very good, but you almost want to praise her for the fact that she is there and encourage her. I've asked the girl and it's: 'Well my Mum says if I don't want to go I don't have to go.' Mum's wrong, but I have to leave the matter there really. There's not much more work I can do than bring in other help. The other help hasn't produced much permanent change. The girl is brought in now and then.
>
> (Form Tutor, Year 10, School 17)

In this case it can be argued that the teacher, and it seems also the school, are attempting to be supportive and catalytic (see Chapter 4).

Among the form tutors in the sample the facilitative approach is less frequently judged to be used, confirming findings by McLaughlin (1989). Facilitative tutors undertook work in form time where the major focus of concern was school issues, and where there was no set programme to follow. The facilitative approach could be difficult to maintain in such circumstances.

Staff were questioned, and publications analysed, for information on the existence of systems that recognized good attendance through a reward scheme. The importance of rewards was considered in Chapter 4, where it was argued that a good reward system could improve behaviour and attendance. Nine of the schools told parents that there were rewards for good attendance (see Table 5.3). Table 5.3, however, does not give information on what these rewards were. The analysis in Table 5.6 provides information on the rewards used regardless of the source of the information. It was clearly common for schools to say that they recorded attendance in the pupils' records, usually in their record of achievement or 'Compact' record. It was much less common for pupils, or groups of pupils, to be praised for their attendance or improved attendance; it is not common to give prizes, or to write special letters home. These actions, suggested by Tattum (1989, p. 155) as commonly used in schools to improve behaviour generally, do not appear to be used by the twenty schools in relation to attendance. Indeed it seems that praise for good attendance was much less frequent than sanctions for poor attendance, and this is supported by the information presented in the final section of Table 5.6. Detention (an authoritative intervention) was the more common way of attempting to improve attendance; counselling (a facilitative intervention) was used in a minority of schools.

It is common for the school to ask the EWO to take action when internal processes have not improved attendance. The following is typical:

Table 5.6 Analysis of elements of the pastoral care system

Topic	amount of tutorial time		programme set for the form group			major focus of concern		form tutor's general style		ways of recognizing good attendance				methods used to improve attendance		
School	am	pm	none set	by form tutor	by school	school issues	pupil issues	authoritative (control)	facilitative (care)	records	praise	prizes	letters home	counselling	detention	EWO
15	**10**	**5**	✓			✓		✓		✓					✓	✓
17	25	5	✓		pse	✓			✓	✓	✓	✓	✓		✓	✓
10	15	5	✓		pse	✓	✓	✓		✓	✓	✓			✓	✓
2	5	5	✓			✓		✓		✓					✓	✓
8	20	5	✓			✓		✓		✓		✓			✓	✓
13	5	15/5	✓			✓			✓	✓					✓	✓
20	20	5	✓			✓				✓					✓	✓
6	25/5	5 end	✓		pse	✓		✓		✓	✓	✓	✓	✓	✓	✓
5	20/5	5 end	✓		pse	✓		✓		✓	✓	✓			✓	✓
7	2/10	2	✓			✓		✓	✓	✓	✓	✓		✓	✓	✓
4	20	20	✓			✓		✓	✓	✓					✓	✓
9	25	5	✓			✓	✓	✓	✓	✓					✓	✓
3	**10**	**5**	✓			✓				✓					✓	✓
14	**10**	**2 cl**	✓			✓				✓				✓	✓	✓
1	20/5	5	✓			✓	✓	✓	✓	✓	✓	✓		✓	✓	✓
19	40	2 cl		+lessons	pse	✓				✓					✓	✓
18	**20**	**10**	✓			✓			✓	✓					✓	✓
12	40/5	5		✓	pse	✓			✓	✓				✓	✓	✓
11	20	5		✓				✓		✓						✓
16	25/10	5		✓				✓							✓	
Total			16			18	3	12	8	19	6	7	2	5	19	18

Table 5.6 *continued*

Notes:
Explanation of **topics**:
amount of tutorial time: the amount of tutorial time, in minutes, that was available for form contact, as reported by the tutor. Where / separates two figures, the time varies within the week
programme set for the form group: indicates the existence, or otherwise, of a set activity taking place within the form period
major focus of concern: the major focus of the form tutor's work with the form group, as judged from their comments on the work undertaken
form tutor's general style: the approach adopted by the form tutor based on the frequency of use of controlling or caring words used in the interview
ways of recognizing good attendance: the responses used by the school; **letters home** = use of special letters praising attendance in addition to the annual report
methods used to improve attendance: when attendance becomes a problem the method(s) used most frequently by the school judged by frequency of mention

Key
end = registration taken at the end of the school day
cl = registration taken in the class by the class teacher and not in the form by the form tutor
+ lessons = additional lessons given to the form based on the tutor's subject specialism
pse = personal and social education periods based on a school-wide curriculum and delivered by the form tutor

> The senior pastoral co-ordinator meets with the year heads, and then each week she
> sits down with the ESW and says, 'These are our problems.' There is a referral sheet
> for each child and he (the EWO) has to write on there what action he's taken.
>
> (Deputy Head, Pastoral Care, School 20)

If non-attendance is seen by the school as a disciplinary matter then it is likely that such a referral will carry with it an implicit request for the EWO to enquire into an apparent breach of discipline. This stands in contrast to the information generally supplied by schools to parents (see Table 5.5), which can fail to identify the attendance function of the EWS, and does not state their enforcement role. The work undertaken by the EWO when dealing with a referral will be considered later in this chapter.

Developing effective relationships with parents of non-attenders

In Chapter 4 it was argued that establishing effective relationships with parents would be to the benefit of their children's academic progress and behaviour in school. It was suggested that parents should be kept well informed, preferably before things went wrong, and that they should know their rights and responsibilities. It was also argued that effective collaboration with parents could be established by staff having time to meet them in school and in the parents' homes. In this chapter it has been shown that some of the sample schools limit information to parents about attendance, and that some only provide information when things go wrong. In order to compete the picture data were gathered to discover what methods were used by the schools to make effective contact with parents over attendance. These data are presented in Table 5.7.

The first point of interest is that it is more likely that direct work with parents on attendance matters will be undertaken by senior school staff. Interviewees suggested that this was a direct result of form tutors not having sufficient time and that senior staff, with less teaching contact time, had more time to deal with parents. This finding is consistent with Galloway (1985, p. 149). One form tutor's response was typical of many:

> All form teachers teach 23 periods out of 25 so there is very little non-contact time in
> the week. Some form teachers if they have five minutes will enquire if a child hasn't
> turned up. Most tutors just don't have the time to do it.
>
> (Form Tutor, School 7)

The significance of having available time is shown by the finding that in nine of the ten schools where home visits were undertaken it was senior staff who reported having a time allocation for parental contact, either directly or by arranging for an EWO visit. It has been stated previously that in many of the sample schools unauthorized absence appears to be seen as a disciplinary issue, and it is possible that many of the home visits made by, or required by, senior staff might be interpreted by the parent as authoritarian. Home visits were seen by some as beneficial in certain circumstances, but not in all. An example of the difficulties that can be encountered was given by one senior pastoral care manager:

> Some parents can be stroppy when we contact them for the first time but 99 per cent come to welcome the contact because it shows our concern, particularly if there is a genuine illness. Visits home can get a clear picture of what is happening and why. Visits are made to homes where there is no phone, and we need an answer. But I don't go round to a house where I don't know what the reception will be. Last week I sent the EWO round with a 3-day absence note, not because the girl was a bad attender but because I wanted her to complete some coursework. The following day she took an overdose. So you go through the motions for good reasons and increase the pressure on the child without realizing. It shocked me.
>
> (School 10)

Showing care for the pupil has to be balanced by an assessment of the likely reception by parents of the demonstration of the caring through a home visit. If a relationship has been established, by previous phone calls or classroom contact, then a judgement on whether to visit, and the likely response to it, can be made. The outcome of visits made in the absence of that information cannot be predicted.

It is clear from Table 5.7 that the most common way of making contact with the parent was by phone or letter, which provides information about the absence and the many reasons for it. It was uncommon for parents to come to school to see form tutors about non-attendance, although this could improve the parent/teacher relationship (Woods, 1989). It is more common for the EWO, rather than a teacher, to make a home visit on the school's behalf in order to gain support. An example of this is given in the quote from the senior pastoral care teacher above. It will be remembered that those schools that commented to parents on the role of the EWS did so in relation to general issues of attendance and support (see Table 5.5). It seems that the majority of schools actually use their EWO in this way even if they do not publish the fact, and would like to develop the function. The following comment illustrates that wish:

> If I had the money I would have a daily visit to the school from the EWO. Then that person would be able to go and speak to the parents. I don't want a conflict. When it takes 3 or 4 days to make contact you are into a conflict situation. If you had someone who could link well with the parents, who has the respect and affection of the parents, then we could create a much better partnership.
>
> (Year Head, School 11)

The three schools that reported on the work of the home/school liaison teacher did so in the context of questions about unauthorized absence. In this limited number of cases the teachers were thought to be particularly helpful in establishing good working relationships with parents where non-attendance was a problem.

The interrelationship of the publication of rules to parents on absence (see Table 5.3) and staff concern about parental actions is interesting. Of the ten schools that publish information nine do so in the context of some staff

Table 5.7 Analysis of teacher/parent contact in relation to non-attendance

Topic →	time given for parent/staff contact				types of school contact used to foster parental support						Table 5.3 item 1.3 imported	parent actions seen as presenting school staff with difficulties			
School	adm.	fm.t	yr.h	PTA	phone calls	letters home, notes to school	visits by parent to form tutor	home visits by staff	home/ school liaison teacher	EWO contact to gain support	rules on un abs provided at registration	late notes from parents	parental indiff-erence	condoned absence: child at home or at work	condoned absence covering for truancy
15			✓		✓	✓			✓					✓	
17	✓	✓	✓		✓	✓				✓		✓			
10			✓		✓	✓		✓			✓	✓	✓	✓	
2			✓		✓	✓		✓		✓				✓	
8		✓			✓	✓				✓					✓
13			✓		✓	✓	✓	✓	✓	✓	✓	✓		✓	✓
20			✓		✓	✓		✓		✓	✓			✓	✓
6			✓		✓	✓		✓		✓	✓				✓
5			✓		✓	✓		✓		✓	✓			✓	✓
7			✓		✓	✓		✓		✓				✓	✓
4		✓	✓		✓	✓		✓	✓	✓	✓	✓			✓
9			✓	✓	✓	✓		✓		✓	✓		✓	✓	✓
3			✓	✓	✓	✓				✓	✓				
14	✓		✓	✓	✓	✓									
1		✓			✓	✓		✓		✓	✓			✓	✓
19			✓		✓	✓				✓	✓	✓			
18					✓	✓				✓					
12		✓			✓	✓								✓	✓
11			✓		✓	✓								✓	
16	✓		✓		✓	✓	✓								✓
Total	3	5	16	3	20	20	2	10	3	14	10	5	2	11	11

Table 5.7 *continued*

Notes:
Explanation of **topics**:
time given for parent/staff contact: indicates that time was made available to administrative staff, form tutors or year heads (or senior teachers)
PTA: ✓ = use of the parent–teacher association, or similar organization, to deal with attendance and unauthorized absence matters
phone calls: ✓ = frequent use of phone calls to authorize absence
letters home, notes to school: ✓ = use of a written notification system to authorize absence
visits by parent to form tutor: ✓ = parents of frequent absentees are encouraged to make visits
home visits by staff: ✓ = practice is for school staff to make home visits to obtain information on absence
home/school liaison teacher: ✓ = practice is for h.s.l.t. to be used to obtain information on absence
EWO contact to gain support: = ✓ practice to use EWO or attendance officer to gain the co-operation of parents
rules on un abs provided at registration: ✓ = responses imported from Table 5.3 as evidence of initial parent contact
parent actions seen as presenting school staff with difficulties = four areas of concern identified by the school staff: ✓✓✓ = concern mentioned in 3 or more interviews; ✓✓ = in 2 interviews; ✓ = in 1 interview

concern about difficult parental actions over the authorization of absence. It might be reasonable to suppose that such an interrelationship was to be expected because schools needed to make the rules clear. However, eight schools where staff find parental actions over authorization present them with difficulty do not publish information to the parents at the time of enrolment on the process of authorization. Furthermore the distribution of both groups within the table appears to be random. Therefore there seems to be no direct relationship between publishing or not publishing information and the incidence of staff concern.

Use made of outside agencies to motivate pupils

As discussed in Chapter 4, schools have limited use of the educational psychologists, Child Guidance clinics or SSDs for the treatment of pupils where unauthorized absence was the major problem. Therefore this section concentrates on the role of the Education Welfare Service, the major agency providing a service to the school relating directly to attendance. Table 5.8 summarizes information from the sample schools on the links made with the EWS, using headings derived from issues discussed in Chapter 4. The table is limited to the processes of co-operation; it does not include information on the professional work undertaken by the EWO with pupils and families following referral. However, some of the findings presented in Table 5.8 will be considered against Halford's findings presented in Table 4.3.

All but one school in the sample knew who their EWO was and had established systems for informing the EWO of pupils thought to be 'at risk', as suggested by the Elton committee (DES, 1989, p. 183). The school that did not know their EWO had the lowest rate of unauthorized absence in the sample, so low as to be officially unrecordable, and considered that they had no need to know. School staff said they knew how to make contact with the appropriate office should the need arise, but the school did not provide that information for parents (see Table 5.5).

Twelve of the sample schools gave indications that they had sufficient confidence in their EWO for that person to represent the school; an example of confidence was give by one senior pastoral care manager:

> We have a good ESW. Unfortunately we have to share him with about 14 other schools. Our access time to him during the week is limited. There has been some talk that we could syndicate an EWO, and share him with some other schools. I can't see that happening with money so tight. I think that the tasks of the EWO are grossly underestimated by the people who oversee the system, and they should be paid a lot more money. If that was the case then the standard of care would be even better. Our EWO has taken part in other activities in the school like parents' evenings, he has met parents and offered to play a much wider role in the school, but that was before his case load was changed and he went from 8 schools to 14.
>
> (School 6)

This view makes it clear that this school not only has confidence in their

Table 5.8 Analysis of schools' contact with their EWO

School	basic information		relationship with the EWO				service agreement		
	named officer	info. on absence	can represent school	access to form tutor	access to senior pastoral staff	direct access to pupils	s.l.a.	skills	time
15	✓	✓			✓				✓
17	✓	✓		✓	✓				✓
10	✓	✓	✓		✓	✓			✓
2	✓	✓	✓	✓	✓	✓			✓
8	✓	✓	✓		✓	✓	✓		✓
13	✓	✓	✓	✓	✓	✓		✓	✓
20	✓	✓			✓				
6	✓	✓	✓		✓				✓
5	✓	✓	✓	✓	✓	✓	✓	✓	✓
7	✓	✓			✓	✓	✓	✓	✓
4	✓	✓			✓				
9	✓	✓	✓	✓	✓	✓			✓
3	✓	✓	✓	✓	✓	✓			✓
14	✓	✓			✓				✓
1	✓	✓	✓		✓				✓
19	✓	✓	✓	✓	✓				✓
18	✓	✓			✓				✓
12	✓	✓	✓	✓	✓	✓		✓	✓
11	✓	✓	✓		✓		✓		✓
16					✓				
Total	19	19	12	8	20	9	4	4	17

Explanation of **topics**:

basic information

named officer ✓ = school knows who their EWO is
info. on absence ✓ = a system exists for informing the EWO of absence

relationship with EWO

can represent school ✓ = school has confidence in EWO presenting school policy
access to form tutor ✓ = EWO has easy access to form tutor
access to senior pastoral staff ✓ = EWO has easy access to senior pastoral staff
direct access to pupils ✓ = EWO can easily see any pupil in school whose absence causes difficulties

service agreement

s.l.a. ✓ = a service level agreement exists and has been provided to the school
skills ✓ = the school knows what skills the EWO can provide
time ✓ = the school knows the time allocated by the EWO to the work generated by the school

EWO but would like to use him more frequently than his time allocation allows.

It is interesting that eight of the schools did not express such a level of confidence in their EWO. Unfortunately, there was insufficient evidence from this study to explore the reasons for this. However, it is worth noting that lack of time for the EWO to take action was a common theme in the responses from the sample as a whole, with considerable frustration at the restrictions this imposed.

Only eight of the sample schools indicated that the EWO had direct access to the form tutor. This finding may be considered as surprisingly low given that the form tutor is the basic unit of the pastoral care system and marks the register. One form tutor described the situation as follows:

> It would be nice to meet the EWO! I'm on the front line, and I'm in a better position to know the reasons for absence. I know the home circumstances better than the Heads of Year who do meet with the EWO. I am looking at the matter from the pastoral aspect and the moral reasons for coming to school, while they are looking at it from the legal aspect.
>
> (Form Tutor, School 4)

Table 5.8 shows that in all the sample schools the EWO met with the senior pastoral staff. It will be recalled that staff at this level have more time for this contact, that they will be dealing with more difficult pupils and are more likely to see unauthorized absence as a disciplinary matter. The EWO may, therefore, be seen by pupils and parents as part of the disciplinary process of the school. This view may well be reinforced by what has already been shown to be the lack of information provided to parents and pupils on the EWO's role in relation to the school.

In nine schools the EWO had direct access to pupils, while they were in school, to talk to them about attendance or related matters. In only two of these schools was it clear that the EWO operated a 'drop-in' or counselling service where pupils could refer themselves. This is very different from the description of the services supplied by EWOs reported by Halford (1991) and described in Chapter 4, in which EWOs in 104 of the 107 local authorities surveyed said they provided counselling to children in schools. While the differences in responses can be accounted for by differences in definitions, it does provide some evidence that there is a need for clarity by all involved as to what services EWOs are providing.

Most schools knew what time their EWO had for work within the school (and, as has been shown, some staff considered it insufficient), but very few staff knew what services the school was supposed to receive from the Education Welfare Service. Neither did schools know what skills their EWO had to bring to those tasks that were undertaken. It appears that the work of the EWO is often known through custom and practice rather than by any formal statement. The following response illustrates the situation:

Question   Is there a written statement of the services that can be provided by the EWO?

Answer   I've not seen one.

Question   So how do you know what his job is?

Answer   Tradition. There ought to be a statement, because confusions have come up this week, about what is policy and what is unstated policy, which causes all sorts of difficulties for us. . . . Also you cannot be absolutely certain what you can demand of them. If it is just door knocking, which was tried and failed, well it would be as well to know that, but it wouldn't be very satisfactory, but it would be as well to know it.

(Year Head, School 18)

It appears that many schools are using whatever skills are made available, but they do not often insist on establishing levels of service, or requesting the skill levels that they consider they need.

Section summary: Methods used to motivate pupils to attend

Attempts to motivate pupils to attend were focused on individuals rather than on class groups, year groups or the whole school. Few schools attempted to motivate large groups of pupils through changes to the curriculum. Most form tutors did not have any programme of study for their tutor group and did not plan the tutorial time in order to improve their motivation to attend. Indeed the main focus of tutorial group work was on school-related issues with a strong organizational and disciplinary element. In these circumstances tutors were required to be authoritarian rather than facilitative.

Giving praise to pupils for good attendance was much less frequent than the use of sanctions for poor attendance. Detention was a common form of punishment for truancy, used with the aim of improving attendance. Counselling, either by teacher or EWO, was used in a minority of schools.

Direct work with parents on attendance matters, including home visits, was undertaken by senior school staff and may have a disciplinary focus initially. Successful home visits were based on personal contact. Home/school liaison teachers were effective in establishing good relationships between home and school. It was unusual for parents to come to school to talk to their child's tutor about poor attendance and how to improve it.

It was common for the school to ask the EWO to make a home visit when action by the school (either punishment, the threat of punishment, or a home visit to the parents) had not improved attendance. Schools did not commonly provide parents with a written explanation of the enforcement role of the EWO. EWOs usually visited parents as a result of referral from the school, schools did not tell the parents of the referral or the purpose of the visit. Schools believed that such visits were effective since they said they would like more of them, but they seemed resigned to the fact that restricted EWO time limited the number of visits made. Despite their wish to have more time provided for home visits, the schools did not know what skills the EWO had or used.

The information provided to some EWOs was limited, coming from senior staff rather than the form tutors who knew more about the pupil. This may result in a disciplinary bias to the purpose and conduct of the referral and could add to misunderstandings about the functions of the service in the minds of parents.

Section 3: A typology of approaches to unauthorized absence

The previous sections in this chapter have analysed issues arising from the way schools communicated with parents on matters relating to absence, and how schools went about motivating individual pupils to attend regularly. The analysis undertaken in those two sections was in the form of frequency of schools' response to specific issues. The result was to form a view of what was common practice within the sample schools. The purpose of this section is to propose a typology by which management approaches used by the schools to deal with unauthorized absence may be better understood. This section presents a perspective which emphasizes what is different rather than what is common; and in so doing identifies four schools from the first stage of data collection that appear to be examples of these differences. A summary of those schools' action in relation to truancy is presented in Chapter 6.

The model proposed in Chapter 1 offered a way of understanding the various motivations of consumers (usually parents), when they send their children to secondary school. The typology discussed below offers a way of understanding the communications that take place between parents, as consumers, and the schools once the child has been registered with the secondary school. The typology is based on the use of transactional analysis, a form of analysis of communication described in *Games People Play* (Berne, 1964, Chapter 2) and proposed for use in understanding organizations in *TA and Training* (Barker, 1980, p. 5).

Berne proposed a way of analysing the social interactions that take place between people based on an understanding of the psychological states of the people involved. He suggested that transactions could be classified as 'complementary or crossed, simple or ulterior, and ulterior transactions may be sub-divided into angular and duplex types' (Berne, 1964, p. 32). Berne states:

> Simple complementary transactions most commonly occur in superficial working relationships and social relationships, and these are easily disturbed by simple crossed transactions. In fact a superficial relationship may be defined as one which is confined to simple complementary transactions. Such relationships occur in activities, rituals and pastimes.
>
> (Berne, 1964, p. 31)

For the purpose of the development of this typology only simple transactions will be considered since the relationships established between parents and teachers in relation to attendance matters are more likely to be 'superficial working relationships' operating at a social level.

Berne suggests that there are three psychological states, or 'systems of feelings accompanied by a related set of behaviour patterns', that an individual can experience. These are 'Parent', 'Adult' or 'Child' ego states; he suggested that the individual can move between these states and combine them in order to respond appropriately in social situations. The transactions between people depend upon the ego states in play between them at any moment and the degree to which they are complementary (that is that the states are 'agreed' by both) or crossed (that is that the states being used are not 'agreed'). The analysis of transactions, and the psychological 'games' that result from crossed transactions, are used in social psychiatry to help improve relationships between people (Berne, 1964, p. 47).

Transactional analysis can also be used in organizations to deal with 'boundary relationships' (Baker, 1980, p. 208), and formed the basis for developing an understanding of the verbal and written interactions that took place between individuals in their performance of the social roles as either a member of school staff or as a parent. The possible complementary (agreed) transactions between the social roles, following Berne's method of presentation, are given in Figure 5.1.

Two adaptations have been made to Berne's hypothesis. The first is that one of the ego states, shown in black in the figure, is not included in the analysis. The reason for this exclusion has to do with the unlikely situation of a member of school staff being required to perform a social role in the ego state of a child. The second adaptation is the partial amalgamation of the adult and parent ego states as far as the parent of the pupil is concerned. This is an attempt to acknowledge that these two states are likely to have strong links when the focus of attention is the schoolchild.

Figure 5.1 shows four simple complementary transactions that could result from the interaction of the ego states. Each of these is now considered; each provided a basis for the selection of the four schools.

In Figure 5.1 the relationship established is Adult-to-Adult; interactions are characterized by effective and efficient exchange of information (termed 'procedures' by Berne): parents and school staff agree on the aims of school, these aims are clearly laid out and form the basis of an accepted contract, explicit or implied. There is mutual trust between the parties based on this agreement. School staff respect parents and their individual differences, the relationship is open with a free flow of information and parents are seen as equals: interactions described by Woods (1989) as prerequisites for an effective partnership. This relationship contains many of the elements that characterized the 'consentient' group discussed in Chapter 1. In relation to attendance, rights and duties are known, the legitimate reasons for absence are agreed and the process for notification understood and used. As a result school staff will trust and accept the parents' phone calls and notes, and will authorize absence without hesitation. However, exchanges based on these

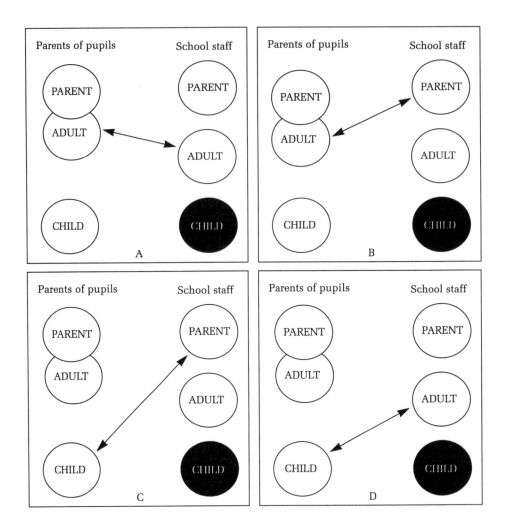

Figure 5.1 Complementary transactions between roles

transactions may include information which allows both sides to use considerable discretion, and decisions may be neither predictable nor stereotyped.

The Adult-to-Adult transactions may appear the ideal; however, there is evidence from the analysis of the data so far collected that many of the sample schools did not provide parents with sufficient information on attendance for there to be a trusting relationship based on a clear agreement. It has already been shown that policy and practices are not always made clear in prospectuses, that the basis for action in dealing with non-attendance at registration is not always clear, that parents may not be provided with attendance information and may not know how to make best use of the Education Welfare Service. These deficits are unlikely to form the basis of an efficient Adult-to-Adult transaction. However, some schools provided a great deal of information and one that did so more consistently than most was School 18. The following is an example of the school's policy in relation to absence.

> The ethos and structure of the school is clearly stated in the staff handbook, and the governors' code of conduct, which goes to all parents. There is a single school rule which reflects that structure ... [and] provides a source of discussion between staff and pupils. There is a policy of raising expectation and achievement in this school. It is only possible to increase teacher expectation and to raise student achievement if we have solid and reliable attendance. If the attendance element is not there it is likely that a number of other elements of the educational equation are not there.
>
> It would mean that something has gone wrong in terms of ensuring family support for learning and an understanding of what the education enterprise is about. It might indicate a health problem, it might indicate a number of problems in the family which require further investigation.
>
> (Deputy Head, School 18)

In Figure 5.1(B) the relationship established is Parent-to-Adult; just as in the Adult-to-Adult ego states, interactions are characterized by what appears to be an effective and efficient exchange of information, and parents and school staff agree on the aims of school. Much of the information required for an Adult-to-Adult transaction is present and often used, and in many transactions there may be little to distinguish between the two forms, but in relation to attendance there are important differences. The tutor's response to absence is to both punish the pupil and seek as much information as possible in order to determine the cause. Where the tutor's enquiry produces evidence that emotional or social difficulties are being experienced by either the parent or the pupil the pastoral care staff's instinctive response is to attempt to provide a form of welfare support. Senior staff move easily into a quasi social work role and make home visits. The staff may not have had training to undertake home visits, but they do so because it is 'the right thing' for a caring school to do. The purpose of the home visits may not be clear. The role of school staff involved in this work is not made clear to parents in published material, so may not be known. Staff may also call on the EWO to assist in the development of the social work task. The pay-off for the parent is that they have authority figures listening to their troubles, and they can establish an understanding with the school staff that protects the child from punishment, and results in sympathetic treatment of problem behaviour. The pay-off for the senior school staff is that it confirms them as coping parents, and the pay-off for the EWO is that it confirms them as social workers. Where absence from school is seen as a by-product of the family's difficulties the pupil is not held wholly responsible, so punishment may not be applied, and if it is the application may be erratic. A number of schools in the sample responded in this way. One that was typical was School 3. The following is an example of the school's approach.

> We have our problem families ... they are well known to the year heads and myself.

For example, we have one girl who comes from an horrendous family, major problems there and our relationship with Social Service is not too good because we have this battle about child protection registers and who should go on them. Education lines up on one side with the idea that they should be on them and Social Service lines up on the other because they are frightened of the parents and don't like working with them. Therefore the child is left without protection.

The girl concerned has had a string of absences and no notes. Now technically it would be unauthorized because no authorization has come from the home, but we know in this case that the girl sees school as a haven. She would be here rather than stay at home; she would do anything to be in school. Therefore we have taken it upon ourselves to authorize those absences, because she is always having to separate her parents from attacking other children. ... Out of 7 children in the family 3 have been assaulted by the parents. All 3 have come through the school, all 3 have been statemented, the girl who is actually here at the moment is fourth in line. The problems are very emotionally draining for the staff who deal with these kids. ... When she is absent we don't know what is happening to her, but we have a pretty good idea. When she comes back she talks to her year head, or she will come and talk to me.

I think we have a staff that has a happy relationship with all the kids, the kids know when they have stepped over a line and we can shout just as well as any other school, but we do care about our kids, and we do spend a lot of time with them. If the kids are upset they tell us. This gives us insight into what is happening. We know more about what is happening on this estate down here than either the Police or the Social Services. ... We talk to parents, we have them coming in and crying on our shoulders. ... You can't put a child in a classroom unless certain needs are met. If a child is in an emotional turmoil it's not going to benefit at all from being in a classroom or even a form lesson. That needs to be dealt with before any learning occurs. ... That child has to feel that they come here and know that that need is going to be addressed, or at least recognized.

(Head of Pastoral Care, School 3)

In Figure 5.1(C) the relationship established is Parent-to-Child. The parent ego state is characterized by ritual behaviour which 'may have lost all procedural validity' (Berne, 1964, p 34); the child ego state is characterized by spontaneity and enjoyment (p. 26). In relation to schools there are no clear statements made to parents about the need for attendance, or the methods of following up and authorizing absence, or the role and function of the EWO. There are clear internal procedures provided to staff which have to be re-enforced periodically because individuals do not follow them. The reaction to absence by school staff is predictable, stereotyped and authoritarian; many parents of absent pupils are seen as non-conforming and wilful, and absentees themselves as deviant, anti-authority and uncontrolled. Absence is always seen as suspicious and unauthorized absence is usually punished, often with the apparent agreement and encouragement of the parent. The pay-off for school staff is that they can act as if they were the responsible parent without having to enquire too deeply into the complex social mores and difficulties of the real parents. Staff transactions may be stereotyped, having become patterned by experience, custom and practice, and are likely to be resistant to any proposed changes. The pay-off for the parent is that as the school's systems and procedures are unclear and inconsistently applied they can usually get their own way within the muddle. A few schools within the sample appeared to make no information available to parents on attendance and very little on the Education Welfare Service, and staff reactions seemed to mirror those described. One such school was School 15. The Deputy Head of Pastoral Care gave a flavour of the approach taken.

> *Question*   What do the School rules and the School behaviour policy have to say about unauthorized absence?
>
> *Answer*   We don't have school rules. It is mentioned in our code of conduct which says that punctuality and attendance are vital. The children know of the sanctions available from our pastoral periods, and in form periods staff will go over certain aspects of the code of conduct.
>
> *Question*   Are parents told what will happen if their child is absent without permission?
>
> *Answer*   This is something that we will have to revise. In 1992 when we revised our discipline policy all parents received the new policy and had to sign as having received it. That included absence. In 1993 the newcomers to the school were given a copy. This year's intake were not given copies . . . .Parents were told about it in a more informal way.
>
> (Deputy Head, Pastoral Care, School 15)

In Figure 5.1(D) the relationship established is Adult-to-Child. It will be recalled that the adult ego state is characterized by effective and efficient exchange of information and the child ego state by spontaneity and enjoyment. In this relationship information may not be routinely available to all parents on matters relating to absence since the view taken of parents by school staff is that they only need information when the pupil's poor attendance seems to warrant it. The school seeks and collects information on the pupil's family and background, possibly over many years as a result of the enrolment of many family members. This information is used by staff to predict and explain all school behaviour including absence. Individual staff contact with parents over many years means that staff judge the truthfulness of notes and phone calls on the basis of previous events, not necessarily on formal agreements. These actions of school staff may at first appear to be from the parental ego state, but the response to absence is not ritualistic or stereotyped, rather it is based on insight and understanding of the parent and pupil. The staff view of parents is that they can be trusted until evidence proves otherwise, the parents' view of the staff is that it is perfectly safe to leave matters to their good judgement, if things go wrong they will be told.

The pay-off for staff is that the school has ultimate control based on custom and practice which implies a trust by the parents in their skills and judgement, thus validating them as professionals. The pay-off for the parents is that they are relieved of some responsibility and can get on with other things, having accepted the 'natural' authority of the school. Some schools in the sample made little information available to parents at enrolment and provided that information only when appropriate, and some had established long histories of contact with parents over many generations. One such school was School 14, whose approach to unauthorized absence was explained by the head teacher as follows:

> If you see unauthorized absence as a school problem then I don't think you are seeing the whole thing at all. You've got to see it in relation to what it is actually telling you about other aspects of the child's life.
> ... We don't publish information on unauthorized absence to parents, I think it is somewhat discredited as a performance indicator, and we wouldn't want to make any comment on it whatsoever. We have views on it. I don't think that it is the panacea that it is supposed to be, nor do I think it's the most valid and reliable data that is coming out of school. The qualitative data that you can't document are far more important to us. Things like unauthorized absences league tables are hardly on the top of our agenda in terms of promoting what we are about.
> ... There isn't a school behaviour policy. ... [T]here isn't a policy that you could pull off the shelf, but if you ask a child he or she will tell you what the policy is, because it is part of the air we breathe here. Good behaviour, punctuality are part of the oral tradition of the school. Discussions with the children reinforce the values of the school.
> ... The basic reason why the majority of parents choose this school is because they know their child will be cared for here. Conversation with the children is the very essence of a good relationship. So talking with children is our bread and butter, as well as teaching them. Parents welcome that as a good basis for working together.
>
> (Head Teacher, School 14)

The four schools were included because some data suggested that their approaches to dealing with absence and unauthorized absence appeared to contain a prevalence of a certain type of social transaction between managers and parents. All four types of transaction are probably exhibited in some degree in all the schools in the sample, and in many other schools. The selection in this study is based on what appeared to be prevalent from the analysis of the data collected from them.

All the tables in sections one and two of this chapter identify the performance of the four selected schools. Table 5.3 shows that the typology resulted in the selection of two high-scoring and two low-scoring schools. The two high-scoring schools emphasize the efficient and effective exchange of information as found in 'adult' forms of transaction. These transactions make people aware of policy and services before they are needed (as indicated in the heading to this chapter). The two low-scoring schools emphasize the ritualistic and traditional exchange of information as found in 'child' transactions. These transactions make people aware of policy and services only when it seems required.

The next chapter summarizes findings from the four selected schools (further detailed analysis can be found in Collins, 1996). In each case the typology discussed in this chapter is used to aid the understanding of the approach taken by the school in its transactions with parents and pupils. The chapter concludes with an analysis of the usefulness of the typology suggested here.

## CHAPTER 6

Transactions in Four Schools

The principal aim of schooling is to prepare children for the adult world. Hands up any adult who has never been late, never forgotten something, never done a bad piece of work, or ever made a humorous quip about someone in authority. Hands up any adult who has ever suffered any deprivation of liberty, or any formal punishment for such actions.

(Dr C. Williams, 'School detention or false imprisonment?', *Childright*, Sept. 1994, no. 109)

During research four schools were selected, as described in Chapter 5, for further investigation; this chapter analyses the information gathered and the usefulness of the typology proposed. Data were gathered on truants selected by the school, on the school's knowledge of their background, on school contacts with their parents and on attempts made to improve their attendance.

There are five parts to this chapter. The first four parts provide a summary of the information obtained, school by school, and include an analysis of the relevance of the transactional hypothesis proposed for that school. The fifth part presents issues common to all four schools, and reviews the value of the typology.

School 18

The school is in an inner city area enrolling pupils from a community with a high proportion of families where Asian languages are spoken at home. The transactional hypothesis was that the school emphasized the 'Adult-to-Adult' in its exchanges with parents.

Review of attendance

The pupils chosen by the school were representative of all years. Two were from Year 11, five from Year 10, five from Year 9, and two each from Years 8 and 7. All attendance data had to be extracted from handwritten registers. Very little information on attendance was available in the pupils' file records. Attendance rates of the 16 selected pupils were not included in the file copies of reports to their parents, although there was space for this on the report form. In the process of collecting the attendance data it became obvious that the method of recording did not conform to the school or the DfE guidelines. It was found that many entries did not distinguish in any way between authorized and unauthorized absence, that notes from parents providing evidence for authorization did not tally with marks in the register, and that the notes were often vague in relation to the dates they covered. There was anecdotal evidence that some absences were retrospectively marked as authorized at the time when the DfE returns were being prepared. There was no evidence that the records had been inspected in relation to their being properly kept. The basic data on which other action might be taken, either by the school or the LEA, were therefore suspect.

Comparison of the sample with the 'average' pupil

Staff were asked for their view of the behaviour of absentee pupils when in school, and the behaviour of their parents, compared to the behaviour of the 'average' pupil and parent.

The teachers said that pupils who were unauthorized absentees liked being in school a little less than their peers and were less happy when they were there. They were less interested in the work, were less likely to complete homework, appeared to be less able and to need more help with their work. They were very unlikely to be involved in extra-curricular activities, were less well-behaved in the playground and much less well-behaved in class. They got on less well with staff, were less easy to talk to, less likely to listen and do what was wanted, and were less reliable. They were no more likely to be bullied than their peers, but were more likely to bully others and were more aggressive.

The staff's views of all parents was that they came into school infrequently, but parents of unauthorized absentees were even less likely to come. Parents of absentees took much less interest in their child's schoolwork, were very unlikely to make sure that homework was done, showed very little support for the school, and were much less likely to attend parents' evenings. They frequently condoned absence whereas other parents seldom did so; they missed appointments and failed to provide notes and other information when asked. They got on less well with staff, were less easy to talk to, but like the 'average' parents were not seen as aggressive.

These opinions suggest that teachers see unauthorized absentees as harder to motivate than the average pupil, and that teachers may believe that parental co-operation will not be forthcoming when they attempt to motivate unauthorized absentees.

Work undertaken with the sample pupils

Teachers provided information on the sample pupils' involvement with the Education Welfare Service, on their known criminal activity, on the involvement of other agencies in dealing with attendance problems, and on the likely prognosis for the improvement of attendance. Teachers also commented on additional family information known to them. A summary of these responses appears as Table 6.1. The table has been arranged in descending order of pupil absence as expressed in the third column.

Teachers' information on the pupils' home background shows that family breakdown, disruption and lack of parental control were common experiences among the sample. Some of the comments made by teachers show that they considered that the parents were directly responsible for the absence (for example #13 and #3), but generally the home background was not 'blamed' for the absence. The connection was implied by the reference to lack of parental control, or there was speculation. For example, one teacher said:

> I believe, but cannot support, that [his] absences tie into his mother's work routines, and that he carries responsibility for looking after younger brothers and sister.
>
> (Year Head on #15)

In this particular case the pupil's file showed that he had been excluded from school for violent behaviour twice within a two-month period at the start of Year 8. It also showed that he was abusive and disruptive in class and was known to leave school without permission. In these respects he fitted the general picture of the absentee pupil considered above. There was a record on file that his mother had been into school to see a senior member of staff to discuss her son's absences, and his moving to a more local school. No record of the content of that meeting had been made. Given the reluctance of parents of absentees to come into school (commented on above), the opportunity presented by this meeting to establish the foundations of co-operation went unrecorded and was possibly lost. There was a letter on file to the mother, written four months after that meeting by another senior member of staff, which asked for her co-operation in telling the school of her son's absences, but this made no reference to anything discussed previously. The Education Welfare Officer told me that the service was considering applying for an education supervision order in this case; however, the school had no information on file about the legal action being contemplated, and it was apparent that the year head did not know.

Returning to the consideration of Table 6.1, it is of interest to note that the Education Welfare Service was not involved with five of the sixteen pupils in the sample. Given the high levels of absence of this group this is surprising. It is also surprising given that the staff had selected out for the study those pupils who gave them concern. It became apparent that the school did not have an automatic system of referral to the service when attendance fell below a certain figure. The absence of a system appeared to be related to the

Table 6.1 Information on pupils at School 18: analysis of the teachers' views of the 16 selected pupils

#	m/f	%abs	%un abs	5	6	7	8	9	précis of additional family information
13	f	73.8	62.9	E	ews *				parents keeping her off to help at home
1	f	51.9	25.5	E	ews thv		ssd	poor	single-parent family, mother mentally ill, child beyond her control
15	m	51.2	48.7	E	ews *		hsl	poor	single-parent family, possibly kept home to look after younger children
5	m	51.0	19.5	Pan	ews				single-parent family, father left family for other 7 wives
12	m	48.0	24.5	Pan			ssd	imprvt	single-parent family, mother cannot cope; recent improvement in behaviour
4	f	43.7	41.6	E	ews tcon	✓	ep ssd	v. poor	parents recently separated, child aggressive, disruptive and out of parents' control
17	f	41.4	16.8	E	tcon ews		hsl		illness used as an excuse for absences
2	m	41.3	22.6	E	ews	✓		poor	mother condones absences; child beyond her control
16	m	40.8	1.3	E	ews				illness used as an excuse for absences
9	f	38.6	16.8	E		✓			no information on family background
3	m	38.6	5.2	E	tcon			poor	mother condones absences; illness used as an excuse for absences
8	f	32.2	23.1	nk	ews		ssd		single-parent family, father died '94, mother near nervous breakdown, child looks after family
7	m	31.4	18.5	Pan	tcon			poor	socializes with a low-achieving group, not motivated, on fringe of crime
10	m	26.0	19.1	Ben	ews				contact with parents difficult, no shared language
6	m	23.7	21.0	Ben	ews				single-parent family, father died last year, child not motivated to learn
14	m	13.8	8.45	Ben	thv	✓	hsl		single-parent family, child does as he pleases, stole while absentee
11									void

Notes:
The table has been presented in descending order of percentage absence (column 3)
= pupil identification number
m/f = male or female
%abs = the total percentage of schooling missed since enrolment
%unabs = the total percentage of schooling missed as a result of unauthorized absence
5 = language believed to be spoken at home: **E** = English, **Pun** = Punjabi, **Ben** = Bengali
6 = forms of contact: **ews** = by Education Welfare Service (* = action being taken to bring about a prosecution), **tcon** = by teacher, **thv** = home visit by teacher
7 ✓ = known involvement in criminal activity
8 = agencies involved: **ep** = educational psychology, **ssd** = social services department, **hsl** = home/school liaison teaching or equivalent
9 = prognosis

way in which the registers were kept in that accurate data on individual, form, or year group were not routinely available. Referrals to the Education Welfare Service were normally by request of the year head on pupils that the form tutors had drawn attention to, or by referral by other staff when behaviour and absences deteriorated.

Four of the sixteen pupils were known to be involved with crime. Only one was known to have committed offences while absent from school. The Education Welfare Service was working with two of these known offenders, but was not working with the one (#14) who had offended while absent. There was evidence on the file of #14, going back over two years, of his being on report for violence and disruption, of being excluded once and warned of permanent exclusion. There was evidence from absence notes that they had probably been written by the pupil himself. This may have been because his mother spoke and wrote little English. There was no evidence of any checks made on the truthfulness of the notes, although some home visits by the year head had been made. There was no information on file of the work being undertaken by the home/school liaison service. The absence of the involvement of the Education Welfare Service in this case may well be explained by the relatively low levels of absence as compared with the others in the sample, and the lack of a referral by the year head. However, as this pupil was still in the early stages of his school career and many difficulties already existed, it is surprising that there was no referral, and that greater attempts to gain the co-operation of the parents had not been made.

Four of the sixteen absentees were known by the school to have contact with the Social Services Department. In these four cases there was no record on file giving information on the social workers involved. One of these cases had been referred to the Social Services Department by the school, but the school file gave no information on any action being taken.

In four cases the teachers knew that either home/school teaching was being provided, or the Educational Psychology Service was involved. The pupils' files showed nothing of these services' involvement. In the case where the educational psychologist was involved (#4), the records showed that transfer to the school had been made as a result of difficult behaviour in her previous school and absence from it. The poor behaviour had continued and she was frequently on report, abusive to teachers and other pupils and disruptive in class. Her year head reported that a programme of individual teaching had been introduced, supported by a specialist teaching team. Nothing on the content of this teaching was in the pupil's record, and there was no record of the parents being told.

Finally, before leaving consideration of Table 6.1, the information supplied on #9 is worthy of note. There had been very little involvement by the school staff with this pupil during the four years of her secondary career, no family details were known and there had been no home contact. She was not being dealt with by the Education Welfare Service although the year head believed that a referral had been made. Her school record contained a copy of last year's end of year report to parents that included mention of absence and underachievement. Her teacher said that she was able, usually good in class when in school, but poor at the provision of homework. The file included evidence of a great deal of lateness, but only one note from the parents excusing a lateness. There were no notes explaining the absences in previous years, and all of the current year's absences (approximately 40 per cent) were unauthorized. There was a note on file that she had been reported for shoplifting. The lack of intervention and action was not typical of the others in the sample. What is of concern is that this pupil had been included in the research sample, and was therefore seen as a cause for concern, but there was no action despite abundant evidence of unauthorized absence, involvement in crime, and lack of proper preparation for GCSEs. This example indicated the need for regular reviews by the school of pupils whose absence is seen as a problem, regular inspections of the register and action by the EWO, and discussions with the parents aimed at gaining their co-operation.

Analysis of teacher time given to improving attendance

Staff were asked for an estimate of the time given to the methods used to improve attendance of the sample group. Table 6.2 gives a summary of the responses made by year heads. The table is presented in descending order of absence since enrolment with the school (see column 2). The responses indicate that there was difficulty in answering this question in terms of time. Few year heads were able to respond with an estimate of the time given either weekly or over a term, and those that did were not confident of their estimate. However, some evidence of the time given can be made from the comments appearing in column 6, which provides a summary of the types of contacts made.

Table 6.2 can be divided into three distinct sections. The first, presented in in bold type in the table and covering 6 pupils, is where there is some evidence that time and effort have been given to a strategy designed to help deal with absence problems. The second, presented in italics and covering 7 pupils, is where there is some evidence that limited time has been given to an attempt to help. The third, presented in normal type and covering 3 pupils, is where no time has been stated and no special methods apparently used. The evidence presented in the table suggests that there is some attempt to target intervention on the very poor attenders, either by additional work from staff, or by the EWO, or both. However, the absence of any strategy or methods used for #5 is surprising. This is an instance where the Education Welfare Service had considered the possibility of prosecution, and made some home enquiries, but no civil or criminal action had been taken. This situation was not known to the form tutor or year head. The fact that the father had recently left home was reported, as was the fact that previous siblings had attended the school without difficulty. There appeared to be no

Table 6.2 Time given to pupils at School 18

1 #	2 %	3 m/f	4 week	5 term	6 comment
13	73.8	f			no time stated, weekly home contact, referral to EWO
1	51.9	f	3		home visits
15	51.2	m		4	home visits
5	51.0	m			no special methods used
12	48.0	m			no time stated, phone calls to parents, talks with EWO
4	43.7	f			no time stated, foster care, police, special teaching programme
17	41.4	f		3	interviews, letters
2	41.3	m			no time stated, one meeting with hsl
16	40.8	m		2	meetings with mother
3	38.6	m			no time stated, referral to EWO
9	38.6	f			'a few minutes from time to time', talking to year head and EWO
8	32.2	f			'a few minutes from time to time', talking to year head and EWO
7	31.4	m			no time stated, contact with parents and EWO
10	26.0	m			no special methods identified by form teacher
6	23.7	m			no special methods used
s 14	13.8	m		4	home visits
s 11					void

recent staff contact with the mother and no visits made by the mother to the school. There was no evidence from information supplied to explain the lack of action; however, the lack of a positive relationship with, and co-operation of, the mother would make it difficult to get an education supervision order in this case. Further, it was believed that the adult court would be unlikely to be able to pass anything more that an absolute or conditional discharge in the circumstances, since the mother had no money to pay a fine. There appeared to be no immediate explanation for the lack of action in a situation where the pupil's unauthorized absence rate during the last year had been nearly 50 per cent.

Summary of data analysis

Initial data collected from the school suggested that the communication with parents at the time of enrolment was clear and set out their rights and duties. However, further investigation provided no evidence that this good start was followed up. Rates of attendance for pupils and year groups were not produced and therefore could not be reported to parents. It follows that there could be no presentation of attendance certificates to individuals or groups, and no letters of congratulation sent home. Neither was there comment to parents about changes in the levels of attendance over years or terms.

The lack of information to parents may be related to the fact that the attendance information was suspect. Also systems used in the school did not allow accurate recording of post-registration truancy. In these circumstances the school might have reduced confidence in anything published, and it would have been possible that rewards and letters home might have gone to poor attenders. There was also evidence that unexplained absences were retrospectively marked at a much later date as authorized.

Notes providing a reason for absence from parents were usually accepted, and the absence authorized. There was evidence that one pupil had written his own note excusing a period of absence and excusing himself from P.E. The reason for this may have been because the parent was not English-speaking, but there was no evidence that the parent had been contacted over the matter and a process of communication agreed with her. A senior member of staff said that communication from the school to the parents was always in English, even when the language spoken at home was known not to be English. It was interesting that all the notes from non-English-speaking parents were in English, and had signatures made up of English characters. Clearly the school's practices invited misunderstanding, and encouraged forgery by the pupil.

Pupils' files contained old report cards issued as punishment or control over poor behaviour and attendance. These cards were required to be read and signed by the parent each evening. Some report cards had not been signed by parents and may not, therefore, have been seen by them, or may not have been understood. No action on the absent signatures appeared to have been taken. Most of the cards indicated that the pupil's behaviour or attendance during the period of monitoring was 'excellent' or 'good', and there were very few critical comments. This lack of critical comment was also evident in the end of year reports written by the form tutor to parents. These reports were usually positive and encouraging, even when the school was dealing with very difficult pupil behaviour. These reports did not normally comment on the pupil's poor attendance.

Meetings were arranged by the senior staff with parents, but the letters sent to parents sometimes read more like a summons than a request; for example, 'Please come and see me between 9 and 9.30 on ... '. Also the letters suggested that the meetings would be to discuss the school's demands, for example: 'We want to see an improvement in attendance and behaviour.' There were no examples of a mutually convenient meeting being arranged to discuss the possible reasons for unexplained absences, or to plan action jointly to deal with it; however, this might have been because the sample pupils were beyond that stage.

The school did not have a system of telling parents that a referral had been made by the school to the Education Welfare Service. However, the service used two standardized letters to send to parents which indicated that information on absence had been passed to it from the school. Both letters threatened legal action if attendance did not improve and assumed that attendance would improve once the warning had been given. One of the letters was sent following unsuccessful home contact. Neither letter gave a clear indication of what help could be given by the service. It has already been noted that court action was rare, therefore the threats made in the letter were usually no more than that. It was possible for parents to receive several letters of each type. The school appeared to have no control over this communication with parents.

The transactions

The evidence suggested that the 'Adult-to-Adult' hypothesis proposed for this school was not appropriate in relation to the communication established with parents of truants for the following reasons:

- There was no attendance policy in operation within the school that gave general guidance to teachers on acting equitably in relation to absence prior to or after registration. Thus authorization of absence was idiosyncratic, giving form tutors considerable discretion which allowed them to respond from their own ego state rather than a corporate one.
- The registration data were suspect, making any communication which used them suspect.
- The contact established by senior staff with the parent of absentees was largely ritualistic, made up of a set of stereotyped responses and 'parental' in origin, tending towards direction and dictation rather than consultation and collaboration.
- There was no single source of reliable information on the sample pupils. The files were not reliable since they did not contain all that was known to be significant. Information exchanges between staff were verbal rather than written and liable to misunderstanding and reinterpretation.
- Reports to parents were bland through omitting mention of problem behaviour and poor attendance. The result was a false impression that things were better than they really were, or conflicting if they had received warning letters during the year. This seemed unlikely to lead to their collaboration in improving matters; it certainly did not invite collaboration.
- Respect for difference was not shown to parents by the use of their native language in formal letters.
- Parents of absentees avoided contact with the school, which is a form of procrastination associated with the 'adapted child' response (Barker, 1980, p. 10).
- The school did not respond with encouragement when contact

was made, responding from the position of 'critical parent' rather than 'nurturing parent'.

The school's initial information to parents may be seen as a wish by senior management to establish a relationship that emphasizes a transactional exchange between 'adult' ego states. The data collection produced evidence that this exchange did not take place in relation to the sample. There is no evidence available that establishes whether reverting to 'adult' transactions would be any more effective in gaining parental co-operation than the 'critical parent' to 'adapted child' methods apparently used.

School 3

The school is in an urban area serving a predominantly white population. The school is popular, has an increasing roll, and takes many extra-district pupils. The transactional hypothesis was that the school emphasized the 'parent' in transaction with the parent as 'adult'.

Review of attendance

The pupils were representative of all years within the school. Four were from Year 11, three from Year 10, two from Year 9, four from Year 8 and two from Year 7.

The school was gradually introducing a computerized register system, so attendance data had to be extracted from computer printout and hand-written registers. The method used to complete the handwritten registers made confident identification of unauthorized absence difficult. All absences were marked with a zero, with the intention of filling in the zero with a code letter indicating the reason for absence at a later date. However, it was possible for the zeros to be left blank either as a result of forgetfulness or the absence of a note from the parent. All zeros without a code letter were counted as authorized absence! For this reason the handwritten registers may have underrecorded unauthorized absence. The introduction of the computerized system did not allow this to happen since the computer program demanded a reason for all absences.

Information contained within the files showed that parents were sometimes informed in annual reports of their children's attendance record, and that letters of congratulation for improved attendance were occasionally sent.

There was no evidence that the registers had been inspected.

Comparison of the sample with the 'average' pupil

The staff were asked for their view of the behaviour of the sample pupils when in school, and the behaviour of their parents, compared to the behaviour of the 'average' pupil and parent. In their view, truants liked being in school less than their peers and were less happy when there. They were much less likely to complete homework, were less attentive in class, less able to do the work and needed more help with it. They were much less likely to be involved in any extra-curricular activities. They were less well-behaved in the playground and in the classroom. They got on less well with staff, were less easy to talk to and less likely to talk about their problems. They were less likely to listen to their teachers and were much less reliable. They were slightly more likely to be bullied and to bully others, but were perceived to be as aggressive as their peers.

In relation to the parents of truants, teachers believed that they came into school about as much as other parents, but took much less interest in their child's schoolwork and were much less likely to make sure homework was done. They showed less support for the school, were less likely to attend parents' evenings and were very unlikely to be involved in the PTA. They got on much less well with the staff, were less easy to talk to and talked less about their problems. They were more difficult to contact, and were much more likely to miss appointments or not to give information when asked. They were a little less likely to provide notes, and were perceived to be as aggressive as other parents.

These findings suggest that teachers saw unauthorized absentees as making less effort in relation to all school activities than the 'average' pupil, and that their parents had insufficient interest to counteract the lack of motivation.

Work undertaken with the sample pupils

Teachers provided information on the sample pupils' involvement with the Education Welfare Service, on their known criminal activity, on the involvement of other agencies in dealing with attendance problems, and on the likely prognosis for the improvement of attendance. Teachers also commented on additional family information known to them. A summary of these responses appears as Table 6.3. The table has been arranged in descending order of pupil absence as expressed in the third column.

The teachers' information on the pupils' home background shows that family breakdown, dysfunction, lack of parental control and adolescent rebellion appear to be a common experience among the sample. In only two cases did the teachers have evidence that the parents condoned their children's absence (see #12 and #15), although there was suspicion that some others might be doing so. The pupils' home background was seen to allow or encourage absence. For example, one teacher wrote:

> Parents are divorced, [she] has lived with her father most of the time. Father is absent most of the time during the week because of work commitments. [She] sees mother regularly and uses her home as a bolt hole. [She] is the youngest of three children and seems to have a good relationship with her eldest sister who has the

Table 6.3 Information on pupils at School 3: analysis of the teachers' views of the 15 selected pupils

#	m f	%abs	%un abs	5	6	7	8	9	précis of additional family information
3	f	55	16	E	ews thv		hsl	poor	limited parental control, school phobic (collected daily from home by staff)
15	f	48	33	E	ews *			poor	single-parent family, mother condones absence, lives a long way from school
13	m	44	31	E	ews	✓	ssd p	poor	taken into care as beyond control, foster care, children's home, lived rough
2	m	43	2	E	tcon				single-parent family, illness used as an excuse for absences
9	m	41	7	E	ews thv			poor	limited parental control, poor health, little motivation
14	f	38	34	E	ews tcon	✓	ep p ssd	v. poor	family breakdown, lived with relations, lived rough, prostitution possible
1	f	37	18	E	ews tcon		ssd		single-parent family, sexually abused, on 'at risk' register, low ability
10	f	33	1	E	ews tcon			poor	single-parent family, absence condoned
12	f	30	8	E	ews	✓		poor	parents divorced and often absent, stays irregularly with both
8	m	22	6	E	ews			poor	single-parent family, can't accept separation, rebellious
11	f	17	1	E	tcon			poor	ran away from home, promiscuous, poor health, looks after siblings
7	f	16	5	E					no information
5	f	13	7	E	ews thv			impr.	school phobia, tantrums, bouts of aggression
6	m	10	1	E	ews		ep	impr.	low ability, sullen, emotionally labile, low motivation
4	f	0 $	0	E	ews		ep	poor	low ability, educated off site

Notes:
The table has been presented in descending order of percentage absence (column 3)
$ data kept by school on attendance recorded presence at off-site provision as authorized absence!
# = pupil identification number
m/f = male or female
%abs = the total percentage of schooling missed since enrolment
%unabs = the total percentage of schooling missed as a result of unauthorized absence
5 = language believed to be spoken at home: **E** = English
6 = forms of contact: **ews** = by Education Welfare Service (***** = action being taken to bring about a prosecution), **tcon** = by teacher, **thv** = home visit by teacher
7 ✓ = known involvement in criminal activity
8 = agencies involved: **ep** = educational psychology, **ssd** = social services department, **hsl** = home/school liaison teaching or equivalent, **p** = well known to the police
9 = prognosis

role of mother to her. [She] is very stubborn and is very unlikely to actually conform. She does what she thinks is correct. She is always full of good intentions which never materialize.

(#12)

In this case the teacher's comments seem to indicate disorganization within the family, which resulted in the pupil being able to please herself. It appears from the methods used to improve her attendance: praise for attendance, meetings with the pupil, and use of attendance reports, that staff had attempted to make her conform without having the agreement and co-operation of the parents. This may have been because, in the staff's view, the parents avoided any form of contact with the school. However, there was no evidence on file that either the staff or the Education Welfare Officer had made any attempts to encourage contact.

The effect of dramatic changes in home circumstances on behaviour and absence was well illustrated by one teacher, who wrote:

[He] lived at home, ran away, then lived in a foster home, then in a children's home, sometimes with friends. Now his place of abode is not known. He has lived on the streets. Levels of attendance, co-operation and motivation varied widely with the different 'home' circumstances. He was a very regular attender when with foster parents, who were very positive. They could no longer put up with lies and stealing, but [he] left of his own accord.

(#13)

In this case the Social Services were clearly heavily involved, although the file record did not indicate the legal backing for that involvement. Despite this involvement, the year head reported spending many hours simply trying to track him down, and at the time of interview the school did not know of his whereabouts. His records showed that he had missed 202 sessions during the last year out of a total of 262, and that 190 of these had been unauthorized; however, no action had been taken to enforce attendance. As he was approaching the end of Year 11 it seemed enforcement action was unlikely.

Returning to the consideration of Table 6.3, it is of interest to note that the Education Welfare Service was involved with twelve of the fifteen pupils in the sample. The remaining three (#2, #7, #11) had very low levels of unauthorized absence and this could have been the reason that no referral to the service had been made. However, in two of the cases (#2 and #7) the year heads indicated that they believed that much of the absence covered by notes from the parents was 'condoned truancy'. It was difficult to understand why, in these cases, the service was not involved, but no reason was provided. In the case of #11 the school had made a number of attempts to deal with absence and problem behaviour by having discussions with her parents, by placing her on report and suspending her for three days for bullying. The staff appeared to be acting as though they were dealing primarily with a disciplinary problem that did not need other intervention.

The EWO for the school was interviewed in relation to the tasks undertaken. Unfortunately the interviewee did not want to discuss the circumstances of the pupils in the sample. The EWO said that the main duties were to enquire of the parents as to the reasons for absence when asked to do so by the school staff, and report back to the year heads on what had been discovered. If during this enquiry it became clear that there were serious concerns about a child's safety, then a referral to the Social Services Department would be made. In those cases which did not warrant such a referral the EWO would offer support to the family or the child through counselling the pupil or parent, and attempting to improve the communication between school and the pupil. During this intervention it was common practice 'to assess whether the absence has a cause which can be removed' (a comment which was not further elaborated). It did not appear to be common practice to make a formal agreement on action with either the parents, the pupil or the school that was based on the assessment. Furthermore, the enforcement function of the LEA operating through the Education Welfare Service was not commonly discussed with parents in the early stages of intervention. In these circumstances it is very possible that some parents lacked a clear idea of what the EWO was attempting to do, and why it was being done.

It will be noted from column 10 of Table 6.3 that enforcement action was not common. In only one case within the sample (#15) had any legal action been taken. In that case the parent had been fined, but the register showed that the pupil's attendance had remained poor, and according to the year head the relationship between parent and school had broken down completely. The EWO said that it was the LEA's policy to prosecute very rarely because it did not result in improvement in attendance of the pupil and it tended to destroy any collaborative relationship there may have been between the school and the parent. The reported results of prosecution in the case of #15 seemed to show this to be the case. But the policy of very infrequent prosecution, when combined with a lack of clarity in relation to the function of the EWO, may have produced misunderstanding in the minds of parents. For example, there was evidence from absence notes sent by some parents that they were unclear that the EWO was employed by the LEA, with notes referring to the EWO as 'a teacher from the school'. Therefore, an explanation offered to the EWO was thought to be sufficient for the school to authorize the absence, for example, one parent wrote to the school in relation to her child's absence, 'X knows all about it' (where X was the name of the EWO), as if that were sufficient in itself. In this confused state of affairs it would be possible for parents to believe that the school was responsible for prosecution, to blame them for the legal action and thereby produce a breakdown in the relationship. Paradoxically, members of staff said they wanted more prosecutions, that they would have liked more control over the activities of the EWO, and would have been much more content if the EWO *had* been a member of staff. In effect, the staff appeared not to be so concerned about the breakdown in the relationship with the parents following prosecution as did the LEA; they believed that more prosecutions would have a general deterrent effect and were therefore worthwhile. The staff agreed with the LEA's policy in that prosecution was unlikely to improve attendance of the individual child, but they believed it would improve attendance generally.

It will be noted from Table 6.3 that three of the fifteen pupils were known to be involved with crime. One of these, #13 (a male), had stolen while in school as well as outside it, and one, #12 (a female), had been caught shoplifting while absent from school. Both pupils were in Year 11, both had large amounts of unauthorized absence in that year, and the staff appeared to have tried all that was possible to be of help. In the case of #14 (a female), also in Year 11, the involvement in crime was known as a result of her having talked openly in school of under-age sex and prostitution while living 'rough'. As can be seen from Table 6.3, a number of different agencies were involved with her. The school had become resigned to being unable to be of any help to her. Her year head wrote:

> [She] was hell bent on abusing everyone and the system. She was determined to be a lost cause. She has an extremely bad reputation, enjoys the attention, loves being the baddy and basks in the glory.

Despite the time and effort of several agencies, the school file showed no evidence of any attempt to assess the reasons for her difficult and aggressive behaviour, and no evidence of collaborative work between the school and other agencies to try to help her. Her file did, however, contain press cuttings associated with her being missing from home for several weeks.

Three of the sample were known to the Social Services Department. One, #1, as a result of being on the 'at risk' register, #13, as a result of being in care, and #14, discussed above. The files indicated who the social worker was for the pupil, but none contained evidence from case reviews held by the SSD.

Table 6.3 shows that the staff considered the prognosis in the majority of the cases to be poor. This is not surprising given the process of selection of the sample. In the two cases where improvement was noted, #5 and #6, it is interesting that they were younger pupils, the staff considered that they had the co-operation of the parents, and they had developed a close relationship with the pupils. There was daily contact between year head and the parent in relation to #6. This pupil was considered to have some learning difficulties, as had other siblings in the family, and poor attendance had been a common feature of them all. It was clear that the year head had acted swiftly and forcefully in this case to stop a habit of absence developing. In relation to #5, the year head had collected the pupil from home every day for the four weeks prior to the data collection and taken her into her first class. During the week of the data collection the pupil had come into school of her own volition, hence the judgement that there had been an improvement.

Table 6.4 Time given to pupils at School 3

1 #	2 %	3 m/f	4 week	5 term	6 comment
3	**55**	**f**			**too much to estimate, home visits, special tuition, open access to f/t**
15	48	f			no special methods used, evidence to EWO
13	*44*	*m*			*no time stated, constant phoning, contact with EWO and SSD*
2	43	m		1	telephone contact with mother
9	**41**	**m**			**too much to estimate, interviews with parents, home visits, counselling**
14	*38*	*f*		*1*	*phone calls and letters home, contact with EWO, SSD and police*
1	**37**	**f**		**5**	**interviews with mother, contact with EWO, case conference**
10	**33**	**f**			**too much to estimate, meetings with staff, EWO, family friends**
12	*30*	*f*		*5*	*letters home, interviews with parents, contact with EWO*
8	*22*	*m*	*2*		*referral to EWO, attendance report, interviews with mother*
11	*17*	*f*			*no time stated, interviews with parents, attendance report*
7	16	f			no special methods used
5	13	f			constant supervision thro' Year 7 and 8, home visits, bringing to school
6	10	m		12	constant supervision, links with e.p.
4	**0**	**f**			**too much to estimate, home visits, home teaching, contact with EWO**

Analysis of teacher time given to improving attendance

Staff were asked for an estimate of the time given to the methods used to improve attendance of the sample group. Table 6.4, above, gives a summary of the responses made by year heads. The table is presented in descending order of absence since enrolment with the school (see column 2).

The responses indicate that there was difficulty in answering this question in terms of time since no record of time spent was made and answers were guesses. Some evidence of the time given can be made from the comments appearing in column 6, which provides a summary of the types of contact made. This table can be divided into three distinct sections. The first, presented in the table in bold type and covering 7 pupils, is where there is some evidence that time and effort have been given to a strategy designed to help deal with absence problems. The second, presented in italics and covering 5 pupils, is where there is some evidence that limited time has been given to an attempt to help. The third, presented in normal type and covering 3 pupils, is where no special methods had apparently been used.

The table shows that time and effort spent in helping pupils appear not to be related to the amount of absence from school. Considerable time has been spent with three pupils who experience the least absence; evidence already presented tends to suggest that this low level of absence is a direct result of the time given to the methods to improve attendance. However, a great deal of time is being spent on those with much higher rates of absence, but to less obvious effect. In relation to those where no apparent methods were being used, #15 shows the effect of the breakdown in the relationship between the school, the pupil and the parent already discussed. The situation in relation to #2, a Year 7 pupil, is quite different. The staff believe that most of the absence is condoned, and that the boy's mother keeps him off school for relatively minor ailments in order to have his company. The mother came into school frequently to talk to staff about trivial matters, and was judged to be very overprotective. There was some concern that a pattern of absences was developing that might lead to greater problems in the future, and that medical problems were overwhelming the educational need. In these circumstances it might have been appropriate to refer the matter to the EWO, but this had not been done. The reason given for the lack of referral was that there was a belief that the EWO was overworked, and would be unlikely to be able to produce any improvement in the case.

Summary of data analysis

Data collected from the school suggested that the communication with parents at the time of enrolment gave clear information on the authorization of absence and the lawful reasons for absence. The governors were provided with information on absence on a termly basis, and the parents on an annual basis, but as far as could be ascertained no comparison over years was made for either group.

Rates of attendance for pupils, classes and year groups were produced from the computer-generated records, but not from the handwritten ones. Where rates were produced they were for school use. There was no system of review of the records that drew absentees to the attention of the year head or the EWO when attendance, as distinct from unauthorized absence, fell below a set figure.

Individual staff had their own way of storing and filing notes or messages received about absences, no school-wide system existed. This meant that there was no reliable way of checking the data entered into the manual or the computer registers, and that notes were not always available if needed as proof of contact. Instead, the registers themselves became that evidence, and these were shown to parents when the need arose. Such evidence might be difficult for parents to challenge successfully if they had not kept copies or records of their own.

Staff tended to accept parents' reasons for absence without question. A phone call was enough to authorize the absence, even in cases where there was apparent cause to be suspicious. Whoever took the phone call, most often the administrative staff, completed a message slip, and on many occasions this was all the evidence there was about the absence. The acceptance of phone calls meant that the caller authorized the absence, which was not in accordance with the school's own policy statements made to parents.

Staff did, however, react to the absence of both the pupil and information in cases where there was a known history of poor attendance or condoned absence. Phone calls home and home visits were common in these cases. One year head said, 'I've got kids out of bed before now!' It was clear that action in relation to a pupil was likely to be different once persistent absence had been noted, but it was not clear how much absence would lead to that action, or what evidence led to the judgement that the absence might be condoned. There appeared to be no formal system for alerting the parents to the possibility of special action or monitoring by school staff other than by putting the pupil on report. There was no evidence of any formal agreements on attendance having been made with the parents of pupils in the sample, and there was no evidence that these parents were routinely informed of their children's attendance. From the teachers' responses to questions they believed that the parents lacked the interest to motivate their children, and it is possible that this may have accounted for the absence of any agreements made with them, or information sent to them. However, this non-action denied the parents the opportunity to respond, if not from interest then from irritation at their being reminded of their duty. Indeed, persistent reminders could have some effect in families where disorganization and lack of routine mean that parental attention is diverted from school matters.

The school had no system for informing parents that they and their child had been referred to the EWO and what action might be taken by the officer. The Education Welfare Service did not appear to have a system of telling parents of their function, responsibilities or action that could be taken following a referral from the school. An unannounced first visit to a disorganized and poorly functioning family from an official 'from the school', whose functions had been learned of by word of mouth and 'history', seems more likely to produce resentment than co-operation.

The school was proud of its reputation for being able to deal successfully with pupils who had a history of behavioural difficulties and poor attendance elsewhere. During the data collection there were many examples of the senior staff using firm and fair controls combined with care to deal with bad behaviour. What was less in evidence, particularly in relation to the sample, was that the work to improve attendance was not based on clear agreements made with parents. Indeed, the making of agreements with parents was, apparently, officially discouraged by the LEA. As a result, many attempts to improve attendance involved dealing with the pupil without reference to the wishes or ideas of the parents.

The transactions

The evidence collected suggests that the 'Parent-to-Adult' hypothesis proposed for this school may not be appropriate in relation to the communication established with parents of absentees. There is evidence to suggest that staff respond from the 'parent', but they do so to the parents' 'adapted child'. The following points seem significant:

- There was no written attendance policy available to parents either at enrolment or when attendance became a problem to give information on what action would be taken by the school.
- This lack of information may have confused some parents as to the role of the school and the EWO in enforcing attendance.
- The lack of a policy meant that there was no system for recognizing and dealing with pupils, or parents, where absence was increasing.
- In some cases the relationship between staff and the parents of the sample pupils was fragile. Very little attempt appeared to be made to improve matters in these cases.
- The staff's judgement of this group of parents was that they lacked interest in their children's education, which meant that there was no requirement to be flexible or creative in interactions with them.
- Contact with these parents was sometimes minimal, ritualistic, predictable or purposeless. This allowed the focus of any action to reduce unauthorized absence to fall on the pupil, whether it be praise, or more commonly, punishment via report or detention.
- Home visits to parents were sometimes made. The authority for these visits was not clear and agreement to them by the parents seemed to be assumed rather than formally requested.

There is evidence that the school acted from both modes of the 'parent' ego state, by 'nurturing' (being caring and understanding), and being 'critical' (being judgemental and moralistic). The parents appeared passive and procrastinating, and did not protest about being ignored, suggesting the 'adapted child'. Staff seemed to take little action that was aimed at these parents' 'adult' ego state.

School 15

The school is in an inner city area, serving, according to the staff, a community with a high proportion of black families. Approximately 70 per cent of the school population has an Asian ethnic background, 25 per cent an Afro-Caribbean background, and 5 per cent have a UK ethnic background. The transactional hypothesis was that the school emphasized the 'parent' in transaction with the parent as 'child'.

Review of attendance

The pupils were representative of Years 9 and 10. No Year 7 or 8 pupils were offered for inclusion in the sample. Also, attendance data for Year 7 were not available for the older pupils included in the sample as the registers could not be located. No Year 11 pupils were included because they were all on study leave during the data collection and the school thought they would be of no interest to the research. These Year 11 pupils were not counted as absent, since the school granted them 'leave' under the provisions of section 199 (3) and (8) of the Education Act 1993.[1] Because their absence from school was legal it was not added into the school's absence returns even in cases where the pupil was absent, with or without authority, on the day the leave started. One effect of this is to reduce absence and authorized absence to zero for that group for that period; another effect, and consequent on the first, is to halt any referral process of absentees to the Education Welfare Service.

There was evidence from the attendance data for Year 9 that there were more truants within the year than was normal for the school. This was confirmed by the pastoral care staff in relation to unauthorized absence and also in relation to many other disciplinary matters. The explanation for this difference was that Year 9 appeared to contain a higher than normal proportion of less able and disaffected pupils, a difference which had been evident from Year 7. The reason for this difference was put down to chance.

Ten of the fourteen pupils in the sample had not started their secondary career with the school. Three of these pupils had been enrolled by the school to give them a fresh start because of poor attendance and behavioural difficulties at their former schools. In these cases the choice to attend the school appeared to be for positive reasons and supported by the parents, but their difficulties had continued and thus they came to be included in the sample. However, a senior member of staff said that the school enrolled many difficult pupils under similar circumstances and often succeeded in improving their attendance and behaviour. This policy applied equally to enrolling difficult pupils into Year 9, despite its problems. In relation to the other seven there was some evidence from the files that their 'late' enrolments into Years 8 and 9 were as a result of changes in family circumstances, often as a result of family breakdown or disruption.

The attendance data for all the sample pupils were available from computer records and handwritten registers, some of which (as previously noted) could not be found. There was evidence that the computer register was maintained accurately, although it was not possible to cross-refer absence notes to register entries, since the notes were not routinely filed. There was a similar problem with the handwritten registers from previous years, with many absences being marked as having a medical reason but there being no note on file as supporting evidence. There was also evidence from observation that phone calls were considered sufficient evidence for the school to authorize absence, although in many cases no report of the call found its way to the files. There was evidence on one file that the report of the home/school liaison teacher on a period of absence appeared to have been used to authorize all absence occurring in the term prior to the investigation. Generally the registers were accurate and could be used as evidence so long as there was no need to have the primary evidence to support the entries.

Comparison of the sample with the 'average' pupil

The staff's view of truants was that they liked being in school less, that they found schoolwork less interesting and needed more help with it, and that they were much less likely to complete homework. Their involvement in school activities was less, they seemed less happy when in school, and paid less attention in and out of class. They got on less well with staff, were much less easy to talk to in general, and about problems in particular, and were a great deal less reliable. They were seen as more aggressive than their peers, and more likely to bully others, but were less likely to be bullied.

The teachers' perception of the parents of truants was less negative than it was for their children. Generally the parents of unauthorized absentees came into school, took an interest in schoolwork, showed support for the school, attended parents' evenings, got on well with the staff, and were easy to talk to. However, they were much less likely to make sure that homework was done. They condoned absence as much as other parents, were slightly more likely to miss appointments and to fail to provide notes; however, they provided information when asked. They were a little more aggressive than other parents.

These findings suggest that teachers consider unauthorized absentees to be low in ability, with no wish to study, difficult to motivate and possibly aggressive. In these respects they appear to be very different from their peers. In contrast, the parents of unauthorized absentees seem to want to work in partnership with the school, but they do not help their children with their studies. A possible explanation for the parents' attitude is they are seeking the school's support in attempting to have some control over their children. The evidence for this explanation is considered below.

Work undertaken with the sample group

Teachers provided information on the sample pupils' involvement with the Education Welfare Service, on their known criminal activity, on the involvement of other agencies in dealing with attendance problems, and on the likely prognosis for the improvement of attendance. Teachers also commented on additional family information known to them. A summary of these responses appears as Table 6.5. The table has been arranged in descending order of pupil absence as expressed in the third column.

Information supplied on the sample pupils' home background suggested

Table 6.5 Information on pupils at School 15: analysis of the teachers' views of the 14 selected pupils

#	m f	%abs	%un abs	5	6	7	8	9	précis of additional family information
2	m	89.0	38.9	E	ews thv *	✓		poor	single-parent family, pupil has not come to school after breaking into it
3	f	82.5	12.5	E	ews		ssd	poor	parents separated, pupil looking after siblings
8	m	62.6	26.3	E	ews		sbs	poor	single-parent family, not motivated to learn
11	f	50.0	16.3	Pan	hsl			poor	beyond parental influence, family fights, family business failed recently
13	m	47.7	10.9	U	hsl tcon		ssd	poor	parents unskilled and unemployed, children out of control, ? black economy
6	m	45.8	17.6	U	ews	✓	ssd sbs	poor	beyond parental influence, mixed-race family not accepted by either culture
1	f	42.1	19.9	E	ews tcon	✓	sbs	poor	anti-authority, pupil has sickle-cell anaemia, severe behaviour problems
14	f	41.0	5.0	E	ews			poor	no information
4	m	33.1	10.0	Pat	ews	✓	ssd p sbs	poor	recently from Jamaica, rejected by stepfather, mother in refuge, now in care
7	m	24.4	14.6	U	hsl		sbs	poor	beyond parental influence, easily influenced by peers, low ability
5	m	22.9	16.5	U	hsl tcon		sbs	poor	out of school interests dominate through involvement in Muslim sub-culture
9	m	22.3	10.5	E	ews		ssd	poor	beyond control of parent, in care of LA
10	f	20.3	1.6	E	ews			poor	parents separated, mother keeps child at home 'for her safety', pupil may work
12	m	19.9	1.0	E	ews		sbs	poor	rejected by stepfather, mother in refuge, lives with uncle, limited control

Notes:
The table has been presented in descending order of percentage absence (column 3).
= pupil identification number
m/f = male or female
%abs = the total percentage of schooling missed since enrolment
%unabs = the total percentage of schooling missed as a result of unauthorized absence
5 = language believed to be spoken at home: **E** = English, **Pun** = Punjabi, **U** = Urdu, **Pat** = Patois
6 = forms of contact: **ews** = by Education Welfare Service (* = prosecution while at another school), **hsl** = involvement of home/school liaison, **tcon** = by teacher, **thv** = home visit by teacher
7 ✓ = known involvement in criminal activity
8 = agencies involved: **ssd** = social services department, **sbs** = special behavioural support, **p** = well known to the police
9 = prognosis

that a common issue identified by the teachers was the parents' lack of control over their children. There are eight pupils where this issue was directly referred to in teachers' answers (#s 1, 4, 6, 7, 9, 11, 12 and 13). There is some evidence from staff that parents turned to the school for support in helping to achieve some control. It was reported by one member of staff that the parents were 'often at their wits' end as to know how to deal with their children' because of a lack of parental authority. The reason for this difficulty was given as a clash of cultural norms for which the parents had no resolution. That same member of staff explained that traditional methods of control used in some of the countries from which the parents came were to threaten to beat older children who would not conform, and to threaten to throw them out of the family in disgrace if their behaviour did not improve. In these countries there were, apparently, sufficient examples of this happening for young people to take the threat seriously. In this country neither of these actions is considered legal or legitimate, and the children know that here the threat cannot be acted on. These parents then turned to the school to support their attempts at retaining control.

There were some cases in the sample where the school and the parents worked together to encourage better attendance. It was common for parents and teachers to meet regularly, for visits to be made to the home by the specialist home/school liaison teacher, and for parents and teachers to monitor hourly or daily attendance. In this respect, this school appears different from the other two so far reviewed in that there was some accord between teachers and parents; and this is reflected in the teachers' views of the parents discussed earlier in this section. There are two cases where this accord did not exist and the school knew that absence was condoned by the parents (#3 and #10, both females). In the case of #3 there was some evidence that the pupil might have been caring for younger children. The family's difficulties seem to have recently become too much for the mother and a number of outside agencies had become involved. In this case the pupil's educational needs seemed to have been almost totally overtaken by the impending family breakdown. In the case of #10 the mother was in dispute with the school in relation to a lack of action over alleged bullying, and it appeared that the mother had withdrawn her daughter from the school in protest. The school believed this to be a pretext to allow the pupil to work in order to supplement the family income.

The records of the three remaining pupils in the sample for whom there was information (#s 2, 5 and 8) seem to suggest that they were not motivated to attend school. In the case of #5 the teacher wrote:

> The father supports the school and wants his children to get on, but the boy's interests out of school are stronger than those in school. Possible involvement in the local Muslim subculture of similarly disaffected youths.

There was evidence in this case that other children in the family were experiencing a clash between Western attitudes and the Muslim faith, which the father could not resolve. The pastoral care staff had attempted to deal with the problem by introducing the pupil to a form of group counselling within the school that aimed to identify cultural differences and produce some personal resolution of them. Staff said that this approach had helped many pupils, and were sorry #5 had failed to attend sufficient sessions for them to have any effect.

In the case of #2, he had been enrolled into Year 9 on transfer from a school where his behaviour and attendance had been poor. The mother had at some time been prosecuted and fined for her son's unauthorized absence, and at the time of transfer there was a further threat of prosecution. The transfer had been arranged by the Education Welfare Service, agreed to by the boy and his mother, and put into effect towards the end of the spring term. Within a few days of transfer the boy was caught breaking into the school canteen. It was reported by the pastoral staff that he had been ashamed of what he had done and 'was too embarrassed to come to school' (apparently this creative piece of rationalization was not discussed further). The school staff considered that he would not return, and reported that the EWS were considering placing him in a special unit for difficult children. From the time of the offence his non-attendance at school had been recorded as authorized.

In the case of #8, he had been transferred to the school via a special unit designed to improve behaviour and attendance. He had been permanently excluded from his previous school for continual disruption of classes. On transfer many attempts had been made to motivate him, but attendance continued to be poor with a great deal of lateness, and his file showed that he was frequently on report for disruption of classes. He and his mother claimed that this behaviour was due to unsuitable GCSE options. These were changed, but there was no improvement in attitude or attendance. A great deal of absence had been authorized by the school following notes from his mother stating that he was unwell. A further referral had been made to the Education Welfare Officer, but no action had been reported as having been taken. There was some suggestion from the manner in which staff discussed his behaviour in school that they were not too displeased with his current absence.

It is significant that in all the cases in the sample the school staff considered the prognosis to be poor; the above case is a good example. The sample contained pupils whose attendance and behavioural problems were among the worst with which the school had to deal. In all cases there had been considerable attempts to improve their attendance, but obviously without success. The school's actions in these cases is now considered.

Analysis of teacher time given to improving attendance

Staff were asked for an estimate of the time given to the methods used to improve attendance of the sample group. Table 6.6, opposite, gives a summary

Table 6.6 Time given to pupils at School 15

1 #	2 %	3 m/f	4 week	5 term	6 comment
2	89.0	m		3	agreement to transfer including home visit by senior staff
3	82.5	f		20	case conferences, transfer from Year 10 to Year 9, meetings with EWO
8	62.6	m		many	agreement to transfer, change to GCSE options, meet with sbs and EWO
11	50.0	f		4	agreement to transfer, meet with hsl and parents
13	47.7	m		5	hsl visits home, staff meet with father, numerous discipline reports
6	45.8	m		4	hsl visits home, discipline reports, school counselling team
1	42.1	f		2	teacher meet with mother and EWO, attendance report, referral to sbs
14	41.0	f		1	attendance report, referral to EWO
4	33.1	m		many	numerous discipline reports, referral to sbs, weekly guidance meetings
7	24.4	m		4	hsl visits home, discipline reports, school counselling team
5	22.9	m	2		hsl visits home, many discipline reports, school counselling team
9	22.3	m		4	numerous discipline reports, fixed exclusion, referral to sbs and EWO
10	20.3	f		1	referral to EWO (withdrawn from school by parents), discipline reports
12	19.9	m		8	referral to sbs and EWO, school counselling team, discipline reports

of the responses made by year heads. The table is presented in descending order of absence since enrolment with the school (see column 2).

The responses indicate that there was much less difficulty in answering this question in terms of time than with the previous two schools, but even then it was clear that some responses were estimates and in some cases it was not possible to quantify the time given at all. The table clearly indicates that a great deal of time has been given to a range of methods in relation to the pupils in the sample.

In only one case, #14, are the methods used somewhat limited. This is also the case where the school had no information on the pupil's home background (see Table 6.5). High levels of lateness and authorized absence had developed during the year and the EWO had been asked to investigate. There had been no outcome from this referral as the EWO had been unable to establish any contact with the parents. The pupil's file did not contain the notes which the school had used to authorize the absences, and all that could be told from the register was that the absences were for non-medical reasons. In this case the school had not asked the home/school liaison teacher to visit, nor had there been any recorded contact between the form tutor and the parents, either by letter or home visit (there was no phone at home). The school appeared to be relying entirely on the Education Welfare Service in this case, for reasons that were unclear.

Table 6.6 shows that in ten of the samples, disciplinary reports had been used to resolve the attendance difficulties. In discussion with staff it emerged that the use of reports was a common method of dealing with lateness, unexplained absence and absence from specific classes. In many of the cases in the sample the pupils had displayed other problems than simply being absent, or late. In these cases the disciplinary procedures had been used to deal with all issues.

Disciplinary methods were not reported as being used in the cases of the pupils who had been transferred recently to the school, #s 2, 8 and 11 (considered previously), and had not been used in relation to #3 who had been transferred to a lower year group. The reason for this appeared to be twofold. First the circumstances surrounding the pupils were well known to all, their behaviour was closely watched, and each had a special timetable. As a result their actions were more closely monitored than if they had been on report. Second, the work being undertaken with them had a rehabilitative aim not a disciplinary one.

In the remaining cases disciplinary action was coupled with various attempts at gaining understanding of the difficulties facing pupils, in getting co-operation from the parents, and in providing specialist group counselling for the pupils. These actions appear to be a combination of control with care, operated in collaboration with the parents.

Summary of data analysis

Data collection from the school suggested that there was very little communication with parents over attendance matters at the time of enrolment. The school emphasized good attendance and punctuality in its code of conduct but did not give rewards for either; there was no attendance policy. Parents were not told of the sanctions that were used for poor attendance and unpunctuality and pupils only learned of them from the pastoral staff. The school did not publish attendance data for parents, and did not discuss the data that were available from DfEE returns with the governors since, as one member of staff said, 'it was not part of our policy to raise the matter with them'. It was found that there was no formal written explanation of the roles of the home/school liaison teacher or the Education Welfare Officer in relation to attendance matters, no explanation of the help available from either, and no information on the approaches taken to prosecution. It emerged that it was the practice of the pastoral staff to review attendance regularly, but there was no agreed criterion for staff action or referral to another agency if attendance fell below a particular level. When action was taken staff tended to use disciplinary procedures to deal with unauthorized absentees as an initial response, usually without reference to the parents. As absences became more frequent so attempts were made to get the co-operation of the parents and some understanding of the pupil's circumstances and motivation. Staff reported that these actions often produced improvement.

The school had a good record of dealing successfully with difficult pupils, including truants, who had been excluded from other schools. However, they had become victims of their own success in that an already difficult Year 9 had taken in most of these pupils, and the addition of more difficult pupils presented a major management challenge.

In relation to the sample of truants selected by the school the staff's combination of control and care appeared to have had little positive effect. In none of the cases in the sample had the pastoral staff made written agreements with the parents on joint action to be taken. Thus parents, form tutors and class teachers had to rely on verbal agreements as the basis of their actions, with all the problems of misunderstanding that this can bring. However, written agreements could have presented other difficulties since many of the parents were not literate. Despite evidence of the willingness of the parents and the school to collaborate, neither the school, nor the parents, nor their acting together, could motivate these pupils.

The transactions

The evidence collected and reviewed suggests that the 'Parent-to-Child' hypothesis proposed for this school in relation to communication with parents was accurate. The following points are significant:

- There was no written attendance policy available to parents either at enrolment, or when attendance became a problem, to give information on what action would and should be taken either by the school or the parents.
- Staff made judgements and took action without the guidance of an attendance policy.
- Pupils, and eventually parents, learned from staff what the sanctions were for poor attendance.
- Praise for good attendance was seldom given.
- Parents were not given information on the services available in, or through, the school to help when attendance or other difficulties were first noticed by them.
- Agreements with parents were not formally recorded, monitored, reviewed or renegotiated.
- Parents sought help from the school to underpin their attempts at regaining control of their children, while the school offered their children counselling for which they did not seek parental consent.
- There was no evidence that parents had been made aware of the

particular difficulties of Year 9, or the considerable amount of work being done by staff to deal with the difficulties.

• The success the school believed it had in dealing with absentees appeared not to have been formally evaluated, yet it continued to take them.

Clearly the staff set limits, if sometimes arbitrarily and without explanation, seldom praised and frequently disciplined. It was clear that power and authority rested with them, and that in some cases they could rely on parental support with this approach. The transactions established appear to be from the 'critical parent' ego state of the staff to the 'adapted child' ego state of the parents.

School 14

The school is on the edge of a city, taking pupils from a wide area including many outlying towns and villages. A large proportion of pupils use school bus services, which are sometimes delayed by bad weather or traffic congestion. The school is popular, has an increasing roll, and specializes in arts-based subjects.

The transactional hypothesis was that the school emphasized the 'adult' in transaction with the parent as 'child'.

Review of attendance

The pupils were representative of four years within the school. No Year 7 pupils were selected. There were four pupils from Year 11, five from Year 10, two from Year 9 and five from Year 8. It is significant that the absence rates for the sample from School 14 were less than half the rates for the samples from the other three schools. If the sample pupils were representative of the worst cases that School 14 dealt with, then it would appear that it has substantially less of an overall problem than do the other schools.

All the attendance data had to be extracted from handwritten registers. The registers were maintained, checked and updated by administrators. The form registers were completed by tutors in the mornings, and a class register was taken in the afternoon. There was some evidence from comments made by staff that both form tutors and class teachers would mark a pupil present if they believed the child to be in school: their physical presence at registration was not needed.

The administrator filled in the register for the afternoon based on information supplied by the class teachers. Class teachers only provided information on pupils absent, or believed absent, from their class; they did not give information on those present. It follows that a pupil had to be in the right place at the right time in the afternoon, or the teacher had to believe that they were in school, to gain a mark. In these circumstances a pupil could be absent from school and marked present, or present in school and marked absent.

The accurate recording of lateness also caused difficulties. Late arrival of buses in the morning, and the system of identifying only absences in the afternoon, could result in late pupils not being registered. Enquiries then had to be made by the administrator, who appeared to have the task of deciding whether a pupil's lateness was the pupil's own fault, or a fault of the transport system, or a fault of the class registration system. The fact that the system worked at all depended largely on the ability of the administrator to keep track of absentees and class registers, and the truthfulness of the pupils. What the system apparently failed to do was to record post-registration 'truancy' accurately.

Following a period of absence, notes were given by the returning pupil to either the form tutor or the administrator. In all observed cases these notes were accepted as sufficient evidence to authorize that absence. Where notes were not provided it was the administrator's task to request them from the pupil, to receive them when brought in, and to mark the register. It appeared that all the notes were kept in the pupils' files. It was common for parents to phone in during a pupil's absence to inform the administrator of the reason for absence and the likely date of return; a note of the call would be taken and placed in the file. These calls were sufficient for the administrator to mark the register and authorize the absence.

The system employed by the school probably underrecorded absence, and possibly underrecorded unauthorized absence. However, staff said that once a pupil's poor attendance came to notice, informal communication between them resulted in checks on presence and absence and greater accuracy in the register entries for those pupils.

There was no information on the files that showed that reports on attendance, or absence, were sent to parents, either as a routine end of year report, or when attendance was being monitored.

There was no evidence that the registers had been inspected.

Comparison of the sample with the 'average' pupil

The teachers' view of the sample pupils compared with their peers was that there were differences but these were not great. Not surprisingly they are judged to like being in school less. They find schoolwork less interesting, are less attentive in class, are thought to be less able to do the work and therefore need a little more help with it. They are less likely to listen and do what is wanted, and are less reliable. They seem slightly less happy, get on less well with staff and are a little less easy to talk to, and are less forthcoming about their problems. They are no more likely to be bullied than their peers, but may bully others a little more, although they are thought to be no more aggressive than their peers. Unauthorized absentees scored poorly on completing homework and in their lack of involvement in extra-curricular activities. In these aspects their peers did not score highly either but the differences are more marked.

The teachers perceived the differences between parents of unauthorized absentees and 'average' parents to be more marked than the differences between the two pupil groups. Parents of absentees were considerably less likely to come into school and took much less interest in their child's schoolwork. They were less likely to make sure homework was done. They showed less support for the school, were much less likely to attend parents' evenings, and never got involved with the PTA. They got on less well with staff, were less easy to talk to and less willing to talk about their problems. They were more difficult to contact, much more likely to condone absence and much more likely to fail to give information when asked. They were a little more likely to miss appointments and fail to provide notes, and a little more aggressive than the average parent.

These findings suggest that teachers see unauthorized absentees as not markedly different from their peers in many aspects of school life, but they struggle more with the work and do not make use of the opportunities offered by the school. It appears that the teachers believe that they cannot count on much help from the parents in whatever is done to motivate their children.

Work undertaken with the sample pupils

Teachers provided information on the sample pupils' involvement with the Education Welfare Service, on their known criminal activity, on the involvement of other agencies in dealing with attendance problems, and on the likely prognosis for the improvement of attendance. Teachers also commented on additional family information known to them. A summary of these responses appears as Table 6.7. The table has been arranged in descending order of pupil absence as expressed in the third column.

The teachers' information on the pupils' family circumstances shows that the sample can be divided into three distinct groups: ambitious parents, weak parents and unco-operative parents. These three groups, and the effects on the pupils, are now considered.

The first and smallest group is where the parents have unrealistic ambitions for their child that create additional pressure which presents itself in poor behaviour of the pupil when at school (#5 and #6). An example of the this difficulty was given in relation to #6, a pupil who was becoming disruptive in class and had been accused of bullying. The head of year wrote:

> The parents have high expectations of him and were invited into school to talk to the head of school, who convinced them that he must be given an opportunity to pursue his own interests, not necessarily academic, and that he was by no means going to be a high flyer. We have had his educational needs assessed and believe that he will leave school with minimum qualifications.

Table 6.7 Information on pupils at School 14: analysis of the teachers' views of the 16 selected pupils

#	m f	%abs	%un abs	5	6	7	8	9	précis of additional family information
11	m	38.1	22.2	E	ews	✓		poor	no contact with parents, no information
7	m	29.8	12.7	E	ews			poor	single-parent family, recent separation, loss of family home, condoned abs.
16	f	23.0	0.0	E	tcon m			fair	father unemployed, older sibling handicapped
10	m	22.7	5.5	E	ts			poor	parents unsupportive, low motivation
9	m	19.1	8.9	E	ts			poor	parents unco-operative, paper round, long distance to school, low ability
13	f	18.2	0.6	E				good	no relevant information
1	m	18.1	0.4	E	ews ts c	✓		fair	parents unco-operative, condoned absences, bully, worked illegally
2	m	18.1	8.9	E	ews tcon	✓		poor	parents unco-operative, no agreement with parents on dealing with absence
5	f	15.7	0.5	E	tcon			good	parents concentrating on child's singing career, late night talent contests
3	m	13.4	6.9	E	ews ts	✓		poor	parents lack control, excluded for violence and aggression, not motivated
15	f	11.9	1.2	E	tcon			poor	little parental control, is 14 has 17-yr-old boyfriend, parents disapprove
4	f	10.4	0.0	E	ews c		m	fair	single-parent family, mother little control, dislikes visits by EWO
12	m	9.3	0.0	E				good	single-parent family, paper round, girlfriend leads to a great deal of lateness
8	f	8.1	0.6	E	t.hv	✓		fair	parents recently separated, manipulates differences, confused
14	m	5.2	1.2	E				good	no relevant information
6	m	2.3	0.1	E	t.con			good	parents overambitious for their adopted child, child average ability

Notes:
The table has been presented in descending order of percentage absence (column 3)
= pupil identification number
m/f = male or female
%abs = the total percentage of schooling missed since enrolment
%unabs = the total percentage of schooling missed as a result of unauthorized absence
5 = language believed to be spoken at home: **E** = English
6 = forms of contact: **ews** = by Education Welfare Service, **ts** = classroom support provided, **tcon** = meeting at school with parents, **m** = referred for medical assessment, **c** = counselling by school staff
7 ✓ = known involvement in criminal activity
8 = agencies involved: **m** = medical
9 = prognosis

> I think that he will probably continue reasonably well after the recent interview
> with parents.

These parents were judged by the staff to be co-operative, supportive of the school, but very busy with their own lives and difficult to contact.

The second group is one where parental control over their children seems to be weak or non-existent (#s 3, 4, 8, 12 and 15). One example of this is #3, a pupil who had been excluded from school for violence and insulting behaviour, of whom the year head wrote:

> His elder brother recently left school at 16. He attended sporadically during his final
> year, and is now unemployed. Now [#3] is involved with him much of the time
> outside school. His parents virtually gave up on the brother and therefore have little
> incentive to try harder with the second one.

These parents were judged to avoid school contact, and meetings arranged between the Education Welfare Officer and the parents had little effect in improving contact. Towards the end of the summer term the head gave the parents a clear statement that the school had reached the limits of the help it could give, writing in the following terms in a letter:

> The school can't put any more resources into chasing him. I am certain that you will
> want to do whatever you can to improve the situation.

This is clearly negative, and given the relationship between the school and the parents it must have been well known that the exhortation to them would have no effect. It is worth noting that this was the only written evidence found during the search of pupil files in the four schools that presented the school's position in this way.

The third and largest group is where the school had not been able to gain the co-operation of the parents, either as a result of limited contact (#s 11, 13 and 14), or as a result of antagonism, or both (#s 1, 2, 7, 9, 10, and 16). One example of this difficulty and its consequences is #2, a pupil whose absence had been encouraged by his parents by taking him on holiday during term-time without the permission of the head. During that term he had been suspended from school for aggressive behaviour, rudeness and bullying. The year head wrote:

> #2, his elder sister and his younger sister all have attendance problems, they are all
> aggressive to staff. The parents are difficult to contact and show no interest in their
> children's behaviour in school.

In order to try to deal with the difficulties the staff drew up a contract with #2 intended to improve his attendance at school, and behaviour within it. This was done without seeking the agreement or co-operation of the parents. Furthermore, because of incomplete coursework and non-attendance at mock exams, the school withdrew him from an examination without any consultation with the parents. The parents were told of this decision after the event and invited to comment if they wished.

Returning to the general consideration of Table 6.7, it is of interest to note that the Education Welfare Service was involved with six of the sixteen pupils in the sample. This is the lowest involvement of the service out of the four schools. The service was involved with nearly all the pupils with high (for this school) levels of unauthorized absence. The circumstances surrounding #11, the pupil with the highest rate of unauthorized absence, are interesting. In the spring term the school had referred the pupil to the service following an alleged incident of theft from the school and his subsequent failure to attend at all. The EWO had visited the parents and taken no further action after being told that they had applied to transfer their son to another school. There were no notes from parents to cover this period of absence so it had been recorded as unauthorized, despite the fact that attempts to register a child at another school might have been considered as authorized absence under the provisions of the Education Act 1993, section 199(4)(b)(iii)[2]. The year head reported that the other school had refused to accept him due to the alleged offence. At the time of the data collection the matter remained unresolved. There was no record on file of the referral to the EWO, no report from the EWO on the contact made, no letters to the parents about the situation, and, judging from the absence of comments from staff, no plan of action to resolve the situation. It seemed that the case had moved into a period of limbo, and in the absence of a policy to guide staff in this situation it seemed destined to stay there. It was clear that this was a case where the parents' inaction could have led to consideration for prosecution, but no such consideration had been made. This lack of action appeared to be due to the service being somewhat uncertain of the legal grounds upon which to take action, and possibly not having the wish to do so, since prosecutions were very rare. Also the school was not pressing for such action in this or any other case. Here, again, this school was different from the others in apparently not demanding more legal action.

It will be noted from Table 6.7 that five of the pupils were involved with crime, the largest number (by one) out of the four schools, and occurring in the school which offered a sample with the lowest rate of unauthorized absence. The known involvement in crime was spread across the sample; for two of these, #1 and #8, the amount of unauthorized absence was very small, for two others, #2 and #3, unauthorized absence was around the mean, and for #11 it was the highest. The types of crime ranged widely. As discussed earlier, #11 was alleged to have committed theft from the school, and so apparently had #1; #2 had offended by driving his own car to get to school when aged fourteen; #3 was believed to be involved with his older brother on the fringe of crime during and after school hours; #8 had been caught shoplifting during a weekend with a group of pupils from the school. From the evidence available to the staff, only one of these pupils, #3, fitted the image portrayed by the government of the 'truant' who commits crime while absent from school, discussed in Chapter 2.

Table 6.7 shows that the staff had not referred any cases to the Social Services Department for help or assessment.

The table shows that the staff considered the prognosis to be good or fair

Table 6.8 Time given to pupils at School 14

1 #	2 %	3 m/f	4 week	5 term	6 comment
11	38.1	m		3	report, EWO
7	29.8	m		2	EWO
16	23.0	f		5	phone calls with parents and talks with pupil
10	22.7	m			timetable changed, work experience
9	19.1	m			timetable changed
13	18.2	f		1	report
1	**18.1**	**m**		**many**	**special teaching, counselling by staff, reviews, home visits, EWO**
2	**18.1**	**m**		**many**	**report, work experience, contract, exclusion, brought to school, EWO**
5	15.7	f		1	one interview by head with parents
3	**13.4**	**m**	**3**		**report, special teaching, EWO**
15	11.9	f		3	parents into school, change of tutor group
4	**10.4**	**f**	**3**		**report, counselling, contract, EWO**
12	9.3	m			
8	8.1	f		1	informal checks
14	5.2	m			
6	2.3	m	1		report, informal checks, special needs assessment

in eight of the sample. These eight are the pupils with the lowest amount of unauthorized absence. The staff rated the prospects of all pupils with an unauthorized absence rate above 1.2 per cent as poor; the school clearly had not given up on trying to help this group, as is indicated by the amount of involvement they had with them. The work undertaken in this respect is now considered.

Analysis of teacher time given to improving attendance

Table 6.8, above, gives a summary of the responses made by year heads. The table is presented in descending order of absence since enrolment with the school (see column 2). The responses indicate that answering this question in terms of time was difficult since no record of time spent was made and some answers were guesses.

The table can be divided into three groups. The first, presented in bold type, and covering four pupils, is where there is evidence that considerable time and effort have been given to a strategy designed to deal with absence problems. The strategies used with these four vary, but a common theme is the use of individual discussions or counselling over a period of time involving both school staff and the EWO. It is noticeable that this group does not contain the pupils with the worst attendance records, and does contain the only two pupils in the sample with whom the school had made contracts. A possible reason for this came from interviews with staff. There was a general expectation within the school that pupils would be 'self-motivated' in relation to all aspects of schoolwork and discipline. In cases where the staff believed that by intervention they could encourage greater self-motivation, or bolster weak motivation, then they had given freely of their time. Further evidence to support this practice comes from analysis of the activity of staff with the second group in the sample. This group, presented in italics in the table and containing seven pupils, shows that limited time had been given to a strategy to improve attendance. Five of this sample are the highest non-attenders, #7, #9, #10, #11 and #16. There was evidence that the staff had made some attempts to motivate these pupils, but that they believed that the parents would not support the work. Their belief was based either on difficulty in making contact with the parents at all, or on the fact that previous attendance patterns by siblings suggested a lack of parental interest. Therefore their work with this group was aimed at containing the situation rather than improving it. This analysis does not hold good for the other two in the group, #6 and #15. In both these cases the school had established a working relationship with the parents. In relation to #15 (aged 13) the school and parents were in some accord about the difficulties, the pupil was becoming increasingly out of their control as a result of her overwhelming interest in her relationship with her 17-year-old boyfriend. It was implied that the relationship was more like one that could have been expected of a much older girl. No direct statements were made that an illegal sexual relationship was taking place, but the suspicion remained that it was possible. Neither the parents nor the staff approved, but neither had sufficient influence to make her change her behaviour and concentrate more on schoolwork. The only intervention the staff had made was to split her from her friends within her registration group. There had been no referral to the EWO, or perhaps more sensibly in the circumstances, to the Social Services Department. The staff believed that attendance would get worse and, as with the other five in the group, their actions appeared to be aimed at containment. The situation in relation to #6 has already been considered, the staff having modified the parents' unrealistic expectation of their son.

The remaining members of the sample form the final group, #5, #8, #12, #13 and #14. Very limited action had been taken in these cases, despite some whose absence record was high for this school. The staff considered that the prognosis for the pupils in reducing absence was good in four cases and fair in the fifth. The lack of time given to these cases was because the staff believed that they could still rely on the pupils' self-motivation.

The staff at School 14 seemed to use a hierarchy of strategies with absentees which was applied with some consistency across the school. Their strategies appear to be based on their views of each pupil's motivation. This was done informally and in the absence of an attendance policy. The consistent use of this informal approach may have been as a result of the staff applying what the head called the school's long-standing 'oral tradition' to helping pupils.

Summary of data analysis

Data collection from the school suggested that there was very little communication with parents over attendance matters at the time of enrolment. Information made available at that stage on the school rules said nothing about the need for good attendance and punctuality, or what sanctions would be used if both deteriorated. Information to parents following enrolment gave information on the school day and when registration took place, on the need for notes from parents on absence or lateness, and on the school's policy on granting holidays during term-time. However, the school's annual report to parents gave no information on attendance or unauthorized absence, and parents could not expect information on attendance in the end of year report on their child. No information was made available to parents on the school's role in authorizing absences, or on what action could be taken by staff in relation to unauthorized absence. No information was provided on what help the staff could give to parents if attendance or behaviour became a problem. There was no information provided to parents on the function and role of the Education Welfare Service.

From observations and reports from staff it was clear that all notes from parents explaining absence were accepted as sufficient to authorize that absence. This was a school tradition that was said to be well known to all parents. However, there was also evidence that the staff would accept a pupil's explanation of another pupil's absence, and that the afternoon class registers remained open all afternoon, which allowed pupils who were late to be marked as present. The result of this was that neither the school nor the parents could be sure of where individual pupils were at any time. This process may have been part of the tradition of the school, but there was no evidence to suggest that the parents knew about it or accepted it, the fact of its illegality notwithstanding. Clearly such a policy could not be published.

Evidence from pupil records showed that the school had made collaborative partnerships with some of the parents in the sample, but not with all. To some extent this difference appeared to be linked to the judgement made by staff on the level of motivation of the parents. In situations where the parents appeared to lack interest in their children's difficulties at school, the staff took on parental responsibilities and made arrangements and contracts with the pupil, sometimes without the parents' knowledge or prior agreement. Subsequent communication with these parents supposed agreement with the action taken.

In those cases where the staff made collaborative partnerships with parents there was some evidence that the power relationship was not equal, staff either taking responsibility for bolstering what they considered to be weak control by parents, or being asked by the parents to supply control.

The transactions

The evidence suggests that the 'Adult-to-Child' hypothesis proposed for this school was not appropriate in relation to the communication established with parents of absentees. There is more evidence to support a 'Parent-to-Child' hypothesis. The following points seem significant.

- There was no written attendance policy available to parents either at enrolment or when attendance became a problem to give information on what action would be taken by the school or the Education Welfare Service.
- The school relied on an oral tradition in relation to many matters, of which absence was apparently one. It was not clear how much of that tradition in respect of attendance was understood and agreed to by parents.
- There was no information to parents on what action might be taken to refer pupils to agencies where absence was associated with difficulties the school could not or did not have the authority to resolve.
- It was not clear to parents that the oral tradition placed heavy emphasis on pupil self-motivation in relation to reliable attendance and punctuality. Parents could not be sure if the school would know about, or inform them of, absence or lateness.
- Information to parents on the school's rates of absence and on their own child's rates of absence was not given. Since the register data were suspect, any communication which used those data was suspect.
- Once staff had identified a pupil as having attendance problems, closer monitoring took place, but it was not made clear to parents what criteria were used to determine that there was a problem, and parents were not routinely informed when their child came under closer and more accurately recorded scrutiny.
- In some cases where the staff judged the parents' motivation to be poor they developed only limited collaboration with them, and little attempt appeared to be made to create opportunities to improve matters. In these circumstances the staff sometimes acted without the knowledge and agreement of the parents.

The absence of formal policies to guide actions, and the reliance by staff on tradition, can be related directly to the 'parent' ego state (see Barker, 1980, p. 60). The relative powerlessness of the parents generally, and the apparent rejection of the school by some, and compliance by others, suggest the 'adapted child' ego state (p. 10).

Conclusion

This conclusion is in two parts. The first part considers three interrelated management issues that arise from the analysis presented in the previous sections of this chapter:

- policy on attendance
- the process of recording presence and acting on absence
- the variety of relationships established between staff and parents of absentees.

The second part is a consideration of the application of the typology in the four schools.

1   *Management issues*

Policy on attendance   None of the four schools had a written behaviour policy, nor did they have a written attendance policy that gave a clear statement of the rights and duties of the school and its pupils and their parents. None had statements of the rewards and sanctions that would be used, and none gave any indication that poor attenders would be monitored more closely than other pupils. The schools did not provide any written statements, nor make written agreements with parents when closer monitoring was taking place. The effects of the absence of a written policy were that parents had no clear statement on what actions might be taken by staff in relation to absence, and staff had no guidance for dealing equitably with absentees and their parents. The schools seemed to rely to some degree on their approach being known to parents through custom and practice, and staff provided information, or reinforced custom, when there was evidence that circumstances warranted it. In acting this way the schools seemed to assume that parents were from the 'consentient' group, an assumption that was likely to be true of many but not all, and an assumption that was less likely to hold good for those selected for inclusion in the research.

The contents of an attendance policy were discussed with staff at the debriefing meetings, using Table 5.2 as a guide. It was clear that the schools had considered the need for a policy but had been unable to give the staff time for developing it. The document set out in the Appendix was offered to staff for use, if they so wished, until a policy had been agreed.

The document includes a brief statement about the role of the Education Welfare Service and provides for a contact name and number. This was included because it was found during the research that in two of the schools there was no information on the caring role of the services in providing help for parents, and no information on their controlling role in enforcing attendance through court action. Also, it was found that there was some evidence of a lack of clarity on the extent of these roles in the other two schools.

There was some evidence from the four schools that parents were not told of other services, external to the school and LEA, that might help with some of the difficulties they faced. Given that there was a large number of dysfunctional families found in the sample, there is a clear need for information to be supplied on how to access skilled help. One effect of not making this information available is that there is no clear statement to parents on the limits to the help available from staff, and no limits set for staff keen to be of service to them. These omissions were discussed at the debriefing meetings within the context of the school's function as a caring institution and the limits that there had to be to those functions. It became clear that senior staff had clear ideas as to the limits of what could be done to help in difficult situations, apparently based on a realistic assessment of the skill levels of their staff and the time that they could make available, but these limits were often not made known to parents. All the schools had policies for referring pupils to other agencies in, for example, cases of suspected child abuse; however, policies for referral for absence, or unauthorized absence, or suspicions of delinquency, had not been considered.

It was acknowledged that, in the majority of cases, unauthorized absence was seen as a discipline problem, and for the school to solve using disciplinary methods, albeit tempered with understanding. The question remained as to whether this was always appropriate given the very great difficulties some pupils faced and the limits to the skills and time of staff. Some senior staff were involved with discussions with Social Services Departments to whom families with difficulties could be referred. However, they had not considered the role that they might play in discussions aimed at developing family support services for children in need, under the provisions of section 17(10) of the Children Act 1989. They had not thought that the definition of 'children in need' could include unauthorized absentees, despite the fact that some were known by the staff to be involved in, or on the fringe of, crime, or at risk of becoming victims of crime.

Recording presence and acting on absence   The accuracy of the entries in the register depends on the honesty of all involved: parents, pupils and teachers, and on the diligence of the form tutors and administrative staff. None of the four schools could have absolute confidence in the register's accuracy; this was acknowledged at the debriefing meetings; senior staff pointed out that attempts to produce absolute accuracy would be too costly and produce very little additional gain on their existing practices.

The introduction of computer-based registers went some way to improving accuracy, but none of the schools had systems for storing and retrieving notes and messages which were the primary evidence for decisions by staff. Where cross-referencing of this evidence with the registers was possible during the data collection, it showed that staff had to use their judgement on the authenticity of the notes, and their knowledge of the family, in order to classify the absence. 'Sorry for her been away, I got a flat tyre and she wasn't feeling well' leaves a lot to the discretion of the form tutor, no matter what system for recording is being used. If the notes cannot be found later, or are not available to the year head, then there is no primary evidence that supports a referral, or discussion with the parents, other than the register entry. Register entries, particularly those produced by computer printout, appear to be incontrovertible evidence, but some entries are the results of judgements made by staff, and should be understood as such.

There was evidence that many referrals to specialist services were made verbally, and informally; this included referrals to the Education Welfare Officer. Records of referrals with supporting evidence were not made, and in many cases it was not clear what the outcome of the referral had been. Such a culture of informality places a high load on memory, and could allow idiosyncratic decision-making that cannot easily be investigated. It may also have the effect of excluding parents from decision-making, providing them only with the effects of decisions once made.

Parents of absentees appeared not to be formally notified of the decision that the staff were carefully monitoring their child's attendance. Neither could they suspect that it might happen, since the schools made no policy statements on monitoring, or on what levels of absence would lead to it being done, or on what improvement was needed to end it. Excluding the parents of absentees in this way had the effect of reducing the ability to enlist their help formally to reduce absences, with the result that efforts often centred on the pupil. This could be a particular problem when the school wanted to deal with the suspected condoning of absence by the parent. There was evidence from all four schools of staff suspicion of condoned absence which had never been raised with the parents.

Staff relationships with parents   Schools not only failed routinely to inform parents when their child came under closer and more accurately recorded scrutiny, but also did not formally record, monitor, review, or renegotiate agreements made with parents, or their children, aimed at reducing absence. Indeed in cases where the staff judged the parents' motivation to be poor, and their relationship with them fragile, they appeared to make no collaborative agreements at all, and there was evidence that little attempt was made to create opportunities to improve matters by senior staff. It was noticeable that the Education Welfare Service did not appear to be used to develop a more collaborative relationship between these parents and the school. In a few cases where the staff considered that the relationship had broken down completely, they acted without the knowledge and agreement of the parents, apparently taking over the parents' role.

Many of the parents of absentees were reported to avoid contact with the school and there is some evidence to suggest that staff did not encourage contact in these situations. There was some evidence from letters on files that staff responses might have been defensive rather than facilitative, or critical rather than encouraging. The prevailing feeling of staff was of resignation: if parents were not motivated, then there was little the school could do to improve matters.

There appeared to be a difference of approach by staff when parents demonstrated motivation by asking for help. Then it was usually willingly given, resulting in a collaborative alliance perhaps designed to regain control over the young person. Such help sometimes resulted in home visits by staff. There seemed to be a need for guidance to staff on the conduct of these visits, which were often made with the best of intentions but without a clear agreement from the parent, and without a plan of action agreed by senior staff. The skill levels of staff may not be sufficient to cope with the circumstances they find, and they are vulnerable to prurient accusation and physical attack. They may be attempting to do work that should be done by the Education Welfare Officer or social worker. This issue was considered at the debriefing sessions, and for some senior staff the policy on visits was going to be reconsidered.

So far consideration has been given to some of the common issues arising from the analysis. In doing so the relationships established between staff and parents have been considered. Attention now turns to an analysis of the relationships based on the transactional hypothesis suggested in Chapter 5.

2   *The application of the typology in the four schools*

A description of the typology and the process of selection of the four schools is given in section three of Chapter 5. The four schools were selected because the information that was collected suggested that a preponderance of particular types of transaction might take place between parents and staff. The typology was used to help formulate a hypothesis that the distinctive transactions that seemed to be demonstrated by the schools would continue to be demonstrated in the transactions established with parents of non-attenders. Figure 6.1 presents the original analysis of the transactions proposed in Figure 5.1 compared with what was found. Figure 6.1 uses the number coding of the schools used earlier in this chapter. The original hypotheses are shown as a dotted arrows and the subsequent findings are shown as solid arrows.

Evidence presented on Schools 18, 3 and 14 suggests that the majority of transactions with the sample parents were not the same as hypothesized following the first round of data collection. Staff in these schools tended to adopt a 'parent' ego state with the parents of absentees, and placed the parents in a 'child' ego state. This was the form of transaction suggested as likely to occur in School 15 and found to hold good there for parents of absentees. Thus all four schools appeared to take somewhat similar actions in relation to parents of absentees, notwithstanding what three had stated previously.

In all four schools there was some evidence to show that many parents

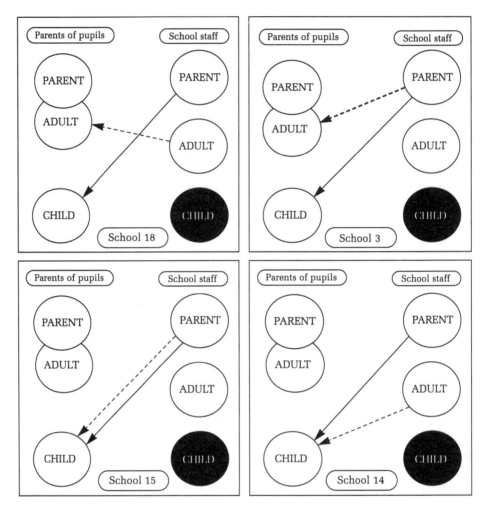

Note: The dotted arrow represents the original hypothesis, the solid arrow represents the subsequent findings.

Figure 6.1 Complementary transactions between ego states

accepted this form of transaction. It was almost as if the parents got what they expected, perhaps because it echoed their own childhood experiences of school staff. This acceptance also seemed to be true of those parents of persistent absentees who avoided contact with the school, for avoidance is a form of procrastination that can be associated with the 'adapted child' ego state. There was also evidence that the interactions often took place in situations which were chosen by the staff, thus emphasizing their power, and which were stereotyped in nature.

Stereotyped responses, conducted from the 'parent' ego state and taking place within defined social boundaries, can be said to fall into two categories. The first are rituals, defined as 'formalised exchanges between people based on social custom' (Barker, 1980, p. 43). The second are games, which may be defined as repetitive, predictable exchanges with a 'covert psychological message' (p. 48). Both forms are highly resistant to change. Both forms were exhibited in the staff's interactions with parents, with ritualized responses predominating.

It can be argued that the typology has brought into focus the significance of rituals, and to a lesser extent games, within those transactions that take place between staff and parents of absentees. Rituals and games, based on tradition, are widely accepted and well understood by those who use them, remain largely unquestioned and are difficult to challenge. Particularly, they support the parental ego state (Berne 1964, p. 34), and do not require much creative energy to keep going. There is some evidence to suggest that the rituals and games established in relation to absentees may be resistant to change and may be stronger than the policies and practices introduced by management that are designed to offer more creative solutions to their problems.

The final chapter will consider issues raised throughout this study using the perspective of rituals and games suggested here.

Notes

1 Now section 444 (3) and (9) of the Education Act 1996.
2 Now section 444 (4) (iii) of the Education Act 1996.

## CHAPTER 7

Six Themes

But Angelo replied, 'We must not make a scarecrow of the law, setting it up to frighten birds of prey, till custom, finding it harmless, makes it their perch, and not their terror.'

(C. and M. Lamb, *Tales from Shakespeare*, 'Measure for Measure', Penguin, 1995, p. 199)

My research reviewed the way in which twenty mainstream English secondary schools dealt with truancy. The schools involved were selected so that the twenty included examples of the major types of school, grant maintained, LEA maintained, selective and non-selective entry, mixed and single-sex schools, with as wide a variation in location and size as possible. There was also a wide range of absence from the schools, from unrecordable amounts to over four times the national average. As a group they experienced levels of absence that was 34 per cent higher than the average for all English schools. The process of selection did not, therefore, produce a sample of schools that were representative of all mainstream secondary schools. For this reason this chapter cannot and does not set out to make generalizations about what happens in all schools; instead it offers some general principles, which it is hoped will be useful to school managers when reviewing management, or developing policy, on truancy.

The general principles are presented in the following six sections:

1. communication with all parents on attendance matters
2. motivation of all pupils to reduce absence
3. recognition, categorization and recording of absences
4. communications with parents of unauthorized absentees
5. measures used by schools to deal with unauthorized absentees
6. engaging help from services outside school to help deal with unauthorized absentees.

1 Communication with all parents on attendance matters

The research for this study found that none of the twenty schools had agreed and published attendance policies. Therefore the parents and school staff had no common, authoritative, statement on which to base their transactions over attendance. Furthermore, some prospectus information to parents on attendance matters was misleading, unclear and incomplete. Some schools did not meet the statutory requirement by publishing attendance data to parents in their annual reports. Therefore some parents knew little of the school's performance in relation to attendance.

Some of the major elements of an attendance policy were considered in Chapter 4 and listed in Chapter 5, Table 5.2. This study has suggested that schools should consider adopting a policy, perhaps based on the contents of Table 5.2, for the following reasons:

- To act as a reminder to school staff of the school's obligations, and their own obligations, under the law.
- To remind all parents and pupils of their rights and duties.
- To provide all parents with a written statement of what actions the school will take in dealing with absence.
- To provide information to all pupils on the school's use of sanctions and rewards in relation to attendance.
- To provide all parents with the information necessary for taking action to seek help or explanation, or for making a complaint.

A policy, therefore, describes and prescribes staff actions, limiting opportunities for idiosyncratic decisions, and it enables parents and pupils to predict action and outcomes accurately.

There may be many reasons for the lack of a written policy. Insufficient staff time was one reason given, perhaps the assumption behind such a reason being that the process of agreeing one was long and complex, and not a priority for the school. Such an attitude may be reinforced by the lack of any recommendations on the need for attendance policies within the Elton committee's report (DES, 1989), but at least such a view can contain the idea that a policy might be desirable, although not essential. By contrast the lack of the need for written policy because of the power of the oral tradition, which was given as another reason for not having a policy, appears to assume that a policy existed and was widely known to parents and consistently operated by staff. In this case the view persisted despite some evidence of inconsistency, and that what was being operated appeared to be contrary to the law.

The lack of a written policy may also be because it is thought to be unnecessary. It is possible that this view is based on the staff's belief that all parents are, or should be, 'consentient', that they know and accept the rules and traditions of the school and consistently support all its activities as an educational and social organization. In this situation the transactions between the ego states of staff and parents may be understood by the staff as complementary, based on a 'Parent-to-Parent' exchange, within which all the rules are tacitly agreed. In such situations the process of dealing with attendance matters may be little more than a bureaucratic ritual.

An attendance policy presents schools with an opportunity to demonstrate openness, providing information on which to continue the development of a working partnership with all parents. It provides a public statement of the principles on which further action to deal with absences is based. If the policy is known and explained to parents at the time of their child's enrolment with the school, then the power of any claims of ignorance is reduced; it also lessens the opportunity for misunderstanding and might provide the environment for improved co-operation. Not having a policy, and only providing the information to parents after the absence has become a problem (in effect on a 'need to know' basis), leaves all the power with the staff; it may also have the effect of leaving a great deal of the responsibility for action with the staff, something that may not be an appropriate use of their time.

2 Motivation of all pupils to reduce absence

Information on the motivation of all pupils was collected from all twenty schools and presented in the first section of Chapter 4. None of the staff interviewed believed that the National Curriculum was a motivating influence in improving attendance; indeed there was some evidence to the contrary. Low-ability, troublesome and 'impulsive' pupils were believed by staff to be absenting themselves once they were presented with evidence of failure to achieve the goals set. However, the evidence must be treated with caution since none of the schools in the study had attempted to correlate attendance rates with curriculum changes, standard testing, or academic success rates.

It is difficult to understand why those schools that could have confidence in their attendance data failed to use attendance as a performance indicator, particularly at a time when absence data and curriculum output measures, in the form of pass rates, have to be published. Published information, together with a commentary on it, could help all parents to improve their understanding of the school's policy on attendance and encourage a greater commitment to it. This in turn could help them to motivate their children to attend. However, it appears that it is much more common for school staff to attempt to motivate the pupils directly, most often by fear of punishment for non-attendance, less frequently by reward for good or improving attendance. Here again the staff appear to be acting from the 'parent' ego state, assuming parental agreement to their ways of dealing with pupils' absences. In so doing they may be sacrificing opportunities for greater co-operation with parents.

Staff use of punishment and reward seems to be based on their belief that either or both are prophylactic. However, this appeared to be unproved by any research they had undertaken.

3 Recognition, categorization and recording of absences

There was evidence that some of the schools experienced difficulty in recording absences at the time of registration, and that the timely and appropriate categorization of that absence by some form tutors was idiosyncratic and possibly inaccurate. This suggests that the long-standing difficulties in producing reliable data, discussed in Chapter 2, may still exist. Schools claimed that the publication of the DfE guidance on categorization of absence (DfE, 1994) had helped to improve consistency within and between schools. However, this appeared to be limited to recording as authorized absentees pupils who were on work experience, or on other off-site activities, or temporarily excluded, rather than recording them as unauthorized absentees as had previously been the case. The introduction of computerized registers, although improving some aspects of accuracy, appears to have made no improvement in relation to categorization, probably because both handwritten and computer register entries are equally dependent on the judgements made by form tutors.

There was evidence that many schools did not have systems to store and retrieve primary evidence (parental notes, notes of phone calls, staff visits home, responses from the EWO, and suchlike), which was the basis for judgements on the categorization of the absence. Some schools, therefore, appear to rely on secondary evidence, such as, for example, the register entries, and/or hearsay, on which to make requests for further action. One effect of this is that their categorization and understanding of the situation cannot easily be questioned, a process which helps to maintain the power of their 'parental' position.

It is possible to conclude from the above that some schools may have developed processes of registration and categorization that have become ritualized. In these schools there may be little time for anything more than cursory enquiry and speedy decision-making which deny investigation from the 'adult' ego state. It appears that form periods in some schools are often routine events, designed to meet the organizational needs of the staff and school. Collectively these processes may be called the 'registration ritual'. One effect of this ritual may be to emphasize the 'parent' ego state of the form tutors in their transactions with the pupils in their form, and in the fleeting contacts made with their parents.

The registration ritual may also be played out in relation to investigations into unexplained absences. When the form tutor wants absence investigated further it is likely that it will be the register, together with a verbal request, that provides the information that is the basis of an enquiry undertaken by a more senior member of staff. Senior staff may well not have the primary evidence on the basis of which the original categorization decisions were taken, or a considered report on prior contacts with the family, on which to act. Thus it seems quite likely that their first approach to pupils and parents will be authoritative and controlling, emphasizing the 'critical parent' ego state. It is possible that their approach will remain controlling if there is a need to uphold the significance of the registration ritual and support the action taken by the form tutor.

Within the context of the registration ritual, and its associated 'parent' behaviour, it is possible to identify two games (or possibly two versions of one game) that can be played by school staff. The first seems to be a version of the game of 'harried' described by Barker (1980, p. 56). In this game a busy senior member of staff enters into a form of damage limitation by retrospective categorization of absences as authorized where no information has been received from parents, thus 'improving' the data that will be published, disguising the true extent of unauthorized absence and condoning the absence. This action may be justified because of the high costs in time of a more thorough process, and because unauthorized absence is not used as a significant performance indicator by the school's managers. The result may well be the maintenance of ritualized behaviour.

The second game is to rationalize taking little action to deal with unauthorized absence by claiming that the school experiences an insignificant amount of it. This view persists although the school avoids efficient collection and proper categorization of attendance and may not know the extent of absence. This game may also be a version of 'harried', but in this case it is played by a number of members of staff, who are rushed off their feet gathering information, some of which may be of doubtful validity.

Both games involve manipulation of data, the first more deliberately than the second, and both have the effect of staff condoning absence. In schools where such games are played, action taken within the school, and by outside agencies, to deal with unauthorized absence is likely to be based on unreliable information.

4 Communications with parents of unauthorized absentees

The need to establish good relationships with parents, as suggested by the Elton committee (DES, 1989), was considered in Chapter 4. It has been suggested above that the absence of an attendance policy may hinder the development of good relationships with parents in general, and can encourage ritualized activity by the staff. It is likely that the absence of a policy will be of more immediate significance when dealing with the parents of pupils whose absence causes the school problems. In these circumstances the staff's initial enquiries into absence cannot be based on the assumption of a mutual understanding of the policy and rules. Initial contacts, usually made by the form tutor by phone, may assume 'consentience' and ask for co-operation with rules that have not been published. There is evidence that this contact by the form tutor is most likely to be rushed. Any subsequent contacts, either by phone or by letter, made by more senior staff aimed at improving attendance, may be based on the view that the parent is a 'problem' and assume 'impulsiveness'. In these situations the opportunity to develop a partnership is limited at a time when it might be assumed that greater effort should be made to gain parental co-operation. There was evidence from the study that staff contact with parents where absence was considered a serious problem tended to be authoritative in tone, and they did not often seek to re-establish co-operation.

There was some evidence that dealing with the parents of unauthorized absentees may become part of an institutional game in which they are understood as unco-operative, and contact is reduced to a minimum. In some cases the end result of the registration ritual is that standard letters are sent, sometimes containing a threat of action that is not carried out, but not requiring any response. End of year reports are sent, but may not contain attendance data or any comment on the effects of absence on learning. Parents are not asked to confirm or refute the school's categorization of absence. This game has the pay-off of making the parents seem inadequate and partnership with them impossible, and it also makes legitimate the staff's attempts to discipline the pupil when in school.

Staff may need to remember that the grudging consent of some parents has only recently been given to compulsory secondary schooling (see Chapter 1). It may be helpful when problems around attendance begin to emerge for an assessment to be made of the level of the parent's co-operation with the process of schooling in general. It may be found that parents of persistent unauthorized absentees may need to have matters clearly and personally stated to them by staff, with information presented and discussed in a way that invites an 'Adult-to-Adult' transaction, as free as possible from rituals and games. One important aspect of this transaction is that, if the parent(s) so wish, it should be conducted in their native language. The outcome of the transaction could be some form of agreement with the parent, possibly based on that given in the Appendix, in which the results of non-compliance for parent and pupil are clearly stated. The breaking of such an agreement could form the basis of further referral, legal action, or removal of the pupil from the school roll.

Staff may also discover, as a result of their enquiries into unauthorized absence, that family breakdown, dysfunction and illness are overtaking the parent's commitment to their child's schooling. This evidence may have the effect of modifying the registration ritual, or other 'parental' modes of transaction, that have been established. For example, there was evidence that staff sometimes authorize absence, thus condoning it, and informally offer help. A sympathetic reaction in these cases is understandable, but informal agreements made in these circumstances may be idiosyncratic and susceptible to game-playing. A policy on how to deal with these issues may need to be added to the school's attendance policy (when adopted), or to the staff handbook, in order to guide staff on appropriate action. The guidance could have, as one outcome, the drawing up of an agreement between the school, parent and pupil, describing the present family difficulties, the likely effects on attendance and lateness, and the actions that could be taken by parent and staff to mitigate the effects of the difficulties. An attempt could be made within this to agree the roles to be played by school staff in relation to the family.

5 Measures used by schools to deal with unauthorized absentees

Consideration of the legal issues concerning absence was presented in Chapter 3. From that consideration it is possible to conclude that unauthorized absence may result in the parent committing an offence. This suggests that the parent has the legal responsibility to control their child and not allow unauthorized absence. However, schools see it as their responsibility to control unauthorized absentees as part of their maintenance of good discipline within the school, usually by a limited range of sanctions following absence. These actions are justified on the grounds that 'Heads and teachers have legal authority to impose reasonable punishment where necessary' (DfE, 1994a, p. 15). Therefore, dealing with unauthorized absentees should be a co-operative enterprise between parent and school; however, reality suggests that this may not be so. It has already been pointed out that there is no written agreement on which to base the co-operative enterprise, and that transactions may be subject to various rituals and games. It has also been suggested that the purpose of the rituals and games appears to be to reduce the need for 'Adult-to-Adult' transactions in a way that allows staff to retain the power within the relationship. Evidence gathered from the four schools suggests that school may frequently adopt a 'parent' ego state in transactions with parents of unauthorized absentees, within which the parents are defined as the 'adapted child'. In such a situation it seems likely that an unequal and flawed partnership will develop, which offers the pupil an opportunity to manipulate differences. In such a situation it seems unsurprising that the school's initial and most common response to unauthorized absence is to discipline, or threaten, the pupil in order to control attendance, to inform the parent of the action taken rather than consult beforehand, and to control the categorization of absence from within the registration ritual. One way in which the pupil can regain some control in this situation is to get the parent to make the absence legitimate by condoning it. Most of the schools within this study recognized the problem of parent-condoned absence, some recognized it as a threat to their authority. None appeared to have recognized that it indicated a breakdown in their relationship with the pupil and the parent that required investigation and action.

The study produced some evidence that the less the parents were able to control their children the more some staff tried to compensate. The method of compensation depended to some extent on the view that the staff took of the reasons for lack of control, and on the attendance history of the pupil. Compensation methods, some of which involved a great deal of staff time, included attempting to limit undesirable social contacts within the school, altering individual teaching programmes, individual counselling and supervision, and providing pupils with special PSE experiences. Some staff appeared to take on the compensation from the 'nurturing parent' ego state, often with the best of intentions, but without the recognition that in so doing they may further weaken the authority of the parents.

While sanctions for unauthorized absence among the sample schools was common, rewarding presence was not so common. Two types of reward systems were identified. Both depend on the maintenance of accurate attendance data; neither appeared to operate where data were suspect.

The first system is one in which attendance data are used in reports to parents and, towards the end of the secondary career, to employers, or colleges (apparently a form of deferred gratification). These rewards appeared to be used to provide evidence of the pupil's general behaviour and suitability for training and employment. This system carried with it the threat of punishment through withdrawal of the reward. The schools involved had not undertaken research to discover whether there had been any effect on the rates of unauthorized absence as a result of implementing the scheme, or of the effect of withdrawal of the reward.

The second system is the more immediate reward of a consumer good or token, perhaps publicly presented to the recipients, for good and improving attendance. Such schemes were in the process of being introduced, and there was some evidence of staff resistance based on a dislike of the use of a bribe to induce behaviour that was expected as normal (a 'parent' response). There was also some evidence that the introduction may not have been discussed with parents prior to its introduction in order to gain their approval and support (a 'parent' mode of behaviour by the school).

Rewards for attendance appear to be harder to give than punishment for absence, suggesting that it is more common for staff to adopt the 'critical parent' ego state rather than one that nurtures or questions. It seems likely that the introduction of a reward scheme will have to overcome the desire of some to maintain 'critical parent' behaviours and the rituals that they have given rise to.

6 Engaging help from services outside school to help deal with unauthorized absentees

The processes of investigation of absence by school staff have been considered above and in Chapter 5. Their investigations usually go no further than phone calls, or brief meetings with parents. If the staff want further investigations made they usually make a referral to the Education Welfare Service. However, the existence of the EWS does not preclude the staff making referrals themselves to other agencies, but evidence suggests that referrals of this sort do not occur for absence alone. Directly referred pupils are more likely to exhibit emotional and behaviour problems, or are considered as being at risk of abuse as well as being absentees.

In referring a pupil to the EWS it seems likely that in the majority of cases the school is requesting contact with the parents and looking for one of three outcomes from that contact.

1. Information as to the cause of absence in order to complete the categorization process.
2. Information as to the cause of absence and a plan of action that will be carried through by the EWO that will result in improved attendance.
3. Information as to the cause of absence followed by a referral made by the EWO to other agencies for them to take action. In this case improved attendance may not be the highest priority.

There was evidence from the sample schools that neither the staff nor the EWO were always clear on whether a referral had been made, what priority it should be given by the EWO, and how much information obtained as a result of the investigation should be made known to the staff. It seemed that in some situations the act of referral was sufficient in itself to satisfy the requirements of the registration ritual, with little or no information on the investigation expected or wanted. There was evidence from the four schools that there was very little written information to the school on action being taken by the EWO aimed at reducing absence. In some cases the school and the EWO held very different views of what was being done as a result of the referral, neither knowing of the view of the other and both without systems for resolving the miscommunication. In these cases the relationship between the staff and the officer, and the officer's service, appeared to be a ritual rather than professional collaboration.

Clearly some schools in the sample had established good working relationships with their EWO and other social workers, but this was usually without benefit of a clear statement of what they could offer to help deal with unauthorized absentees. Successful co-operation appeared to be dependent on personality rather than policy. In some cases schools' interaction with these services was based on custom and practice which appeared to be in need of review and a refreshment of policy. In some situations rituals had become established in which the particular problems of the unauthorized absentees and their parents appeared not to be important.

Conclusion

The six themes identified have as a common element the development and application of an attendance policy which could prepare the ground for more collaborative relationships with all parents, and particularly with parents of unauthorized absentees. A policy, determined by agreement with staff and parents, offers the chance of reducing the rituals and games that stem from transactions based on the 'parent' or 'child' ego states. A policy offers more adult transactional opportunities. Clearly such a policy cannot be introduced without an attendant behaviour policy, of which it would form an element. The success of both would rest, in part, on the way in which they were introduced into the school. That introduction could provide the basis for adult transactions by including parents in the discussion that precedes its development. If possible, not all those parents should be from the 'consentient' group.

Schools also need to bear in mind that policy statements do not always translate into adult transactions, as evidence from this study shows. A behaviour policy, and the attendance element of it, will require careful monitoring and evaluation if it, too, is not to become ritualized.

Information to parents

The law requires that all children between 5 and 16 must receive an education. Thank you for fulfilling your legal duty by sending your child to this school. Part of your duty is to make sure that your child attends school for the whole of the school day. In doing this you are obeying the law, and you are also making it possible for your child to get a good education. We have made the following arrangements to help you fulfil your duty.

We provide a calendar of school dates each year that shows when your child should be in school. Your child should be in school every day shown on the calendar unless there are good reasons why they cannot come.

The school recognizes that there are good, and legal, reasons for your child not coming to school. These are:
being too ill to attend,
having a medical or dental appointment,
attending a family bereavement,
attending days of religious observance,
going for job, or other interview.

If any of these applies then a note from you to tell us about it, beforehand if possible, will usually be enough for us to agree the absence. In an emergency a telephone call will do until you have time to provide a note.

The school can allow absence for other reasons. Please write to the Head, beforehand if possible, to get agreement to the absence. The law allows you to take your child away from school for two weeks' holiday in any school year. This should be agreed with the Head before taking the holiday, and should be arranged so that it does not disrupt study or examinations.

You are **NOT** doing your duty if you keep your child off school to run errands, go shopping, help with younger children, or help around the house. The law says this is truancy. It is the school's policy to record all truancy on school reports and employer references, and we have to notify the Education Authority.

If your child has missed some school time, or comes late to school or classes, and we have heard **nothing** from you, then we will either phone you or write to you for an explanation. If your child's absence was unknown to you, then we will arrange to talk to you and your child and try to work out how to put matters right. The law says that it is up to the school staff to decide whether to accept your explanation about the absence or not. If we do not accept the explanation the absence is recorded as truancy and the Education Authority informed. The Education Authority may decide to send an Education Welfare Officer round to see you to find out the reasons for the absences. If the Education Authority is not satisfied with what they find they may decide to prosecute you.

If there are difficulties at home that result in poor school attendance then you may like to make contact with the Education Welfare Officer who deals with children from this school. She/he is (name), (address), (telephone).

Please talk to your child's form tutor or year head about any school matters that concern you. If you think that there are things happening at school that are making it difficult for your child to attend, then please let them know. They are there to work with you to resolve any problems.

Finally, if truancy persists and we receive no explanation or co-operation from you, then we reserve the right to take your child off the school register. If that happens we will tell the Education Authority, and a new school will have to be found by them for your child.

If you want further information on matters raised in this note, please contact your child's year head.

Definitions and Abbreviations

DES   Department for Education and Science
DfE   Department for Education
DfEE   Department for Education and Employment
EBD   Emotional and behavioural difficulties (identifies pupils with special needs)
ESW   Education Social Worker, an alternative title for EWO
ESWS   Education Social Work Service, an alternative title for EWS
EWO   Education Welfare Officer, a person employed in the EWS
EWS   Education Welfare Service, a service supplied by the LEA to deal with absence from school
GEST   Grants for Education Support and Training. One element was the Truancy and Disaffected Pupils programme first offered by the DfE in 1993; 60 per cent of LEA expenditure was paid by grant. From 1998/9 it became the Standards Fund, one element of which is the Improving Attendance and Behaviour programme, funded at 50 per cent of LEA expenditure, total available £21m
HMCIS   Her Majesty's Chief Inspector of Schools
LEA   Local Education Authority, providing education services to an area
NACEWO   National Association of Chief Education Welfare Officers, an association that represented the interests of the managers of EWOs, now called the Association of Managers in Education Welfare
OMR   Optical mark reader
PSE   Personal and Social Education, a curriculum intended to develop social knowledge and skills in addition to the academic curriculum
SIMS   Schools Information Management System
SSD   Social Services Department
Truancy   Unauthorized absence from compulsory schooling. Authorization can only be given by the school
Truant   Unauthorized absentee

Bibliography

Audit Commission (1996) *Misspent Youth: Young People and Crime*, London, Audit Commission Publications.

Barker, D. (1980) *TA and Training: The Theory and Use of Transactional Analysis in Organisations*, Farnborough, Gower Press.

Berne, E. (1964) *Games People Play: The Psychology of Human Relationships*, Harmondsworth, Penguin (1976 reprint).

Best, R., Ribbins, P., Jarvis, C. and Oddy, D. (1983) *Education and Care: The Study of a School and its Pastoral Organisation*, London, Heinemann Educational.

Billington, B. J. (1979) 'Truants: some personality characteristics', *Durham and Newcastle Review*, no. 43, Autumn 1979.

Blackburn, R. M. and Marsh, C. (1991) 'Education and social class: revisiting the 1944 education act with fixed marginals', *British Journal of Sociology*, vol. 42, no. 4, December 1991.

Blythe, E. and Milner, J. (1991) 'Evaluating effectiveness in education social work', *Practice*, vol. 5, no. 3.

Bolam, R., McMahon, A., Pocklington, K. and Weindling, D. (1993) *Effective Management in Schools*, Report for the Department of Education via the School Management Task Force Professional Working Party, London, HMSO.

Brown, P. (1987) *Schooling Ordinary Kids*, London, Tavistock.

Carlen, P. Gleeson, D., Wardhaugh, J. (1992) *Truancy: The Politics of Compulsory Schooling*, Buckingham, Open University Press.

Carroll, H. (1996) 'The role of the educational psychologist in dealing with pupil absenteeism', in I. Berg and J. P. Nursten (eds) *Unwillingly to School* (1996), London, Gaskell.

Central Statistical Office (1991) *Regional Trends*, London, HMSO.

Children Act 1989 (1989) c. 41, London, HMSO.

Children Act 1989, Guidance and Regulations (vol. 1), Court Orders, London, HMSO, 1991.

Children Act 1989, Guidance and Regulations (vol. 7), Guardians Ad Litem and Other Court Related Issues, London, HMSO, 1991.

Children and Young Persons Act 1933, 1933 c. 12.

Children and Young Persons Act 1969, 1969 c. 54.

Clarke, Hall and Morrison (1993) *Law Relating to Children* (10th edn, ed. A. H. White), London, Butterworths.

Collins, D. (1993) 'Developing a Service Level Agreement', *Journal of Education Social Work*, Summer 1993, issue 2, Centre for Education Welfare Studies, Huddersfield University.

Collins, D. (1996) 'Enforcement of school attendance: a critical path analysis', *Education Management and Administration*, January 1996, London, Sage.

Collins, D. (1996a) *Helping Secondary Schools with their Management of Unauthorised Absence*, unpublished Ph.D. thesis, Birmingham University Faculty of Education.

Criminal Statistics, England and Wales, 1991, Cm 2134, London, HMSO.

Department of Education and Science (1978) *Truancy and Behavioural Problems in Some Urban Schools*, HMI report, London, HMSO.

Department of Education and Science (1984) *The Education Welfare Service: An HMI Enquiry into Eight LEAs*, London, HMSO.

Department of Education and Science (1989) *Discipline in Schools*, Report of the Committee of Enquiry chaired by Lord Elton (Elton Report), London, HMSO.

Department of Education and Science (1989a) *Education Observed, no. 13: Attendance at School*, HMI report, London, HMSO.

Department of Education and Science (1991) *The Education (Pupils' Attendance Records) Regulations 1991*, circular 11/91, London, DES.

Department for Education (1992) *Choice and Diversity* (white paper), London, HMSO, Cm 2021.

Department for Education (1992a) *School Reports to the Court*, London, DfE.

Department for Education (1993) *Secondary School Performance Tables*, London, DfE.

Department for Education (1994) *School Attendance: Policy and Practice on Categorisation of Absence*, London, DfE.

Department for Education (1994a) *Pupil Behaviour and Discipline*, circular 8/94, London, DfE.

Department for Education (1994b) *Our Children's Education: The Updated Parent's Charter*, London, HMSO.

Department for Education and Employment (1995) *The Education (Pupil Registration) Regulations 1995*, London, HMSO.

Department for Education and Employment (1996) *Youth Cohort Study: Trends in the Activities and Experiences of 16–18 year olds, England and Wales 1985–1994*, London, HMSO.

Department for Education and Employment (1997) *Excellence in Schools* (white paper), Cm 3681, London, HMSO.

Department of Health (July 1991) *Children Act 1989: Guidance on Education Supervision Orders*, London, HMSO.

Department of Health (1993) *Children Act Report, 1992*, cm 2144, London, HMSO.

Dickens, C. (1848) *Dombey and Son*, Oxford Illustrated Dickens (1970 edn), London, Oxford University Press.

Education Act 1870, 33 and 34 Vic. c. 75.

Education Act 1891, 54 and 55 Vic. c. 56.

Education Act 1902, 2 Edw. c. 42.

Education Act 1944, 1944 c. 31.

Education (Miscellaneous Provisions) Act 1948, 1948 c. 40.

Education (Work Experience) Act 1973, 1973 c. 16.

Education Act 1980, 1980 c. 20.

Education Act 1981, 1981 c. 60.

Education (Schools and Further Education) Regulations 1981, statutory instrument.

Education (No. 2) Act 1986, 1986 c. 61.

Education Act 1993, 1993 c. 35.

Education Act 1996, 1996 c. 56.

Education Act 1997, 1997 c. 44.

Education Otherwise (1983) *School is Not Compulsory: A Guide to Your Rights*, Cambridge, Education Otherwise.

Education (Pupils' Attendance Records) Regulations 1991, statutory instrument 1991/1582.

Education (Schools and Further Education) Regulations 1981, statutory instrument 1981/630.

Education (Pupil Registration) Regulations 1995, statutory instrument 1995/2089.

Education (School Leaving Date) Order 1997, statutory instrument 1997/1970.

Education Reform Act 1988, 1988 c. 40.

Education Rights Handbook, 1987, Children's Legal Centre, 20 Compton Terrace, London N1 2UN.

Farrington, D. (1992) 'Juvenile delinquency', in Coleman, J. (ed.) *Current Issues in the Socialisation of Young People* (2nd edn) London, Routledge.

Farrington, D. and West, D. (1990) 'The Cambridge Study in Delinquent Development: A long-term follow-up of 411 London males', in Kerner, H. J. and Kaiser, G. (eds) *Criminality, Behaviour, Life History*, Berlin, Springer Verlag.

Flynn, N. (1990) *Public Sector Management*, Hertfordshire, Harvester.

Fogelman, K. (1996) 'Early adult sequelae of truancy: the National Child Development Study', in I. Berg and J. P. Nursten (eds) *Unwillingly to School* (1996), London, Gaskell.

Fogelman, K. and Richardson, K. (1974) 'School attendance: some results from the National Child Development Study', in B. Turner (ed.) *Truancy*, London, Ward Lock.

Galloway, D. (1985) *Schools and Persistent Absentees*, Oxford, Pergamon.

Gillborn, D., Nixon, J. and Ruddick, J. (1993) *Dimensions of Discipline: Rethinking Practice in Secondary Schools*, London, HMSO (DfE).

Graham, J. (1988) *Schools, Disruptive Behaviour and Delinquency, A Review of Research*. Home Office Research Study 96, London, HMSO.

Graham, J. and Bowling, B. (1995) *Young People and Crime*, London, Home Office Research Study 145.

Gray, J. and Jesson, D. (1990) *Truancy in Secondary Schools amongst Fifth-Year Pupils*, QQSE Research Group Education Research Centre, Sheffield University.

Green, A. (1990) *Education and State Formation*, London, Macmillan.

Gunter, H. (1997) *Rethinking Education: The Consequences of Jurassic Management*, London, Cassell.

Halford, P. (1991) *National Survey of the Education Welfare/Education Social Work Service in LEAs in England and Wales*, unpublished M.Phil. thesis, University of Southampton.

Hansard (1996) *Parliamentary Debates*, 5th series, vol. DLXXII, House of Lords Official Report, London, HMSO.

Hansard (1997) *House of Commons Proceedings, 1 July 1997*, 'School Absenteeism' bill (bill 35 first reading), Harry Cohen MP, Issue no. 1759, vol. 297, no. 31, London, HMSO.

Hastings, M. 'Truancy in Britain: a TV-am major investigation', *CEWS Newsletter*, no. 7. (1991), Centre for Education Welfare Studies, Polytechnic of Huddersfield.

Hibbett, A., Fogelman, K. and Manor, O. (1990) 'Occupational outcomes of truancy', *British Journal of Educational Psychology*, vol. 60, pt 1.

Howe, D. (1993) *Absent from School*, Tamworth, Bracken.

Hurt, J. S. (1979) *Elementary Schooling and the Working Classes, 1860–1918*, London, Routledge and Kegan Paul.

Johnson, D. (ed.) with Ransom, E., Packwood, T., Bowden, K. and Kogan, M. (1980) *Secondary Schools and the Welfare Network*, London, Allen & Unwin.

Jones, J. (1995) *Truancy: A Quick Guide*, Cambridge, Daniels.

Jowett, S. and Baginsky, M. (1991) *Building Bridges: Parental Involvement in Schools*, DES commissioned research, Oxford, NFER-Nelson.

Learmonth, J. (1995) *More Willingly to School: An Independent Evaluation of the Truancy and Disaffected Pupils GEST Programme*, London, DfEE Publications.

Le Riche, E. (1995) *Combating Truancy in Schools*, London, Fulton.

Lewis, E. (1995) *Truancy: the Partnership Approach*, Police Research Group, Stoke on Trent, Smith Davis Press.

Liell, P., Coleman, J. and Poole, K. (1997) *The Law of Education*, (9th edn, issue 35), London, Butterworths.

Liell, P. and Saunders, J. B. (1993) *The Law of Education* (9th edn, issue 22), London, Butterworths.

McCann, P. (ed.) (1977) *Popular Education and Socialisation in the Nineteenth Century*, London, Methuen.

McLaughlin, C. (1989) 'School management and disaffection', in K. Reid (ed.) *Helping Troubled Pupils in Secondary Schools* (vol. 2), Oxford, Blackwell.

Maclure, J. Stuart (1986) *Educational Documents: England and Wales 1816 to the Present Day* (5th edn), London, Methuen.

MacMillan, K. (1977) *Education Welfare: Strategy and Structure*, New York, Longman.

Mann, K. (1994) 'Watching the defectives: Observers of the underclass in the USA, Britain and Australia', *Critical Social Policy*, vol. 14, no. 2, Autumn 1994, Essex, Longman.

Middleton, N. and Weitzman, S. (1976) *A Place for Everyone: A History of State Education from the End of the 18th Century to the 1970s*, London, Gollancz.

Morris, R., Reid, E. and Fowler, J. (1993) *Education Act, 1993: A Critical Guide*, AMA, London.

Morrison, K. (1992) 'Using truancy rates as PIs', *Forum*, vol. 34, no. 3.

Mortimore, P. (1977) 'Schools as institutions', *Educational Research*, vol. 20, no. 1.

Murphy, J. (1972) *The Education Act, 1870*, Newton Abbot, Holman.

National Association for the Care and Resettlement of Offenders (1989) *School Reports in the Juvenile Court: A Second Look*, London, NACRO.

National Association for the Care and Resettlement of Offenders (1997) *Families and Crime*, London, NACRO.

National Association of Chief Education Welfare Officers (1974) *These We Serve*, working party report.

National Association of Social Workers in Education (1990) *Education Welfare National Gradings Survey, 1990*, working party report, unpublished.

OECD (1995) *Public Expectations of the Final Stages of Compulsory Education*, Centre for Educational Research and Innovation, Paris, OECD.

OFSTED (1993) *Framework for the Inspection of Schools*, London, OFSTED.

OFSTED (1993a) *Education for Disaffected Pupils*, London, OFSTED.

OFSTED (1993b) *Achieving Good Behaviour in Schools*, London, OFSTED.

OFSTED (1994) *Assessing School Effectiveness* (summary), London, OFSTED.

OFSTED (1995) *The Challenge for Education Welfare*, London, OFSTED.

OFSTED (1995a) *The Education of Children Looked After by Local Authorities* (jointly with the Social Service Inspectorate), London, OFSTED.

OFSTED (1995b) *Access, Achievement and Attendance in Secondary Schools*, London, OFSTED.

OFSTED (1995c) *Pupil Referral Units: The First Twelve Inspections*, London, OFSTED.

OFSTED (1995d) *Inspection Resource Pack: Guidance on Recording Inspection Evidence and Summarising Judgments*, London, HMSO.

OFSTED (1997) *Annual Report of Her Majesty's Chief Inspector of Schools*, London, OFSTED.

O'Keeffe, D. J. (1994) *Truancy in English Secondary Schools*, report for the DfE by the University of North London Truancy Unit, London, DfE.

Peters, T. and Austin, N. (1985) *A Passion for Excellence: The Leadership Difference*, Glasgow, Fontana/Collins (third impression, 1988).

Pik, R. (1987) 'Confrontation situations and teacher support systems', in L. Cohen and A. Cohen (eds) *Disruptive Behaviour: A Source Book for Teachers*, London, Harper and Row.

Pitts, J. (1988) *The Politics of Juvenile Crime*, London, Sage.

Pond, C. and Searle, A. (1991) *The Hidden Army: Children at Work in the 1990s*, London, Low Pay Unit Pamphlet no. 55.

Reid, I. (1989) *Social Class Differences in Britain* (3rd edn), London, Fontana.

Reynolds, D. (1996) 'School factors', in I. Berg and J. P. Nursten (eds) *Unwillingly to School*, London, Gaskell.

Reynolds, D., Sullivan, M. and Murgatroyd, S. (1987) *The Comprehensive Experiment*, Lewes, Falmer.

Roderick, G. and Stephens, M. (1982) *The British Malaise*, Lewes, Falmer.

Rubenstein, D. (1977) 'Socialisation and the London School Board 1870–1904: aims, methods and public opinion', in P. McCann (ed.) *Popular Education and Socialisation in the Nineteenth Century*, London, Methuen.

Rutter, M., Maughan, B., Mortimore, P. and Ouston, J. (1979) *Fifteen Thousand Hours: Secondary Schools and Their Effects on Children*, London, Open Books.

Skinner, A., Platts, H. and Hill, B. (1983) *Disaffection from School: Issues and Interagency Responses*, National Youth Bureau, Leicester.

SOED (1992) *Using Ethos Indicators in Secondary School Self-Evaluation: Taking Account of the Views of Pupils, Parents, and Teachers*, Scotland, SOED.

Sone, K. (1995) 'School scandal', *Community Care*, 4–10 May 1995.

Spooner, R. (1979) 'Tackling truancy', *Education*, 26 January 1979.

Stoll, P. (1994) 'Truancy and the law', *Childright*, May 1994, no. 106.

Tattum, D. (1989) 'Disruptive behaviour: a whole school approach', in K. Reid (ed.) *Helping Troubled Pupils in Secondary Schools* (vol. 2), Oxford, Blackwell.

Terry, F. (1975) 'Absence from school', *Youth in Society*, no. 11, pp. 7–10.

Utting, D. (1997) *Reducing Criminality among Young People: A Sample of Relevant Programmes in the United Kingdom*, London, Home Office Research Study 161.

Warnock, M. (1976) 'Education and its purposes', *New Society*, 18 November 1976.

Whitney, B. (1994) *The Truth about Truancy*, London, Kogan Page.

Woods, P. (1989) 'Treating parents as partners', in K. Reid (ed.) *Helping Troubled Pupils in Secondary Schools* (vol. 2), Oxford, Blackwell.

Index